Between Worlds

Second Language Acquisition in Changing Times

David E. Freeman • Yvonne S. Freeman • Mary Soto

FOURTH EDITION

HEINEMANN
Portsmouth, NH

Heinemann

145 Maplewood Avenue, Suite 300

Portsmouth, NH 03801

www.heinemann.com

Offices and agents throughout the world

The authors and publisher wish to thank those who have generously given permission to reprint borrowed material:

List (on p. 81) from "Stephen Krashen's Seven Tips for Teaching Language During Covid-19" by Stephen Krashen. Published May 8, 2020 on languagemagazine.com by Language Magazine. Reprinted with permission of the publisher.

Acknowledgments for borrowed material continue on p. 226.

Library of Congress Cataloging-in-Publication Data

Names: Freeman, David E., author. | Freeman, Yvonne S., author. | Soto, Mary, author.
Title: Between worlds : second language acquisition in changing times / David E. Freeman, Yvonne S. Freeman, and Mary Soto.
Description: Fourth edition. | Portsmouth, NH : Heinemann, [2021] | Includes bibliographical references and index.
Identifiers: LCCN 2020052738 | ISBN 9780325112763
Subjects: LCSH: Second language acquisition.
Classification: LCC P118.2 .F74 2021 | DDC 418.0071—dc23
LC record available at https://lccn.loc.gov/2020052738

Editor: *Holly Kim Price*
Production: *Vicki Kasabian*
Cover and text designs: *Suzanne Heiser*
Typesetting: *Kim Arney*
Manufacturing: *Val Cooper*

Printed in the United States of America on acid-free paper
1 2 3 4 5 RWP 26 25 24 23 22 21
April 2021 Printing

We dedicate this book to our grandchildren, Maya, Christiana, Romero, and Alexander, who provide us with very personal lessons about acquiring language and learning to live between worlds.

—Yvonne and David Freeman

I dedicate this book to my husband, Francisco, a dual language teacher who has devoted his twenty-four-year teaching career to making sure that his students are proud to be bilingual and to know that they are a great asset to this country.

—Mary Soto

Contents

Acknowledgments

This fourth edition of *Between Worlds: Second Language Acquisition in Changing Times* is a result of our reading current theory and research as well as articles on online teaching, our interactions with colleagues, and especially our experiences with teachers who are committed to improving the lives of their students. Our goal when we write is to translate theory and research into practice, but we couldn't do it without the real classroom examples that talented educators have provided us. Their input has been especially important during the time of the COVID-19 pandemic, racial tensions, and political unrest.

We wish to acknowledge the teachers with whom we have worked and especially the following outstanding educators, whose work we share in this book: Khristel Allen, Loretta Aragón, Katie Bausch-Ude, Ann Ebe, Desiree McDougal, Sandra Mercuri, Kathy Smith, Francisco Soto, Marcela Richardson Pinzón, Monica Rojas, Elizabeth Stevens, Kristene Vaux, Helen Milliorn, Christa Bryan, Evelyn Yañez, Gustavo Yañez, Juan Carlos Yañez, and Marta Yoshimura.

We would like to thank our editor, Holly Kim Price, who has supported our writing and always provides important feedback and suggestions to improve our texts. A special thanks to Vicki Kasabian, a longtime friend who oversaw the production of this book despite her busy schedule. We worked with Vicki in the past on several other books. She is a true professional. A special thanks to Elizabeth Tripp, who did the copyediting. She caught many errors and improved the writing style of the book, something we appreciate a great deal. As always, the Heinemann staff is a pleasure to work with. We appreciate their efforts to promote our work. The production team includes Krysten Lebel, the editorial coordinator who carefully checked permissions and the figures. In addition, we wish to thank Kim Arney, who was the typesetter, and Suzanne Heiser, who created the striking cover and designed the interior of the book. Heinemann has been our main publisher over the years, and we appreciate their professionalism and their dedication to teachers. As a publisher, they have made a difference not only for teachers but for millions of children in schools.

Introduction

The focus of this book, as the subtitle indicates, is to provide readers with an understanding of second language acquisition. Our goal is to make acquisition theory understandable and to suggest the implications for teaching students who are living between worlds. To accomplish this goal, we look carefully at a number of factors that influence the acquisition of a second language. One factor that we consider is how the COVID-19 pandemic is affecting schooling for English learners. As we write this book, schools are taking a variety of approaches to deliver instruction safely, but clearly the changes are having a significant impact on schooling for English learners.

Our Audience for This Fourth Edition of Between Worlds

The idea for writing the first edition of this book in 1994 came to us as we taught a course called Language Acquisition and Cross-Cultural Communication. The teachers in our graduate program needed a text that described different theories of language acquisition and also provided examples for putting theory into practice.

In addition, as we worked with teachers in schools, we were reminded daily that teaching multilingual/multicultural learners (MMLs) involves much more than having an understanding of theory, methods, and materials. We realized that this text needed to address linguistic, social, political, and cultural factors that influence students' learning. Our goals for this fourth edition are not different. We bring to readers what we now understand even more deeply as the result of our own work, the work of teachers around us, and the work of other researchers and theorists.

Our national, state, and local communities are constantly becoming more diverse, and both mainstream teachers and language specialists need to be able to respond to the changes in their student populations. When we wrote the first edition of this book, there were only a few states that had large numbers of English language learners (ELLs), and in those areas, schools were only beginning to recognize the need to adapt their instruction to these students. The context has changed dramatically since 1994.

Now ELLs are attending schools across the country. Teachers and administrators need to know about their English learners (ELs) and the practices that will support their language acquisition. Even when second language students have been exited from limited English proficient (LEP) classification, they need extra support in mainstream classes. For that reason, we do not intend that the audience for this book be restricted to students taking formal coursework or to designated English as a second language (ESL) or bilingual teachers. We hope that mainstream teachers will also find this book useful. In fact, we wrote this book with several possible audiences in mind.

It is our hope that teacher educators continue to find this book useful in courses dealing with learning theory, second language acquisition, and the various factors that influence learning. These courses might be part of a preservice program for prospective teachers, part of a program for teachers wishing to continue their professional development, or part of a graduate program of study.

We have also written this book for school administrators, counselors, paraprofessionals, and parents. Administrators provide leadership in curriculum, and they support the efforts of classroom teachers. In many schools, language-minority students have become the numerical majority. For administrators to carry out their role, they need to be aware of the factors that influence the academic performance of second language students as well as their curriculum needs. Counselors with a good understanding of second language acquisition can better advise students and ensure that their schedules are appropriate for their level of English and academic proficiency.

In many classes, paraprofessionals play a key role in providing support for students learning English, especially paraprofessionals who speak these students' home languages, and the more they understand about language acquisition, the more support they can provide. Finally, we have written this book for parents and for community members interested in school improvement. Parents and other community members play a key role in the academic success of ELs. Successful programs must involve knowledgeable parents and other community members.

As we explain various theories, discuss current research, and describe classroom practice, we will provide you with opportunities to reflect on what you are reading and consider implications for application to your own situations. Since we believe that learning takes place in social interaction, we have often suggested that the reflections be completed in pairs or small groups.

The Need for a Fourth Edition

We have updated this text because of all the changes that have affected the teaching of English learners since we wrote the third edition in 2011. The current period, to quote Charles Dickens (2009), is the best of times and the worst of times, especially for ELs, their teachers, and the schools where they are being educated.

In many ways, this is the best of times. Federal government agencies and the different states have responded to the increase in the number of English learners by enacting new laws and regulations that have resulted in school districts implementing more effective programs and methods for teaching these students. These changes have come in response to greater demands for accountability. The Every Student Succeeds Act (ESSA) legislation that replaced the No Child Left Behind (NCLB) initiative states that every teacher must attend to teaching academic language as well as academic content to all students, including English learners. In addition, states like California and Massachusetts have adopted new legislation to promote bilingual education and overturn English-only laws.

Other positive changes have come as the result of new research. A good example has been the increased implementation of dual language bilingual programs in response to research showing their effectiveness. The use of translanguaging strategies in both bilingual and ESL settings is also the result of recent research being done with translanguaging in schools. A growing awareness of the benefits of bilingualism and biliteracy in the twenty-first century has led many states to adopt the Seal of Biliteracy and to promote global education.

However, in other ways, this is the worst of times for many English learners in America. Many live in poverty, have suffered from trauma, or are homeless. For this reason, as Suárez-Orozco (2018) and others point out, social–emotional learning (SEL) is a crucial component of the curriculum of any school with ELs and other immigrant students. As Suárez-Orozco states, SEL development is

> *an essential part of pre-K–12 education that can transform schools into places that foster academic excellence, collaboration, and communication, creativity, and innovation, empathy and respect, civic engagement, and other skills and dispositions needed for success in the 21st Century.* (6)

Social–emotional factors become particularly important during times of stress. As we write this edition, many schools across the country are closed to in-classroom teaching because of the COVID-19 pandemic. Schools are struggling to provide on-line education for students, and social inequities are increasingly noticeable. Many ELs do not have access to the internet, and families have neither the devices students need to access online platforms like Google Classroom, nor an understanding of how to use them. These factors from outside the school can have a greater impact on our students than factors within the school.

Further, the current political climate has created an atmosphere in which racist at-titudes and divisions among groups of people have increased. The Black Lives Matter movement has brought renewed attention to the racist policies and practices that affect persons of color. Immigration policies have resulted in the separation of children from their parents. DACA students and other undocumented immigrants live in fear of deportation even when they complete school and find good jobs.

As the number of English learners has increased, schools in many parts of the coun-try cannot find teachers with proper certification to teach them. In states like Cali-fornia and New York, the increase in dual language programs has not been matched by an increase in qualified bilingual teachers. Further, in many schools, rapid changes in the EL school population have made it difficult to develop and maintain effective programs. For example, a school with a large number of Spanish-speaking English learners may establish an effective Spanish–English dual language program and then see the population of English learners in the school community change as Burmese students or Somalis move into the neighborhood in large numbers.

With concerns about the coronavirus, some teachers worry that returning to the classroom is dangerous for their students and for themselves, especially older teach-ers and teachers with underlying health issues. Many teachers have chosen early retirement. Even with the development of vaccines, the possibility of virus spread is likely, given that many people may refuse to be vaccinated or to follow health recommendations.

As a result of all these changes, good and bad, we have decided to update this text in order to provide the latest thinking about language acquisition. Educators should be able to apply current learning theory as well as articulate research and theory on language acquisition, bilingualism, literacy, and academic language. This knowledge enables teachers to teach effectively and to advocate for best practices for both in-class and online teaching with colleagues at their school, as well as with parents and com-munity members.

As we have worked with educators in different states, we have seen many more teachers working to prepare themselves to work effectively with ELs. Teachers in small communities as well as cities in Iowa, Nebraska, Oregon, Alaska, Alabama, North Carolina, Georgia, and Kansas are learning about effective approaches to teaching their multilingual and multicultural students.

While teachers are becoming better informed, misconceptions among the general public about new immigrants and their needs have also grown. Immigrants have been blamed for economic and social ills, and there have been strong movements to limit immigration to the United States. Throughout the country anti-immigrant movements have been a concern for all those teaching second language students. We believe that it is perhaps more important now than ever before for educators to be aware of the many issues affecting the academic performance of immigrant students in our schools so that they can be advocates for all their students.

Certainly, no magic formula will ensure the academic success of any group of learners, and while this book offers examples of theory-based practices that have proved effective with a variety of students, we are aware that each learning situation is different. What works in one classroom may not apply down the hall, much less in another part of the country. We hope, however, that by identifying and discussing the factors that impact students who are learning academic content in their second or third or fourth language, we can help professionals examine their programs and their classroom practices to ensure that they are providing what is best for all their students.

In addition to continuing our own research through our reading and school visits, for this edition we have added a new coauthor, Dr. Mary Soto, who teaches in the teacher education program at California State University East Bay. This university has the most diverse student body of any university in the continental United States. Mary teaches classes for preservice and graduate inservice teachers. In addition, she works with them, observing in schools and discussing their progress with their master teachers. Since Mary works every day with teacher candidates working in classes with English learners, she provides many current examples of the contexts and practices schools are using to teach English learners. Her insights were valuable as we wrote this new edition.

Our Title

The title for this book, *Between Worlds*, reflects our conviction that in providing the best education for English learners, we must understand the different worlds students negotiate. They often move between their native countries and the United States as well as moving between the worlds of their families and communities and the world of school.

In a sense, school is a place that is between worlds for all students. Students entering school are leaving the smaller world of their home and entering the larger world of their community. For English language learners, these two worlds are often very different. In schools, they are often surrounded by other students who speak English and whose experiences have been limited to the mainstream culture and whose attitudes and values have been shaped by mainstream views. Even in schools where the majority of the student body includes linguistically and culturally diverse students, there are few teachers or administrators who share their students' cultural or linguistic backgrounds.

Many ELs who live between worlds never fully enter the mainstream school community, and they are no longer fully part of the home culture. They may be marginalized in schools by the instruction they receive and the attitudes they encounter. In their home communities, they are often in a state of cultural ambivalence, because they are now living in a context that is no longer their home country. They struggle with maintaining their home language as they acquire English, and their home culture's values and customs often clash with those of their new country. Rather than experiencing the best of both worlds, many English learners cannot participate fully in either one.

Students who enter school as monolingual Spanish, Arabic, or Korean speakers often leave school as monolingual English speakers. They may succeed in school but find themselves no longer able to communicate fully with family and friends in the home community. These students often distance themselves from their heritage language and culture in order to become part of the mainstream. They leave behind the world of their heritage and trade that world for another.

The subtitle of our book, *Second Language Acquisition in Changing Times*, is important because, as we have already indicated, there are a number of factors that either support or limit students' access to the acquisition of English in these changing and often chaotic times. However, the subtitle also has another purpose. This book also gives those involved with English language learners access to second language acquisition research theories and examples of classroom practices that promote the acquisition of an additional language.

We hope to bring the research and theories alive for you by providing numerous examples of ways teachers have successfully supported emergent bilinguals. Educators who understand research, theory, and the real needs of their students can provide ELs with access to their new language. With knowledge and understanding, teachers can help students living between worlds to develop the academic English proficiency and academic content knowledge they need to succeed in school.

Terms to Describe Students

We wish to comment on the terminology we use to refer to the students we write about in this book. It is always difficult to choose a descriptive term for any group because the words used may, in fact, label or limit the people in that group (Wink 1993). For example, the label used by the federal government office is *limited English proficient* (or *proficiency*) *students*. This term focuses attention on what students cannot do. All of us have limited (or no) proficiency in a number of languages.

In this introduction, we have referred to students in our schools who do not speak English as their home language as *English learners* or *English language learners*. Another term is *languages other than English (LOTE) speakers*. A commonly used term is *second language learners*. This term makes the point that these students already have another language, and English is an additional language. However, we are aware that many English learners are, in fact, adding a third, fourth, or even fifth language to their repertoire. As a result, some people use the term *multilingual learners (MLLs)*. New York has adopted the term *multilingual learner/English language learner (MLL/ELL)*.

Additional labels used in some parts of the country are *English for speakers of other language (ESOL) students* and *culturally and linguistically diverse (CLD) students*. All of these designations focus on what these students are trying to do—what they have in common—so we use these terms at times. In addition, preschool students who start school speaking a language other than English are referred to as *dual language learners (DLLs)* since they are continuing to develop their home language as they acquire English. This term does not refer to children in dual language programs. In federally funded preschool programs such as Head Start, the language of instruction is English.

The terms *emergent bilinguals* and *experienced bilinguals* (EBs) have been proposed by García (2009). Emergent bilinguals are students who are in the early stages of developing an additional language while experienced bilinguals are those who have developed higher levels of proficiency in an additional language. These terms refer to students who come to school speaking English and are studying in a program that teaches them an additional language as well as students who come to school speaking languages other than English. *Emergent* and *experienced bilinguals* are positive labels that focus on the fact that these students are becoming bilingual and biliterate as they learn the academic content of school subjects.

Undoubtedly, other terms are being used to refer to students who speak languages other than English. We varied our use of these terms as we wrote this book, always being aware that it is important to be cautious about the use of any label. We also sometimes refer to students' *home language* and their *new* or *additional language*. These terms reflect the complex language resources (or linguistic repertoires) that all students develop and are preferable to first and second language. In addition, since the majority of emergent bilinguals are from Spanish-speaking countries, we use the term *Latinx* to refer to them. This newer term was coined to create a more gender-neutral word to refer to both Latinos and Latinas.

Overview of the Chapters in This Book

The six chapters in this book focus on the factors that contribute to the performance of English learners in schools, the characteristics of English learners, theories of second language acquisition, the factors that influence teachers who teach English learners, new views of bilingualism and models that have been developed for teaching English learners, and the issue of how best to provide English learners with an equitable education.

One feature that we have added to this book is a list of key points to serve as an overview for each chapter. We have also added to each chapter invitations for readers to reflect or turn and talk with other readers on sections they have read. Since we believe that learning occurs during social interaction, we encourage you to discuss the reading with others. If you are reading this for a class or as a professional learning community book study, you could use these prompts as you read and discuss the chapters. In other cases you will simply be reading the book for your own professional learning, and we offer these suggestions as a way to reflect as you read each chapter.

The first chapter explains a contextual interaction model that includes factors that influence the education of emergent bilinguals at different levels. We discuss factors at the national, state, and community levels that impact the education of emergent bilinguals in our schools.

Chapter 2 poses the question, Who are our English language learners and what factors affect them? We begin by reviewing different context-free single-cause explanations for the academic performance of ELs. Next we explain the importance of conducting case studies to learn about our emergent bilinguals. We give examples of case studies of several different types of English learners. We conclude by describing five categories of English learners and showing how the different case study students fit one of these categories.

Chapter 3 reviews theories of learning and theories of second language acquisition. We begin with current theories of learning. We review key understandings, including Vygotsky's zone of proximal development (ZPD) and his distinction between spontaneous and scientific concepts. We also explain Goodman and Goodman's description of learning as a tension between invention and convention.

Next, we turn to second language acquisition. We review Cummins' research on the difference between conversational and academic language. We also discuss how linguistic competence includes both grammatical competence and communicative competence. We describe in detail Krashen's monitor model of second language acquisition. We also discuss Swain's theory of comprehensible output. We conclude by outlining Van Lier's model of language acquisition that includes both input and output.

Chapter 4 considers factors that influence how teachers teach. We review legislative changes at the federal and state levels that affect teaching. Next, we explain different orientations toward language that have resulted in different approaches to teaching ELs. We then consider the importance of teachers' attitudes on students' success and how changes are stressful for teachers. We tell Yvonne's story of how one teacher has changed over many years of teaching in response to new research and theory. We conclude by arguing for the importance of teachers taking a principled orientation toward teaching.

We begin Chapter 5 by discussing how widespread bilingualism is in the world. Then we turn to theory and research on educating bilinguals. Changing views of bilingualism have led to changes in bilingual programs. We discuss these changes and explain how teachers can use translanguaging strategies to draw on the home languages of emergent bilinguals as they acquire English and learn academic content knowledge in English. Finally, we discuss the different program models for emergent bilinguals, including ESL and bilingual programs.

Chapter 6 considers ways teachers can provide emergent bilinguals with an equitable education. We begin by distinguishing between equity and equality. Then we explain how schools can take an intercultural orientation and promote equity by providing linguistic and cultural equity as well as equity in materials, in signs and daily routines, in grouping, and in academic language development.

We hope that the information in this book will be useful to teachers, counselors, paraprofessionals, administrators, parents, and others involved in the education of emergent bilinguals. We are convinced that by developing a good understanding of the factors that affect second language acquisition, educators can work with parents and community members to provide an equitable education for all students, especially for the many emergent bilinguals in our schools.

increase of white supremacist groups, including neo-Nazis, anti-Muslim groups, and anti-immigrant groups (Beirich and Buchanan 2018).

The immigrant children in schools have had other reasons to fear beyond acts of racism and hate. Many are constantly worried about deportation. The Deferred Action for Childhood Arrivals (DACA), an American immigration policy that allowed over seven hundred thousand immigrants who were brought to the country as children of undocumented parents to receive a renewable two-year period of deferred action from deportation, was announced by President Barack Obama in June 2012. Although the bipartisan Dream Act allowing those in DACA a path to citizenship was submitted to Congress, it did not pass. Although in 2017 Trump's Attorney General declared the Act unconstitutional and illegal, the Supreme Court blocked this move. In 2021, President Biden is moving to provide Dreamers with a path to citizenship.

Other Trump immigration policies included the deportation of parents and sometimes families who have lived in this country for years without legal status. Many of these deportees have contributed in important ways to their communities. In addition, refugee children were separated from their parents as the families tried to enter the United States. In 2018, three thousand children were separated from their parents, and when the public outcry demanded a stop to the policy, the administration could not find information on many of the children to reunite them. As recently as 2019 *The New Yorker* (Gessen 2019) reported that the administration had continued to separate over 1,500 children and parents without public knowledge. The constant bombardment of this kind of news instills fear in students in schools and creates challenges for teachers trying to support these students' learning.

A clear example of this comes from Francisco's third-grade dual language bilingual classroom. In his classroom students read and write daily and discuss a variety of topics including current events based on what the children see on television and in articles they read together from online sources, including Newsela (https://newsela.com/). Francisco has his students write in journals and create their own stories for books to publish for the class library. His students choose their own topics for their writing. During Spanish language arts time his student Noemi worked on the beginning of a book that clearly showed how the news about parents and children being separated was on her mind. Figures 1–2a, b, c, and d are her unedited drafts describing a girl anxiously awaiting a visit with her parents, who were separated from her at the border when she was a baby.

One day Analiyah was very emotional. She was going to visit her parents after a long separation. Her parents had abandoned her soon after she was recently born. But, don't worry. They didn't abandon her because they didn't love her. They had to leave her because of the immigration officials. Her parents were not from the United States. They were from Mexico. They were packing their things [to take]. Books, clothes, crayons, towels, telephone, paper and more. And most important their passport.

Figure 1–2a–d • Noemi's Story

Gessen wrote, "The Trump Presidency is, in its way, like Halloween, but the R-rated, slasher-movie version: a festival of violence, cruelty, and fear" (2019, 1). Trump's politics built on different fears including immigrants committing crimes in cities, non-Christian groups invading the country, and "most of all, fear of immigrants who take your jobs and disadvantage your children and future hopes" (2). A truly frightening example showing how Trump opposed immigration was the help-build-the-wall activity at a yearly White House Halloween party. Children of White House staff members were invited to add bricks of paper with their names on them on a construction paper wall that represented the border wall built to separate the United States and Mexico and keep out immigrants (Gessen 2019). These actions instill fear in students in schools and make it difficult for teachers to know how to support their students' learning when they are concerned about these issues.

National Context: Educational Mandates

Legal mandates on education at the national level also provide a context that influences the schooling of emergent bilinguals. The Every Student Succeeds Act (ESSA) of 2020 requires that schools test ELs after only a short time in the United States. The act has had the positive effect of drawing attention to the needs of emergent bilinguals. There is a better understanding that every teacher is a teacher of language and content. ESSA replaced the NCLB act, which relied on "scientifically based" research that often resulted in drilling of students on grammar and phonics without giving them instruction in meaningful academic content. However, the new standards of the ESSA are very rigorous, and the testing is difficult even for native English speakers.

National and State Levels: Legal Mandates

In 2016, because of ESSA, programs for English learners were placed in Title I instead of Title III and the emphasis of language instruction educational programs (LIEPs) changed so that programs were directed to help students develop academic language in the content areas to compete with native English speakers. In addition, each state was required to develop language proficiency standards for ELs that included speaking, listening, reading, and writing, and were aligned with the challenging state academic standards (US Department of Education 2016). LIEP also called for instruction to take into account varying proficiency levels of English learners.

The language proficiency standards and the emphasis on effective programs have led to an improvement in instruction of English learners. However, emergent bilinguals are still required to be tested after only one year in schools, too short a time for newcomers to catch up with native English speakers.

REFLECT OR TURN AND TALK

Are you aware of the language proficiency standards for English learners in your state? How is your school or a school you are familiar with working to help emergent bilinguals meet the language proficiency standards? If you are not aware, how can you find out more?

State-Level Legal Mandates

Legal mandates at the state level have also impacted schooling for emergent bilinguals. In 1998, 2000, and 2002, respectively, California, Arizona, and Massachusetts passed laws restricting the use of students' home languages for instruction despite research showing the benefits of home-language instruction for academic success (August and Shanahan 2006). As a result, 40 percent of the English learners in the country were restricted from receiving home-language support in their instruction (Mitchell 2019). In addition, Arizona's Proposition 203 restricted the method of English instruction, requiring four hours of sheltered English immersion (SEI) instruction for English learners, which segregated them from native English speakers. In the last few years, all three states have made major changes in their views of bilinguals and how to educate them.

CALIFORNIA

In 2011, California approved a bill to recognize a State Seal of Biliteracy, marked by a gold seal on students' diplomas or transcripts. The seal recognizes high school graduates who have attained a high level of proficiency in speaking, reading, and writing one or more languages in addition to English (CDE 2020). Currently, thirty-nine states and the District of Columbia offer the seal.

Then in 2016, Californians passed Proposition 58, a bill that allowed California schools to offer multilingual programs to ensure students could become proficient in English and, at the same time, be allowed to learn in other languages. Dual language bilingual programs are on the rise in the state, and the California Department of Education has set goals in the Global California 2030 Initiative of having half of all K–12 students participate in programs leading to proficiency in two or more languages and by 2040 having three in four students reach proficiency (CDE 2019b). The state suggests that schools provide one or more of six types of programs to develop proficiency, including dual language bilingual as the first option.

MASSACHUSETTS

Since the passage of Question 2 in Massachusetts in 2002, which called for all public schoolchildren, with limited exceptions, to be taught all subjects in English and placed in English language classrooms, emergent bilinguals in the state have scored low on standardized tests. Many English learners have performed below grade level and only 64 percent were graduating in four years, compared with 88 percent of native English speakers. Because of the success in other states with dual language education and programs that allowed the use of students' home languages and the popularity across the country of the Seal of Biliteracy, which puts a high value on bilingualism, the state changed its English-only stance. In 2017 the Massachusetts legislature passed a bilingual education bill, Language Opportunity for Our Kids (LOOK), that allows local school districts flexibility in tailoring programs for the more than ninety thousand students who are not fluent in English (Glatter 2017). This has led to high interest in dual language bilingual education and the implementation of new programs.

ARIZONA

After the passage of Arizona's English-only law, Proposition 203, in 2000, academic growth for English learners continually declined. The law required that all emergent bilinguals be segregated for four hours each day for SEI instruction. This practice not only segregated ELs from native English speakers but kept them from receiving important academic content instruction.

By 2008 state officials began to see that states with English-only initiatives had a greater achievement gap than states that did not, and doubts as to the effectiveness of Proposition 203 began to arise, but it wasn't until California passed Proposition 58 and Massachusetts passed the LOOK act that state educators began to look closely at the approach the state was taking for educating emergent bilinguals.

Business leaders, educators, and legislators were influenced by the Seal of Biliteracy movement as they began to see the value of bilingualism. In 2017, Arizona had the lowest graduation rates for English learners in the country. Only 18 percent graduated, compared with 75.7 percent of all other graduates (Sanchez 2017). That was 25 percent below the national average (Mitchell 2019). By 2019 it was clear that attitudes toward teaching English learners had changed, as reflected in a quote from the state superintendent of schools: "Our best examples of teaching English well do so with great respect to, and use of, the native language" (Mitchell 2019, 11). At the time of this writing, HCR 2026, the proposition to repeal Proposition 203, has passed both houses of the Arizona legislature but has not been approved by the voters because it was not on the 2020 ballot.

Research has shown that Spanish speakers, who make up the majority of English learners, succeed academically at higher rates when they are placed in bilingual or dual language programs where they can draw on their home language as they learn English and other academic content subjects. As a result, there has been an increase of these programs available.

REFLECT OR TURN AND TALK

How do you feel about teaching English learners using their home language(s)? How do you respond to the fact that two states have rescinded their English-only stance? How do you think teachers and the community you live in feel about teaching using students' home languages?

However, there are other factors that influence the success of Latinx students in schools. Gándara (2017) points out that Latinx students make up 25 percent of the K–12 school population in the United States, a growth from 8 percent in 1980. This growth is not primarily the result of immigration, but simply of the explosion of the population of Latinx already living in the country. For example, more than 90 percent of Latinx children were born in this country. While two-thirds of the Spanish-speaking Latinx are of Mexican origin, the rest come from a variety of countries, including Puerto Rico, Cuba, the Dominican Republic, and Central and South America.

While most of the Latinx population live in the traditional states of California, Arizona, New York, New Jersey, Illinois, and Texas, there has been a dramatic shift in where they live. In 1980, 1.1 percent lived in the southern states of Alabama, Arkansas, Georgia, North and South Carolina, and Tennessee. By 2015, 12.1 percent lived in those states, changing communities and schools. These states are new to the issues related to these students, and schools are often overwhelmed when they try to meet the needs of an influx of emergent bilinguals. These students "tend to share many demographic characteristics, such as low educational attainment, high rates of poverty, and a longtime presence in the continental United States" (Gándara 2017, 5).

REFLECT OR TURN AND TALK

Is your state a state that has always had many English learners, or is the growth of the emergent bilingual population relatively new? Do you believe your state and your school have responded with support for teachers who work with English learners? What kinds of supports are available?

Family and Community Contexts

Researchers point out that the effects of the community and family contexts lead to academic struggles for Latinx students, by far the largest group of English learners (Gándara and Contreras 2009). Many live in neighborhoods where there is a prevalence of poverty and limited availability of preschools, social services, and recreational facilities. Children in these communities often do not have access to extracurricular school activities either. Evidence suggests that children who participate in high-quality after-school programs spend more time on educational activities and perform better academically (Lauer et al. 2006; Miller 2003). Extracurricular activities, however, are often difficult for English learners to participate in because of the cost, lack of transportation, after-school jobs, or family responsibilities, or simply because they do not feel welcome.

Often Latinx students live in neighborhoods with underperforming schools. Research has shown that "many parents may not have the time or knowledge to evaluate the quality of their children's education" and may not feel empowered to press schools to improve the education of their children (Gándara 2017, 6). In addition, Latinx students and English learners from other ethnic groups are isolated from mainstream society. As a result, they seldom encounter peers who are knowledgeable about opportunities outside their neighborhoods or who go on to postsecondary education.

Both Gándara and Contreras (2009) and Suárez-Orozco and colleagues (2008) are concerned about the segregation that new immigrants and other English learners experience at school. Gándara and Contreras point out that "approximately half of all Latino students in Texas and California attend intensely segregated (90 to 100 percent minority) schools, and more than three-quarters of these schools are also high-poverty schools" (2009, 113).

This applies to all immigrants, including emergent bilinguals. As Suárez-Orozco and colleagues write, "The new segregation tends to be not just about color or race, but about poverty and linguistic isolation—so-called triple segregation" (2008, 89). Within these schools emergent bilinguals generally spend time with other English learners, rarely interacting with native-born students, even those of their same ethnic groups.

Gándara and Contreras and Suárez-Orozco and colleagues discuss how neighborhood schools can be dangerous places for immigrants. Safety, in particular, was an issue cited by both sets of authors. Gándara and Contreras found that 10 percent of Latinx students do not feel safe at school or on their way to school. In describing the schools they studied, Suárez-Orozco and colleagues state that "rather than providing 'fields of opportunity,' all too many were 'fields of endangerment'" (2008, 89). For example, they describe in detail a large, poorly cared-for school in a run-down neighborhood with buildings covered with graffiti announcing the presence of five different gangs. The school has students who are Latinx, Blacks, Asians, Filipinos, Pacific Islanders, Native People, and a few who are white, but the racial groups stay separated. As the authors point out, "when the groups come together, it is usually to fight" (98). A murder suspect was arrested on campus, and on one section of the school grounds an Asian boy was beaten up by a Mexican boy who saw the Asian boy talking to his girlfriend. In another incident, a girl was gang-raped there. No school guards ever watched that part of campus. It is clear that this campus was not a safe place for learning.

IMMIGRATION

Suárez-Orozco and colleagues (2008) investigated factors related to the difficulties of the process of migration for new immigrants, including Latinx but also Asians, and the profound effect that both family separations and then later reunifications have on newcomers. Immigrant children often have to adjust not only to a new language, a new school, and a new country but also to a new family.

For example, our son-in-law Francisco, from El Salvador, was separated from his mother for seven years, from the time he was seven until he was fourteen. While she established a home in the United States, Francisco's grandmother took care of him and his older brother, with only two short visits from his mother. When the time came to move to the United States, Francisco felt he was going to live with a stranger. Francisco's experience is not unusual among immigrant children in our schools.

Immigrant families and communities where they live exert a strong influence on the success or failure of emergent bilinguals in schools. It is critical, then, that the schools be aware of these factors as they plan for programs to meet the needs of their students. It is important for schools to consider how to meet the specific needs of the students in their communities.

School Context

Cortés (1986) points out several factors that should be part of any approach to teaching English learners in schools. Teacher knowledge and skills as well as teacher attitudes impact the school context. Emergent bilinguals have a greater chance for success in a school with adequate numbers of highly qualified teachers with background in second language acquisition, second language teaching, linguistics, and cross-cultural communication. The presence of counselors with training in working with second language students is also essential. School resources, including bilingual libraries and adequate technology access, are important for success as well. As is true in all schools with strong parent involvement, programs that include the parents of culturally and linguistically diverse students result in better outcomes for emergent bilingual students.

REFLECT OR TURN AND TALK

How prepared to work with emergent bilinguals are the teachers, counselors, and administrators in your school or in a school you are familiar with? What resources are available for emergent bilinguals? Are parents of the English learners in the school involved in meaningful ways?

Contextual Interactions in Different Schools

In order to show how the interaction of different factors influences our emergent bilinguals in schools, we describe the factors impacting emergent bilinguals in six schools in different parts of the country. We describe an elementary school, a middle school, a dual language elementary school and a dual language high school, a school district, and an entire state. As we have worked with educators across the country, we have constantly been impressed by how differently English learners are perceived and served. As you read over these scenarios, think about the schools in your area. How are these stories similar to what you have observed? How are they different? What factors are influencing these students, the teachers, and the schools themselves?

Texas Border Elementary School

An elementary school located next to the old town plaza of a border city in Texas is a neighborhood school with a student population of almost all children of Mexican origin. The school is a meeting place for this community, and Spanish is heard everywhere around the school. This area is one of the highest poverty districts in the state. There is constant tension felt in this neighborhood because of continuous gang problems directly across the border, stricter immigration policies leading to deportations of undocumented family members and friends, and the presence of a new migrant detention center a few blocks away.

The school's dedicated teachers, who are themselves bilingual, struggle to help the 71 percent of the student body who are designated as English learners. Some first language support is provided, but the district's philosophy is one of English immersion, so most instruction is delivered through English as a second language or transitional bilingual education (TBE) for newcomers and students not yet proficient in English. Students are exited out of any home language support as soon as possible or taught only in English. Despite the dedication and the good intentions of the staff, students struggle with the state's standardized tests, and 84 percent of the students are identified as at risk of dropping out.

New York City Middle School

An ethnically diverse middle school in Brooklyn, New York, has approximately three hundred students from over twenty-one countries and is a microcosm of the surrounding community, which is predominantly African and Caribbean. Several of the students are refugees from areas of Africa that have experienced the violence of ethnic wars. Many of the students are undocumented and have suffered trauma. The principal of the school reported that thirty of the students are homeless, and many others live in challenging home situations (Ebe and Chapman-Santiago 2016).

Students in the school speak nine different languages in addition to English. The largest numbers are native Spanish, Haitian Creole, and Fulani speakers. Other language groups include French, Arabic, Bengali, Mandinka, Sonike, and Twi. Around one-fourth of the students have been identified as emergent bilinguals. Quite a few of these have also been classified as students with interrupted formal education (SIFE). The school's program for emergent bilinguals was originally a Spanish–English bilingual program, but because the school's population has shifted to include so many diverse languages, the school now has implemented an ESL push-in model where ESL specialists work with content teachers to support ESL students in mainstream classrooms. Teachers in the school realize that their students face many challenges so they "have gotten to know their students well in order to tailor the curriculum to build on the backgrounds, knowledge, and strengths they bring to the classroom" (Ebe and Chapman-Santiago 2016, 58).

Dual Language School in Houston, Texas

Cedar Brook is an elementary dual language bilingual school in a large district in Houston, Texas. The district has forty-seven schools and 35,022 students. Fifty-six percent of the students in the district are economically disadvantaged and 34 percent are emergent bilinguals. The students speak over seventy-two different home languages other than English, but the majority home language of the emergent bilinguals in the district is Spanish.

Because of the large numbers of Spanish speakers, both one-way and two-way dual language programs are offered in several schools. One-way dual language programs are for students from Spanish-speaking backgrounds who come to school speaking Spanish, English, or both with various degrees of proficiency. Two-way dual language programs have an equal number of native English and native Spanish speakers. In both programs, the content is taught in both Spanish and English with the goal of having students become bilingual and biliterate in Spanish and English (Freeman, Freeman, and Mercuri 2018).

At Cedar Brook, almost 79 percent of the students are identified as at risk and 77.3 percent as economically disadvantaged. Of the almost nine hundred students, over 80 percent are served in one of the two dual language programs (one-way or two-way). The dual language programs are helping students at Cedar Brook succeed. The school profile shows that student achievement in 2017 was up 10 percent, student progress increased by 35 percent, and performance gaps were closed by 25 percent. However, the leadership of the school and the central office have changed. In addition, the population in the neighborhood is in constant flux. These kinds of changes influence everything that takes place at Cedar Brook, and the future of the effective dual language programs is not clear.

High School in Chicago Suburbs

Highland Park High School is located in an affluent suburb of Chicago. It is a large high school with a population of over two thousand students. The school population has stayed stable, but the demographics of the school has changed fairly recently with an influx of Latinx students. While the school is still 71 percent white, 26 percent of the present student body is now Latinx.

The district has implemented dual language programs in elementary and middle schools over the past several years, and parents of students in the dual language programs have been eager for their children to continue their studies in two languages into high school. This parental support and the change of demographics have prompted school administrators and faculty to take a hard look at their programs. One of the things they noticed was that although only 3.4 percent of the Latinx students in the school were identified as needing home-language support, many other seemingly English proficient Latinx were not succeeding in school. They could speak and understand English, but they struggled to read and write at grade level, all characteristics of long-term English learners.

The principal of the school advocated to his faculty and the community for a dual language program at the high school to help these students succeed. He pointed out to faculty that the demographic data demonstrated the increase of Spanish-speaking families in their community, and he shared research that showed that dual language is the only program that effectively eliminates the achievement gap for those emergent bilingual learners. To convince the community that dual language was an option, he presented the vision of what twenty-first-century students need in order to be successful in an increasingly globalized, interconnected world (Partnership for 21st Century Learning 2019). The school is only beginning to implement dual language, and the program already has a reputation for high academic rigor, and early results show that all students are succeeding academically (Freeman, Freeman, and Mercuri 2018). However, as with the school in Houston, leadership changes have taken place. The principal who advocated for the dual language program has left. As the contextual interaction model indicates, these changes may affect the program either positively or negatively.

A Large School District in the Midwest

While one expects to find multilingual students from many different countries in metropolitan centers like New York City and Chicago or border states like Texas and California, the Midwest is not usually thought of as a place where one might find lots of diversity. Omaha Public Schools (OPS) defies this assumption. OPS is the largest school district in the state of Nebraska, with over fifty-three thousand students reported in the 2019–2020 year. Of these students, 75 percent were students of color. The English learner population was 9,540 (https://district.ops.org). The English learner population grew 500 percent in the last twenty-three years and makes up almost 18 percent of all the students in the district (Muñiz 2019).

While most emergent bilinguals in the district are US-born, 11 percent of the entire district population is foreign-born and 5 percent are refugees. The majority of emergent bilinguals in schools are Spanish speakers, and the refugee population has grown 123 percent between 2009 and 2019. There are over 120 different languages spoken by students in the district, including Karen, Somali, Nuer, and Nepali. In addition to Nepal and Somalia, refugee students come from places like Bhutan, Ethiopia, Kenya, Myanmar, Sudan, and Thailand (Muñiz 2019). The support system is well developed in the district, and attitudes toward refugees are positive. Muñiz (2019) described refugee students as bringing "enormous strengths to their new classrooms, including extraordinary resilience, high educational aspirations, and diverse cultural backgrounds" (para 1).

The district provides multiple supports for the EL populations and their families. At the district level, EL teacher leaders and teacher trainers, a refugee specialist, and dual language supervisors work together to ensure a coordination of efforts in the sixty-two elementary schools, twelve middle schools, seven high schools, and thirteen alternative programs. To meet student needs there are dual language programs and both elementary and secondary ESL programs.

Closely connected to the ESL program is the Yates Community Center. The Omaha Public Schools is part of the Yates Educational Community Partnership, which helps newcomers adjust to life in Nebraska. The district provides full- and part-time personnel for the center including a student and family advocate, bilingual liaisons, interpreters, and childcare workers. Veronica Hill, the teacher leader based at the center, explains the goals of the center: "We help families to integrate successfully and to mitigate some of the stress, change, and trauma involved in being in a new place so that parents can be happy and successful and they can pass that on to their kids" (Muñiz 2019, para 5). The center provides ESL, citizenship, computer, and sewing courses for refugees in the community. In addition, they connect families with resources within the community to help make their difficult transition to life in this country less stressful.

The district is committed to meeting the needs of its diverse student body. The English learner core beliefs include giving students opportunities to practice and produce academic language, ensure that ELs can participate fully in rigorous lessons and achieve high academic standards." Students' languages and cultures are nurtured, and English language proficiency standards guide the culturally responsive curriculum (https://district.ops.org).

Testing results as well as graduation rates show that this commitment is helping the district's emergent bilingual students reach grade-level proficiency and graduate.

Omaha Public Schools is dedicated to meeting the needs of a linguistically and culturally diverse student body, and the district's advocacy approach to the academic and social needs of students and families has led to success for emergent bilinguals there.

California

We mentioned California earlier, but because this state has the most emergent bilinguals, with 29 percent of all the English learners in the country (Sanchez 2017), it seemed important to give more details about what is being done in the state to try to meet the needs of English learners. As of the spring of 2019, the California State Department of Education reported that a total of 1,195,988 students in California schools were classified as English learners. The number represents 19.3 percent of the total school population for the state. Almost 42 percent of all students in California's very diverse state speak a language other than English at home. While 82 percent of these emergent bilinguals speak Spanish as a first language, there are over sixty-seven home languages reported for students in the schools. Other top-ten languages spoken in schools include Vietnamese (2.21 percent), Mandarin (1.87 percent), Arabic (1.53 percent), Filipino (1.25 percent), Cantonese (1.21 percent), Korean (.81 percent), Punjabi (.77 percent), Russian (.75 percent), and Hmong (.69 percent) (CDE 2019a).

The majority of emergent bilinguals in California, 70.2 percent, are in elementary schools in grades kindergarten through sixth grade, yet the remaining older learners also have important needs to be met. Types of ELs in the state are diverse, including newcomers, long-term English learners, students with interrupted formal schooling, students with disabilities, and gifted students.

In 1998, California voters passed Proposition 277, the English for the Children initiative. This proposition curtailed bilingual education and stipulated English immersion for one year for ELs. However, these mandates did not result in positive academic outcomes for ELs. An increased attention to Common Core State Standards led California to develop an ELA/ELD (English language arts/English language development) framework in 2015 that called for the development of academic language across the subject areas for English learners (CDE 2015).

Two years later the new federal ESSA requirements calling for accountability for all students including emergent bilinguals inspired educators in the state to develop the *California English Learner Roadmap: Strengthening Comprehensive Educational Policies, Programs, and Practices for English Learners* (Hakuta 2018). This document lays out in detail research-based policies, programs, and practices for the states' ELs.

Other important supports for English learners include the passage in 2016 of Proposition 58, the California Education for a Global Economy Initiative, and the Seal of Biliteracy, a multilingual initiative that gives recognition to students who have studied and attained proficiency in two or more languages by high school graduation. Proposition 58, approved by 73.5 percent of California voters, repealed some of the restrictions on bilingual education and provided districts with flexibility in the programs they offer, including dual language bilingual programs.

The *California English Learner Roadmap* (Hakuta 2018) calls on California schools to welcome and respond to the diversity emergent bilinguals bring. The mission of schools should also be "to prepare graduates with the linguistic, academic and social skills and competencies they require for college, career, and civic participation in a global, diverse and multilingual world" (50).

The document lays out four key principles that schools should follow. These principles are research based and promote success for emergent bilinguals everywhere. Principle 1 states that schools should value emergent bilinguals' cultural and linguistic abilities. In addition, schools should value and build strong partnerships with families and communities. Principle 2 calls for schools to provide ELs with meaningful access to the full curriculum and give them the opportunity to develop English and other languages. Principle 3 requires that every level of the school system have both leaders and educators who are knowledgeable of and responsive to the needs of English learners and their communities and that assessments inform instruction and lead to school improvement. Principle 4 expresses the need for a coherent and well-articulated set of practices across grade levels that lead to college and career readiness and participation in a global, multilingual twenty-first-century world.

In "Facts About English Learners in California," the California Department of Education sets goals to ensure that English learners acquire full proficiency in English and attain parity with native speakers of English, and that ELs meet the same grade-level academic standards expected of native speakers (CDE 2019a). The CDE suggests the following programs to meet those goals: dual language immersion programs, transitional developmental programs, or structured English immersion. We provide a detailed description of these programs for emergent bilinguals and others in Chapter 5 on bilingualism. California has laid out detailed information about EBs and developed standards and goals that are critical in a state where there is so much cultural and linguistic diversity and there are so many students that need organized support.

Despite these efforts, the coronavirus pandemic has impacted California schools in unexpected ways. The Californians Together organization conducted a survey of 650 teachers. They concluded that

> the results were sobering. Just 17 percent of respondents reported that most of their ELs were regularly participating in distance learning each week. More than half of the respondents said that the majority of their ELs weren't participating weekly, which could be due at least in part to the fact that ELs' families are disproportionately likely to be marginalized by digital divides and reliable internet connectivity. One-third of survey respondents said their districts hadn't ensured that all ELs had access to the internet this spring for virtual learning through school closures. (Hernandez 2020)

The article provides ten helpful tips for providing effective instruction for ELs, but clearly, as this report shows, ELs in California are falling behind in learning despite the state having made many efforts to improve learning for emergent bilinguals.

REFLECT OR TURN AND TALK

The examples in this chapter are meant to provide a snapshot of the diverse school settings of emergent bilinguals and the programs that serve these students. How are these vignettes similar to what you have observed in your school or in schools you know about? How does California's commitment to ELs compare with your state's commitment? What do you see as differences? What factors in schools in your area are influencing emergent bilinguals, the teachers, and the schools themselves?

Conclusion

The contextual interaction model is dynamic. Societal and educational contexts constantly change as new families enter the community and the school. For example, when we visited the Midwest, educators were talking about the impact large numbers of refugees from Somalia were having on their classrooms. These educators had adjusted for their immigrants from Mexico, but immigrants from another part of the world brought new challenges. Teachers in the Southeast had questions about the growing numbers of Latinx and Hmong students in their schools. There had been some Mexican students in the past, but now their Latinx population was changing, and the Southeast Asians brought new cultural and educational challenges.

Cortés' model is a two-way model. The school context is influenced by the larger social context at different levels, from national to family. It is also important to understand that the social context is impacted by attitudes, knowledge, and skills of the students who graduate and achieve some economic success. Some do return to their neighborhoods, where they serve as role models for students still in schools, but many move away. These immigrants change the mainstream community, but their departure from the neighborhoods where they attended school negatively impacts the immigrant communities. Parents and grandparents often feel abandoned. On the other hand, if educated immigrants return to their communities, they often present a challenge to traditional values.

The children of educated immigrants may feel conflicted because they are not sure of their own values or identities. Suárez-Orozco and colleagues (2008) describe poignantly the feelings of the immigrant Chinese and Haitian parents whose children are succeeding academically but losing some of their Chinese and Haitian roots.

Students' success or failure results from complex interactions of dynamic contexts. No single factor can explain success or failure, but change in any one area may alter the dynamics of the whole system in such a way that success is more or less likely.

2

Who Are Our English Learners and What Factors Affect Them?

The contextual interaction model shows that factors at different levels—the national and state levels, the community and family levels, and the school level—affect EBs. Our focus in this book is primarily on the school context. Teachers do not have control of all the factors in or outside of the school that affect student learning, but it is important for teachers to be aware of these factors. By studying the particular influences that affect their emergent bilinguals, teachers begin to take on new attitudes and are more willing to try new teaching strategies to support their English learners and to build on the strengths they see in their students.

We recognize, then, that the success or failure of a particular student may be more related to

Key Points

- Three single-cause context-free explanations of school failure for English learners have been proposed: genetic inferiority, cultural deficit, and cultural mismatch.

- Case studies can help teachers identify different factors that affect the school performance of emergent bilinguals.

- There are five types of emergent bilinguals: newly arrived with adequate schooling, newly arrived with limited formal schooling (SIFE), long-term English learners, potential long-term ELs, and academically successful students.

what goes on outside the classroom than what goes on inside school. As Stanley and Padilla comment,

> there is no question that English proficiency is essential to educational success, occupational achievement, and socio-economic mobility, but these occur in a sociocultural context. Understanding this context can help to explain educational attainments of ethnic minority students and to provide alternatives that can lead to improved educational outcomes for these students. (1986, 35)

An understanding of the various elements that influence student school performance can help teachers in several ways. First, it can keep teachers from blaming themselves, the curriculum, or student ability if emergent bilinguals are not doing well. Second, when teachers understand the role of external factors, they can begin to work for changes that would benefit their students in areas beyond the classroom. They can do this by working with families and community organizations. Finally, teachers can resist the acceptance of negative stereotypes about minorities, and they can help their students develop positive attitudes toward school and toward themselves. They can do this by discussing with students the various factors that contribute to their academic success or failure, including the negative attitudes others may hold toward them because they are members of culturally and linguistically diverse (CLD) groups. They can become advocates and enlist the support of students, parents, politicians, and community members as they work toward creating positive environments for learning.

Perspectives on Failure

Stanley and Padilla (1986) and Díaz, Moll, and Mehan (1986) point out that there are many generally accepted explanations for CLD group failure that simplify complex issues. These explanations tend to be context free. That is, the explanation is applied to all CLD students who fail, without considering any specifics about the individual students, including their background and experiences in and out of school, factors we discussed in Chapter 1. Context-free explanations, then, are applied to a group of students and assumed to fit all situations and all students in the group. This type of explanation is exactly the opposite of what we discussed as we presented the contextual interaction model. Context-free explanations are also usually single-cause explanations. In other words, they put forward one sole reason for behavior or results and do not consider alternatives.

Cortés (1986) notes that we often attribute success or failure to single causes because we confuse cause and correlation. Just because two things occur together, we cannot conclude that one causes the other. For example, students who speak English as an additional language may have low levels of academic achievement in school, but speaking a second language is not the only factor that causes school failure.

Cortés notes this "tendency to decontextualize explanations" (16). Often, factors such as race, language, or socioeconomic status may contribute to school success or failure, but looking at any one of these factors, or even some combination, out of context may lead to false conclusions. For example, there are numerous examples of successful outcomes for low-income Latinx students who enter school as emergent bilinguals even though others struggle. According to Cortés, the question we need to ask is, "Under what conditions do students with similar socio-cultural characteristics succeed educationally and under what conditions do they perform poorly in school? In other words, within what contexts—educational and societal—do students of similar backgrounds succeed and within what contexts do they do less well?" (17).

Single-Cause Context-Free Explanations

Even though multiple factors contribute to students' school success or failure, many explanations for the low achievement of emergent bilinguals attribute a single-cause context-free. The three most common such explanations are genetic inferiority, cultural deficit, and cultural mismatch. Even though these perspectives have been discredited, some people assume they are the reason for the low performance of English learners. These perspectives are summarized in Figure 2–1.

Single-Cause Context-Free Explanations		
Genetic Inferiority	**Cultural Deficit**	**Cultural Mismatch**
Certain groups fail to do well because they are genetically inferior (single cause) not because of any factors in the environment (context free).	Certain cultural groups fail to do well because their culture is seen as deficient (single cause) not because of any factors in the environment (context free).	Certain cultures fail to achieve because their culture is different from the mainstream culture (single cause) not because of any factors in the environment (context free).

Figure 2–1 • Perspectives on Failure   Adapted from Stanley and Padilla 1986

GENETIC INFERIORITY

A context-free interpretation that was once widely accepted is genetic inferiority. The argument has been that certain ethnic groups do better than others because of genetic factors. Oftentimes the groups labeled as inferior have been the newest immigrants to arrive; so, for example, at one time, the Irish received this label, at another time, the Polish immigrants did, and more recently, the Latinx have. Unfortunately, this view has not entirely disappeared. A Hmong leader who publishes a Hmong-English newspaper described the kinds of calls the paper sometimes receives in an interview:

> Some of the people who called me at my office were terrifying, telling me that American people don't need the Hmong; Hmong people came to America to collect American tax dollars; Hmong people are lazy, just like the Hispanic and African-American people. Hmong people just want to produce babies after babies and they don't want to work. (Yang 1992, 9)

The calls this publisher received reflect a genetic inferiority perspective, which blames a group's genetic makeup for their failure to succeed. It precludes any possibility for change, since hereditary genetic factors are permanent. No consideration is given to Hmong individuals, such as the newspaper publisher, who is obviously succeeding, nor to the factors that affect the Hmong or Latinx or Blacks in society.

REFLECT OR TURN AND TALK

Too often hereditary factors of people from one cultural, ethnic, or linguistic group are blamed for their low academic or economic achievement. What examples of this can you think of? Have you seen evidence of people in schools blaming a certain ethnic group for their own failure?

CULTURAL DEFICIT

Cultural deficit explanations differ from explanations based on genetic inferiority because here the focus is on cultural factors rather than hereditary factors. Comments such as "What did you expect? José is from mañana land" or "You can't trust those people—in their culture, it's OK to cheat" are examples of cultural deficit attitudes. The cultural deficit view is another single-cause context-free explanation of failure.

Student failure is understood to result from a deficient culture, and no other factors are seen as relevant. This view also assumes that the mainstream culture has no deficiencies and that any deviation from mainstream practices represents a cultural deficit that schools should somehow fix.

A field supervisor at a university where we worked wrote an evaluation of a student teacher in which he commended her for working "hard to challenge and reward her pupils, especially those with learning or cultural handicaps." The supervisor's comments revealed that he held a cultural deficit view of the students, many of whom were English language learners. This is a stance that labels certain cultures as flawed and students who come from those cultures as handicapped. The comment on the evaluation sent a negative message to the student teacher about those students and what her expectations for them should be. It also might have kept the student teacher from examining other factors that were affecting her students' school performance.

One way to respond to a cultural deficit interpretation of school performance would be to attempt to change what are regarded as deficient cultural conditions or practices. Parent or family intervention programs are an example. However, we must consider some caveats. Valdés (1996) studied ten Mexican migrant families in depth. She discusses the culture of the families and the concerns she has for intervention programs that are based on a cultural deficit view. Valdés comments:

> It is true that the families were not producing successful schoolchildren. It is true that there were many things they did not know about American schools and American teachers. It is also true that they were poor, and they were struggling to survive. What is not true is that the parents in the study were bad parents, or that they did not know how to parent well, or that they did it poorly. (200)

In her study, Valdés identified many important values that the families passed on to their children, values that should not be lost. She is worried about programs that attempt to "cure" the "problems" that "deprived" students have in order to make them more like the mainstream population.

A context-free interpretation would assume that "fixing" the parents so that they reflected the mainstream culture was the solution. Valdés would call for a more context-specific approach in which the schools and parents would work together to draw on the strengths within the culture and validate the values and abilities children brought to school in order to lead them toward academic success.

What Valdés advocates is acculturation, not assimilation. Cultural assimilation is a process of becoming similar to the mainstream culture by adopting the language, practices, and values of the mainstream. All groups assimilate to some degree to the mainstream culture, since they are immersed in that culture, but rather than give up their own language, customs, and values, it is better for the ethnic group to acculturate. Acculturation involves taking on some attributes of the mainstream culture while still maintaining one's own culture. In the case of language, emergent bilinguals can acquire an additional language and still maintain and develop their home language.

REFLECT OR TURN AND TALK

Often, teachers hear complaints at a school because the parents of immigrant groups do not participate in school events or do not help their children with their school assignments. What might be some reasons for this other than the single-cause solution that their ethnic or cultural group is deficient?

CULTURAL MISMATCH

More recently, rather than speaking of a cultural deficit, some researchers have presented the idea of a cultural mismatch. The word *mismatch* may refer to differences between the language of the home and the school or differences in how cultures typically interact. While the term *cultural mismatch* seems more positive than *cultural deficit*, the underlying assumptions are usually the same. According to the cultural mismatch view, something must be done to change the culture so that it can be more like the mainstream, which is assumed to be superior. As with the previous two perspectives, this viewpoint may be used as a single-cause explanation to account for failure and is often applied in a context-free manner.

If teachers or other school personnel take the view that a cultural mismatch is the cause of students' poor academic performance, they may send the message that something is wrong with the students' culture and stress the importance of the student adopting school norms at the expense of their home language and culture. Loretta, a Mexican American high school administrator, has struggled with how she had to give up so much of her culture to get where she is now. In response to reading about how the denial of the first language at school confuses students about their identity, she wrote:

> In the book, we read about the idea of "language mismatch," where the language at home is different from the language of the school. I understood this concept as what we, my family, called Spanglish. I feel that I fall under this category. My spoken and written English is not as good as I would like it to be, and my Spanish is even poorer. As a Mexican American, I used to feel alienated from both groups of kids. I really did not fit in with the Anglo Americans because we did things differently at our home (for example, we ate with a tortilla instead of using a fork). Also, I did not fit in with the Mexican American students who spoke Spanish and were more traditional in their customs than my family. As a student, I was not proud of my culture because I felt I did not belong to any group. As an adult, I feel I was deprived of my language and of being proud of my culture. Presently, my goal is to become proficient in Spanish.

The most obvious kind of mismatch occurs when students enter school speaking a language other than English. Teachers generally recognize that English learners need to develop a new language to function in school. What is frequently overlooked is that these students may also need to learn new ways to use language. Heath writes, "Not only is there the general expectation that all children will learn to speak English but also the assumption that they have internalized before they start school the norms of language used in academic life" (1986, 148).

Schools require children to use language in certain ways. If children's patterns of language use at home are different in significant ways from the uses at school, children may experience difficulties. Heath (1983) has written extensively about differences between uses of language, or ways with words, between homes and schools. She points out that "for all children, academic success depends less on the specific language they know than on the ways of using language they know" (144). For example, in school students are expected to answer questions that a teacher asks, even when it is obvious to them that the teacher already knows the answer. Outside of school, people seldom ask questions to which they already know the answer.

When children don't know the ways of using language that the school expects, they may fail. However, this does not necessarily imply that home-language use must change. Heath also argues that "the school can promote academic and vocational success for all children, regardless of their first language background, by providing the greatest possible range of oral and written language uses" (1983, 144).

None of the three single-cause explanations of school failure—genetic inferiority, cultural deficit, or cultural mismatch—should be used to explain the school performance of CLD students. All three views have been discredited by research. A better approach is to recognize that school performance depends on the interaction of a number of factors both inside and outside of school.

Case Studies

Teachers who wish to understand the complex interaction of factors that affect the performance of their students can benefit from conducting case studies on emergent bilinguals. These studies help show the different factors that influence the academic performance of second language students. Case studies provide a good starting point for understanding the research, theory, and practice described in this book, and this knowledge can help educators respond in an informed way as they work with their emergent bilinguals.

To provide examples, we present case studies based on real students in a real school setting. Since we have lived in several multilingual communities, some of the case studies reflect our personal experiences with English language learners. Others are based on our observations of schools and our conversations with teachers, students, and parents as we have worked across the country. The remaining case studies were conducted by teachers studying second language acquisition in the graduate education programs at universities where we have taught.

To help our graduate students discover the strengths of their second language students, we have them read about perspectives on failure and discuss second language acquisition (SLA) theory and the importance of students' home languages and cultures. They also study the contextual interaction model and the ways different contexts affect schools and students. Teachers choose one emergent bilingual to work with closely. When teachers take the time to study one student carefully, they gain a new perspective on all their English learners. Desiree, an elementary teacher in one of our classes, wrote:

> *I am now a strong advocate for case studies. It is too bad that a case study is not mandatory for all teachers. A case study forces you to really get to know the children. I know that what I have learned will help to make me a much better teacher.*

Another teacher, Katie, listed exactly how her case study experience would influence her in the future:

- I will expend more effort in getting to know my students personally.
- I will provide individual time for each student as often as possible.
- I will never again assume that "what I hear" is "what they know."
- I will arrange my classroom/curriculum around whole, real, purposeful, meaning-filled experiences.
- I will find, value, and exploit each student's contributions and talents.

While we realize that no two students are alike and that no two students have the same needs, there are commonalities among learners that help us approach our teaching in a more informed way. We include here the case studies of students at different grade levels and with different educational, cultural, and linguistic backgrounds. It is important to be aware of the different forces involved and consider them as we work to provide our students who are between worlds access to SLA and content area knowledge. Our students need both for academic success.

We ask you to compare the students in these case studies with emergent bilinguals with whom you have worked and to think about the differences and similarities in the factors that may have influenced them.

Elena

Five-year-old Elena attended school in a small rural community in the Central Valley of California. She came to the United States when she was five months old with her parents, who were undocumented. For four years her parents were seasonal field laborers, moving often and leaving the children with relatives in Mexico at times, but after both parents got jobs in a canning factory, the family settled down near a large central California city.

Though neither of Elena's parents spoke English, and neither had much formal education, both parents believed that education was very important. They saw school as the hope for their children's future. They made sure to attend school programs in which Elena participated and attended parent conferences with the translator the school provided.

When she entered school Elena had acquired some conversational English and was proficient in Spanish because of her parents and her times living in Mexico. The school she attended had just started a dual language bilingual program where she could learn in both languages. Through the program, Elena learned to read and write in both English and Spanish and was taught academic content in math, science, language arts, and social studies in both Spanish and English as well. When Elena entered middle school, she was bilingual and biliterate. Although there was not a dual language program at her new school, Elena could take advanced Spanish with other students who had been in the dual language program, so she continued with her Spanish literacy development.

In high school, she took Advanced Placement Spanish, which gave her college credit when she entered college. Elena's grades were good, and in high school a Latina counselor encouraged Elena to join clubs and take part in community service projects. She also helped Elena when she applied for college. However, as Elena began to apply for college scholarships, her lack of legal status became a problem.

Because she was undocumented, she was not eligible for federal loans and many scholarships. Elena did not give up. Taking her counselor's advice, she applied for DACA (Deferred Action for Childhood Arrivals) and was given temporary status that allowed her to work. She attended the local community college studying prenursing and supported herself by working. Once she transferred to the local state college, she found a scholarship through one of the community service groups she had worked with, and this support helped her finish college and a nursing program.

When Elena graduated in 2019, she reapplied for DACA status and was given permission to remain in the United States for two more years until the Supreme Court would make a decision about the 660,000 DACA recipients in the United States (Svajlenka 2019). She was hired as a nurse working in a hospital emergency room. When the COVID-19 pandemic hit the state of California in 2020, Elena did not hesitate to volunteer in Sacramento to work with the nearly thirty thousand frontline health-care workers fighting the virus across the country. One report stated, "Despite the daily terrors of becoming infected themselves or infecting family," DACA health-care personnel "equally live in fear that they could lose their right to work and be vulnerable to deportation" (Sager 2020, 1). At the writing of this book, Elena was one of those health-care workers hoping that new immigration legislation might offer a path to citizenship.

Ler Moo

Ler Moo's family came to the United States in 2014 as refugees from Myanmar (formerly Burma). The family is from the largest ethnic minority Karen group and speaks

Sgaw Karen, the language of 70 percent of the Karen people. The Karen are among several ethnic groups in Myanmar that have suffered persecution by the Bamar majority in the country. When the British rule ended in 1948, the new government refused to give ethnic minorities, especially the Rohingya, citizenship status or rights. The Karen are one of the Rohingya ethnic groups, who are considered the most persecuted peoples in the world. The government claims they are terrorists and justifies the violence against them with this claim.

Ler Moo's family escaped the violence and lived several years in a refugee camp on the border of Thailand and Myanmar. In 2014, when he was in preschool, his family, including four other siblings, was resettled in the United States. The family moved to Omaha, Nebraska. His father has worked in a meatpacking plant since that time, and his mother works part-time cleaning houses.

Ler Moo's older brothers and sisters had attended school in the refugee camps, but Ler Moo had been too young for school. Although the education in Thailand was very strict and consisted of rote learning, the older siblings were literate upon arrival and had studied math, cultural history, geography, science, Burmese, and English.

When they arrived from Thailand, the older brothers and sisters spoke English as well as their home language and Burmese. Because of their camp schooling and the cultural norms of being respectful and quiet in adult presence, they were very shy and quiet at first. However, they now are generally doing well both socially and academically (Carpeño and Feldman 2015; Gilhooly 2015). Two received scholarships and were planning to attend Midwest universities.

The school district in Omaha has an excellent program for refugee families and children of the families. They provide ESL classes for adults and other refugee support programs. Teachers in the schools are provided professional development and learn about the culture of different immigrant groups. However, they were not as well prepared for students like Ler Moo as they were for the newly arrived refugees who had received some schooling.

Ler Moo entered school in kindergarten. His spoken English was quite good because he had spoken with his siblings and neighbors before entering school. Even so, entering a US school was a shock. He soon developed feelings that he was neither Burmese nor American. He was lost at school in the beginning, something teachers didn't realize because he seemed to speak English quite well, and his older brothers and sisters had been successful. As a result, Ler Moo lost a lot of important basic education in his first years in the United States. He has just completed elementary school in Omaha and entered middle school. He speaks and understands English well. He communicates with his parents in Sgaw Karen about some household matters and does not read or write in Burmese. Ler Moo is struggling in school. His reading comprehension is low as well as his writing abilities in English. His teachers are concerned about his academic progress.

Osman

Osman is a Muslim refugee who has experienced the violence of war in his home country and racism in the United States. When he entered middle school at age twelve, it was the first formal schooling experience Osman had ever had. He and his mother left Somalia with his uncle and aunt and four cousins when he was five. His father was killed during one of the many clan conflicts within the country.

Osman and his family lived in a refugee camp in Kenya where schooling was extremely limited. At times, children attended classes during the morning, sitting on the ground and repeating lessons after the teacher. However, most of the time in the camps was spent trying to obtain the basic necessities to stay alive. Osman and his cousins stood in line for food and water for many hours. Famines all around the refugee camps often made food scarce.

Osman is one of over a million Somalis who have been displaced since the late 1980s. In 2016 officials estimated around two million people born in Somalia were migrants living abroad (Connor and Krogstad 2016). Many had emigrated to Europe, Canada, and the United States. After a short stay in San Diego, California, Osman's family immigrated to the Minneapolis–St. Paul area, home to the largest number of Somali refugees in the United States. In 2017 it was estimated that over fifty-two thousand Somalis lived in the state of Minnesota (Rao 2019). In 2015, between 140,000 and 150,000 Somalis lived in the United States (Connor and Krogstad 2016). The family, like many Somali refugees, moved to Minnesota because of the availability of jobs and the general welcome given to refugees. Recently, that welcome has cooled because the white communities of the state are feeling that their culture and way of life are threatened by these Muslim refugees from Africa (Herndon 2019).

For Osman and many other refugee children, life in the big city is overwhelming. Moving from a refugee camp where thousands of people slept on the ground with no modern conveniences to a large US city with tall buildings, public transportation, and modern technology has been a shock. For the first time in his life, Osman held a pen and kept his own books in a locker.

The challenges for Osman are daunting. He has to learn English and learn the subject area content at the same time. Although he brought many experiences with him, they do not help him understand the school system and the expectations the system has of him. His family cannot help him much because they also have so many adjustments to make in coming to a new country, looking for jobs, and finding a new home. In addition, they had very limited formal education in Somalia and are trying to learn enough English to survive in the United States.

In addition to struggles in school, Osman finds that the climate and the customs are very different in this new place. The cold is hard for Osman and his family to get used to, and they have to learn how to adapt to dressing, eating, and cooking differently. The religious holidays and customs in his new country are very different from the Muslim traditions Osman was raised with. Stories of communities across the country who do not welcome Somalis and mistrust Muslims concern the Somalis in Minneapolis–St. Paul despite the fact that there is an effort in local schools and the community to understand their refugee populations.

Although Osman worked hard and learned quite a bit of English in his first year in school, he realizes that he is significantly behind his native English-speaking peers. Because he didn't have access to school during his time in the refugee camp, he is behind in all subject areas. Now, in this new country, he often doesn't understand what is being taught. Even though his teachers mean well, they struggle to know how to help these older students who arrive with little to no formal schooling experiences.

Tou

Kathy, a junior high school English teacher, chose Tou, a Hmong student, for a case study because he was typical of other middle school students she had. The population at Kathy's school was approximately 75 percent Latinx, 10 percent Asian, 8 percent Black, and 7 percent Caucasian. Tou, like many of Kathy's students, spoke English well, but he tested substantially below the fiftieth percentile on reading and struggled academically.

Tou attended school in the United States from first grade. At fourteen, Tou was the youngest of seven children in a refugee Hmong family. The family fled from Laos because of war and stayed in a refugee camp in Thailand. When the refugee camps closed in Thailand, the family came to the United States with the hope of finding a better life. His family moved to the largest city in the agricultural valley of California, where Tou was born. Economic and emotional problems, however, kept them from achieving their goals. Tou's father, who was a farmer in Laos, did not speak English, was not literate in Hmong, and did not have any job skills appropriate to his inner-city neighborhood. Most of the families in Tou's neighborhood were low-income families living in run-down apartment complexes.

Tou lived with his father and two of his older brothers, who were married with children. His mother lived with a daughter and her family in another city several hours away. Separation of parents is difficult for any child, but because the Hmong place great value on family unity, Tou was deeply affected because his family stood out as an exception.

Tou was generally an extremely reluctant participant in most class activities. Kathy described his frequent pattern of absences:

> He often would come to school toward the middle of the week and then start his weekend early—kind of a two-day school week, five-day weekend model! When he was there, his antisocial behavior was more obvious, and students began to ask me not to seat them close to Tou.

This behavior eventually led to an emotional conference in which Tou's father, with the help of a Hmong-speaking aide, told of his hopes and dreams, of what America meant to him, and of his aspirations for his children. He told how one older brother had dropped out of high school because of involvement in gang activity and how worried he was that Tou was following the same failed path.

After that conference, Kathy saw that there was a change in Tou's behavior, though not a transformation. "Truthfully, it was old-fashioned parental hovering, teacher monitoring, and weekly progress reports sent home requiring Dad's signature that kept Tou in school the last two months of school." His teachers and father did manage to get him through seventh grade, and he was promoted to eighth, an event Kathy explained as "not lifelong success, exactly, but an achievement nonetheless." However, in eighth grade it became obvious that Tou had become part of a gang. He attended school but was in trouble outside of school. He was eventually transferred to a continuation school.

Maritza

Maritza arrived at the United States border from Honduras at age ten with her seventeen-year-old brother, Roberto. They made the journey from a barrio in San Pedro Sula, in the northeastern part of Honduras. This area has been called by some the murder capital of the world (Ahmed 2019). Local warring gangs were a constant threat to Maritza and her family. Roberto knew that local girls were being raped and murdered, some apprehended on the way home from school and some even taken from school. He and his family were threatened if he didn't join a gang. Although Roberto reported threats to the local police, nothing was done about them, and finally his father told him he should leave and take his sister with him to save their lives and those of his parents.

The journey took them several months and was full of hardships and was often extremely dangerous. In Mexico, they rode the infamous *tren de la muerte* (death train) or *La Bestia* (The Beast) and crossed over into the United States illegally. Their journey is like Enrique's harrowing story of his travels from Honduras to the United States, reported by investigative journalist Sonia Nazario (2014) in the book *Enrique's Journey*. Like Enrique, many people from the Northern Triangle attempt the trip several times before finally making it. Too many never make it. It is estimated that two hundred to three hundred die annually, and many more are seriously injured in their attempts.

Maritza and her brother were apprehended at the border but taken to different detention centers because of their age difference. After several months at the detention center, Maritza was eventually united with her aunt's family in New Jersey right outside of New York City and was enrolled in school there. By this time, Maritza had experienced a great deal of trauma both during her journey and while waiting alone in the detention camp. School officials had no records of her sporadic previous schooling. Because of her age, she was placed in a sixth-grade classroom in a large middle school. The school was nothing like the barrio school she remembered in Honduras. There were several floors and many classrooms in the school, and the students in the school were from many different countries and spoke many languages. She was placed in ESL for two periods of the day and in regular classrooms for the rest of the day.

Maritza started behind academically because of her limited schooling in Honduras. Now, she is overwhelmed by the English-speaking environment, the very different school system, and the academic work she is confronted with. On top of these challenges, she struggles with her home environment, where she feels like a stranger living with her aunt's family and doesn't know where her brother is or when she will see him or the rest of her family again, if ever.

José Luis, Guillermo, and Patricia

We first met teenagers José Luis, Guillermo, and Patricia in 1984, less than a week after they arrived in Tucson, Arizona, from El Salvador. A few days before they flew to Tucson, they had watched as their father, an important military official, was assassinated in front of their home in San Salvador. The three had narrowly escaped being arrested and perhaps even murdered themselves. In fact, sixteen-year-old Guillermo had two bullet wounds in his leg when he arrived in the United States.

Their stepmother in El Salvador distanced herself from the three teens for her own safety and that of a two-year-old daughter, who was their stepsister. José Luis, Guillermo, and Patricia, alone in a country that had suddenly become hostile, sought asylum with their aunt, a fellow doctoral student and friend of ours at the university. Through that connection, we often had the opportunity to spend time with these remarkable teens over the next six years. We have maintained contact up to the present, over thirty-five years later.

Although they had studied English at private bilingual schools in San Salvador, their comprehension of English and their ability to communicate in English were extremely limited when they first arrived. Their aunt, a dedicated academic, was eager to get them into school and working toward school success. She enrolled all three in a local high school almost immediately and admonished them that they must do well in all their subjects. She warned them that there was no time to be wasted, and that she would not tolerate irresponsibility.

The aunt, who had an older, ailing husband, found them an apartment near her and supported the three financially the best she could. They also received some sporadic financial help from aging grandparents in El Salvador. The teenagers were soon almost entirely on their own, trying to cope with a new culture and language. Each handled the situation in a different way.

The oldest at seventeen, José Luis felt responsible for the other two. He also felt somehow at fault for not having saved his father and wrestled with that guilt. He studied day and night, smiling little, and taking almost no time for relaxation. English was a struggle for him, and he spent hours with a dictionary, translating his textbooks and studying for tests. He ignored jokes his classmates made about the fact that he studied all the time. Classes in algebra, calculus, and physics were less linguistically demanding, so he soon concentrated on them as a possible specialization. He graduated from high school with a President's Award for excellent academic scholarship just two years after arriving.

Guillermo responded in a totally different way to his new surroundings. He was the most outgoing of the three. He worked hard to make friends and joined high school clubs almost immediately. He talked to anyone who made an effort to understand him, even when they made fun of his accent, and he soon became involved in school government. His grades were not high, but he studied enough to earn a B-minus average and qualify to attend the university.

Patricia depended more on our family for emotional and personal support at first. At thirteen, she was the youngest of the three and the only female. Her aunt wanted her to be responsible for cooking and cleaning the apartment the three siblings shared, but those responsibilities and the adjustment to the new language and culture were often too much for her. Her brothers seemed to understand. They helped with household chores. She studied and made friends but in some ways was the most affected by the move and the loss of her father. English probably came faster to Patricia than to her brothers. She spent more time with our family, and our two daughters helped introduce her to customs and fads in the United States.

The three teens and their aunt became involved in our church shortly after their escape from El Salvador. The church family was especially important when they applied for asylum in the United States. At that time, refugees from El Salvador had to prove their lives were endangered to be granted asylum. Even though they had newspaper articles about the assassination of their father, it was difficult to establish that the three children were in danger. When the hearing for their asylum was held, church members took time off from work to attend. That show of support impressed the judge and probably was instrumental in his filing a positive report with the federal government.

All three eventually attended the University of Arizona and graduated. José Luis completed a master's degree in engineering and is presently working for the City of Los Angeles. Guillermo studied engineering and international economics as an undergraduate and completed a master's degree in architecture at the University of Southern California. Patricia finished a degree in chemistry and is now living in the San Francisco area, where she works in a supervisory position for a large pharmaceutical firm. They are now all financially secure professionals. The three enjoy traveling in the United States and Europe and have returned to El Salvador several times to visit family and friends. They consider the United States home and probably will not return to El Salvador to live, despite intentions to do so when they first arrived.

REFLECT OR TURN AND TALK

Consider the different case studies we described. Which of the case studies did you find the most intriguing? Why? Describe the factors that influenced and may continue to influence that student.

Types of Students

All the case study students we described were emergent bilinguals. They all had to learn in a new language, and many had to adjust to schooling and to life in a country with different customs. However, there are some important differences in their backgrounds that influenced their chances for academic success in this country. These differences are related to their previous educational experiences and to their life experiences both before and after they began their schooling here. It is important that educators understand the factors that affect the academic performance of emergent bilinguals so that they can best meet their students' needs and help them succeed in school.

Researchers (Custodio and O'Loughlin 2017; Freeman et al. 2016; Freeman and Freeman 2002; Horwitz et al. 2009; Menken and Kleyn 2009; Olsen 2010; Samway, Pease-Alvarez, and Alvarez 2020) have categorized English language learners into different groups depending on their academic backgrounds, language proficiency levels, and experiences.

Many emergent bilinguals were born in the United States or came here at an early age. They often entered school speaking little or no English and were given some support in ESL or bilingual classes. If they are still classified as LEP after six or more years, they are considered long-term English learners (LTELs). Often, LTELs drop out of school because the school system has failed to meet their academic needs.

A second related group are the potential LTELs. These emergent bilinguals have attended school for fewer than six years and are classified as LEP. They started school speaking a language other than English and were not placed in appropriate programs to help them acquire academic English or grade-level content knowledge. As a result, they are in danger of becoming LTELs.

In planning for instruction, teachers should be aware of the major differences among English learners. Figure 2–2 lists some key characteristics of five types of students. In the following sections we describe the characteristics of each group. We also refer to our case students to give readers examples of real students who fit into the various categories.

The first two types of emergent bilinguals are both recent arrivals. There are important differences between these two types of newcomer students. Samway, Pease-Alvarez, and Alvarez (2020) have contrasted in detail the educational experiences among newcomer students. They explain differences between students who were well educated in their home countries and those from rural areas or war-torn countries

Types of English Learners	
Newly Arrived with Adequate Schooling	• recently arrived (less than five years in the country) • typically are in grades two through twelve • received adequate schooling in home country • may have studied some English in their home country • soon catch up academically • may still score low on standardized tests given in English • can be influenced positively or negatively by social and economic factors
Newly Arrived with Limited Formal Schooling or SIFE	• recently arrived (less than five years in the country) • typically are in grades two through twelve • received interrupted or limited schooling in their native country • have limited home language literacy • are below grade level in math • attain poor academic achievement • can be influenced positively or negatively by social and economic factors
Long-Term English Learners	• have been in the country for six or more years • are not reclassified as fluent English speakers • typically are in grades six through twelve • have limited literacy in both native language and English • may get adequate grades but score low on tests • struggle with content classes • often have been retained and are at risk of dropping out • have received inconsistent or subtractive schooling or are *vaivén* (go and come) students
Potential Long-Term English Learners	• have lived in the United States most of their lives • begin their schooling speaking a language other than English • typically are in kindergarten through fifth grade • have parents with low levels of education • have parents who struggle financially, socially, or both

(continues)

(continued)

Types of English Learners	
Academically Successful Emergent Bilinguals	• enter school speaking a home language other than English • receive adequate home language support as they learn English • receive comprehensible ESL (or ELD) instruction through academic content based on standards and organized around themes • receive curriculum organized with language objectives to teach the academic language of English • have strong parental or family support for education • often have strong mentors within and/or outside the schools • often experience a culturally sustaining pedagogy

Figure 2–2 • Types of English Learners

who have had little opportunity for formal education. They also contrast newcomers who are literate in their home languages with students who have limited literacy in their home language or in a language other than their home language. They discuss children who studied English in refugee camps and children educated in Spanish or English or the official language of a country but whose home language is different from the language used in school. For example, children in Mexico may speak an indigenous language, such as Zapotek, at home but may be educated in Spanish at school. Students in Hong Kong often speak Cantonese at home but are taught in Mandarin at school.

Still another distinction for consideration of newcomer education background is the script used in the language they can read and write. Some students may be literate in a language that uses an alphabetic system and a Roman alphabet like Spanish or Portuguese, while others may have developed literacy in a writing system using different characters that may or may not be alphabetic, such as Arabic, Thai, or Japanese. These differences in students' general education level and literacy level affect their school performance.

Recent Arrivals with Adequate Schooling

Newcomers who fall under the category of recent arrivals with adequate schooling have come to the United States within the last five years. When they arrive, these students bring with them the schooling experiences of their native country. They are literate in their first language, and their content knowledge is at grade level. While these students may catch up academically fairly quickly, they still struggle with standardized tests and exit exams because they have not fully developed English, and there may be gaps in their understanding and knowledge because tests are written with the assumption that all students have the background of native English speakers.

Recent arrivals with adequate schooling may or may not adjust well socially. The school and community factors that influence them are extremely important. The economic situation their families find themselves in also makes a difference in whether or not they succeed academically. Looking at the case study example below helps us understand these students and assess their chances for achieving academic success.

JOSÉ LUIS, GUILLERMO, AND PATRICIA

The siblings José Luis, Guillermo, and Patricia fit the description of recent arrivals with adequate schooling. All three teenagers arrived in this country at grade level academically. In fact, because of their private schooling, they were probably more advanced in some subject areas than their English-speaking classmates. In addition, their international travel had given these students life experiences that helped them adjust to a new country and a new school. They had even studied and practiced a little bit of English before arriving in the U.S. While their English ability was not equal to school tasks, they could communicate minimally socially.

Certainly, the three young people suffered trauma as they watched their father's assassination and had to flee as refugees. However, they had academic, community, and social support. Their aunt was a graduate student and understood what was necessary for her niece and nephews to succeed academically. She encouraged them to study hard. Our family was also connected to the university and provided academic support. In fact, David was José Luis' composition teacher when he reached the university. We also provided important social support. Our two daughters, although younger than the three teens, introduced them to US culture and traditions. Because our daughters were younger, their indirect lessons were perhaps less threatening than having to learn from peers. Their church community also was important. These young people never felt alone in a new country.

Recent Arrivals with Limited or Interrupted Formal Schooling

A second type of newcomer emergent bilingual is the recent arrival with limited or interrupted formal schooling. Students in this group are also referred to as students with interrupted formal education (SIFE) because of their inconsistent schooling. These students face all the problems of any new immigrants, but they are much less prepared academically than students like the Salvadorans. When they arrive, they have either had little or no schooling or schooling that was so often interrupted that they are significantly behind their peers in literacy development and academic content knowledge.

Custodio and O'Loughlin (2017) detail the characteristics of SIFE students. Most are overage for their grade-level placement. Many have social–emotional needs as a result of trauma that regular ESL and bilingual programs cannot usually meet. SIFE students often have limited or no literacy in the home language or English. Almost all of them lack grade-level academic content knowledge. In addition, SIFE students may be socially and psychologically isolated from mainstream students. They require specific approaches and materials to help them catch up academically and are in danger of dropping out of school.

Sometimes teachers can tell if a newcomer has had limited formal schooling either by the student's poorly developed handwriting or by the student's inability to do even basic math computation, such as addition or subtraction. Because of their limited experiences in school, they lack basic concepts in the different subject areas and are often at least two to three years below grade level in the content areas.

Limited formal schooling students are faced with the complex task of developing conversational English, becoming literate in English, and gaining the academic knowledge and skills they need to compete with native English speakers. Because they do not have the academic background to draw upon in their home languages, they often struggle with coursework in English and receive low scores on standardized tests. Many also lack an understanding of how schools are organized and how students are expected to act in schools. Further, in most cases, they live in families that struggle economically as they try to adjust to living in a new culture.

OSMAN AND MARITZA

Osman is an example of a limited formal schooling student. He escaped the terrorism of his country at age five and spent the next seven years of his life in refugee camps in Kenya. In Minneapolis–St. Paul his family is struggling to adjust to living in a new country. Osman's academic challenges seem overwhelming. He had no previous schooling and cannot read or write in his home language. He is living in a new country, trying to learn a new language, and also trying to learn school subjects at the middle school level. He is starting school at age twelve. He does not have very much time to develop the academic content knowledge and academic English he will need to graduate from high school in five years. His teachers will need to give him specific kinds of support so that he can learn English and the content he needs, but even with the best instruction, the chances of his succeeding academically are slim.

Other challenges are also daunting. Osman lived in a warm, dry climate; now he is living in a state known for its ten thousand lakes, forests, and snowy winters. While Minneapolis–St. Paul has refugees from many parts of the world, it is a traditional Midwestern US city. Osman has always lived in a Muslim world, and now he needs to adjust to different holidays and customs. He is determined to do well in school, but there are many factors that will make academic success difficult for him.

Maritza is another example of a SIFE student. She suffered trauma in her violent home barrio and in both the trip to the United States and the detention center. Starting school in an urban area of New Jersey was terrifying for her. She didn't speak much English beyond the conversational English she had picked up in the detention center and from her stepbrothers and stepsisters in her aunt's home. She had often missed school in Honduras and when she did attend, the quality of instruction and lack of materials left her behind in content knowledge. Although she reads and writes some Spanish, her abilities in reading, writing, and math are probably at about the second-grade level. School officials placed her in sixth grade because of her age, but she needs a great deal of extra support to catch up academically and to develop English.

Long-Term English Learners

Long-term English learners (LTELs) have been a concern for educators across the country for over twenty years. The 2000 census revealed that over half of the LEP secondary school children were born in the United States (Fix and Capps 2005). This is disturbing because LTELs are students who have been attending school in this country for at least six years and yet are still struggling academically and are still classified as limited English proficient.

Menken and Kleyn (2009) have studied long-term English learners with colleagues in New York City and identified common characteristics of this student population. LTELs are typically found in grades six to twelve, speak different languages, and come from different countries. They are often orally bilingual and speak English like a native speaker, but they have limited literacy skills in English and in their home languages. LTELs perform below grade level in reading and writing and, as a result, struggle with their content area classes. Usually, these students have low grades, often they have been retained at some point, and they are at high risk of dropping out. The needs of these students are different from those of secondary newcomer ELLs, "yet the language programming at the secondary level is typically for new arrivals [because] most educators are unfamiliar with the specialized needs of this population" (Menken and Kleyn 2009, 2).

In 2010 Olsen authored a report about long-term English learners in California. This report, *Reparable Harm*, is referred to in the executive summary as "a wake-up call to California educators and policymakers." Olsen expressed the concern that so many secondary students, despite many years in California schools and "despite being close to the age in which they should be able to graduate, are still not English proficient and have indeed incurred major academic deficits" (2010b, iii). California is the first state to have required schools to identify and track the progress of LTELs and to develop programs designed specifically to meet the needs of this group (Olsen 2012, 2014). Despite increased attention in California in particular, results continue to be dismal. The number of LTELs in California secondary schools grew 20 percentage points, from 344,862 students in 2008–9 to 380,995 in 2015–16 (Chen-Gaddini and Burr 2016).

Researchers have published reports about long-term English learners in other states, including Arizona, Texas, Colorado, and New York (Horwitz et al. 2009; Huang et al. 2016; McNeil et al. 2008; Menken, Kleyn, and Chae 2012). These students are generally misunderstood or overlooked. Reports continue to highlight LTELs because of the growing concern about them. In a report on large urban school districts across the country, Horwitz and her colleagues state:

> Leaders and staff in each district were quick to point out the specialized needs of adolescent, newcomer students, yet they acknowledge that a majority of the students falling through the cracks are long-term ELLs who have been in the system for years. (2009, 29)

A useful summary of research on LTELs has been published by CUNY-NYSIEB and is available online (see Carpenter, Espinet, and Pratt n.d.). This report summarizes a great deal of information on background information on LTELs and specific ways to support them.

TWO CATEGORIES OF LTELS

Menken and Kleyn (2009) and Menken, Kleyn, and Chae (2012) have listed two main types of LTELs: students with inconsistent or subtractive US schooling and *vaivén* (go and come) students.

Students with inconsistent schooling become LTELs for a variety of reasons. Some newcomer emergent bilinguals may be placed in transitional bilingual programs when they first enter schools in the United States. However, as soon as they develop some conversational English, they are mainstreamed. Others are only given ESL classes, often taught traditionally with rote learning and the emphasis on grammar instruction. In states like Arizona, where structured English immersion programs were promoted, emergent bilinguals were separated from other students for four hours each day and drilled in English grammar and phonics. Traditional ESL and English immersion programs are considered subtractive (Valenzuela 1999) because many ELs in these programs often lose their first language as they learn English. In other cases, emergent bilinguals are placed in schools that aren't prepared for their arrival and know too little about their languages and cultures.

The second group that Menken, Kleyn, and Chae discussed is referred to as the *vaivén* transnational students because, as the label indicates when translated from Spanish, they "go and come." *Vaivén* students, though primarily educated in the United States, move back and forth between the United States and their country of origin. Many of these students also fit the category of students with the interrupted formal education designation since their schooling is interrupted as they move back and forth between countries.

Vaivén long-term English learners are students who have had inconsistent schooling because they go between countries frequently during their schooling. Many students in New York, for example, have spent time in Puerto Rico or the Dominican Republic during their years of schooling. These moves involve a change in school systems and languages of instruction. Haitian Creole speakers in Florida and Massachusetts travel between the United States and Haiti. In the Southwest students may travel back and forth to Mexico. As a result of being in different schools with different systems and languages as well as missing school in the transitions, many of these students do not develop grade-level English proficiency or academic content knowledge.

LER MOO

Ler Moo came to the United States when he was in preschool. He had only attended school in the Thai refugee camp in the mornings for one year. When he arrived in the United States, he stayed at home at first and only started school in Omaha in first grade. While his older siblings had had very rote learning in the refugee camp school, they did learn a fair amount of English, they learned to read in their home language, and they had studied the various subject areas. The district made an attempt to welcome the newcomers, and they were supported by other students, teachers, and administrators. Ler Moo's siblings studied hard and by the time they got to high school were doing well in school.

Ler Moo, however, struggled in school. He spoke mainly English at home with his brothers and sisters and only used his home language with his parents to talk about everyday things. He watched a lot of television and soon spoke English without an accent. In school, his teachers assumed that he didn't need any special support because of his ability to speak English, but by third grade it was clear that he was struggling in reading and writing.

Although Ler Moo took part in cultural events held in the community, he never developed his home language literacy and saw himself as more American than Burmese. He didn't completely fit into US culture either. He is an example of a student who is culturally ambivalent. Students like Ler Moo leave teachers with special challenges. Traditional ESL for newcomers is not the program that fits them and bilingual support is not really available.

TOU

Tou is a classic example of a long-term English learner and shares some of the same characteristics of Ler Moo in that he is from a refugee family and started school in the United States at an early age. At the time he entered school there was minimal understanding of the language needs of Hmong students and very little home-language support. In addition, teachers did not understand that Tou needed the same support as newcomers, because he spoke and understood enough English to understand what they were saying. The teachers did not realize that he had developed conversational English proficiency, but he lacked the academic language proficiency that he needed to understand, read, and write about the subjects they were teaching.

Tou had some other challenges too. His family struggled economically, and his parents divorced, causing disruption in the traditional strong family ties. By the time Tou's family arrived in the inner-city neighborhood where Tou lived, Hmong teens were beginning to form gangs in middle and high school and were rivals with other ethnic gangs in the city. These influences and the lack of a specific program to meet the needs of young Hmong students like Tou in school got Tou off to a poor start in school. Each year he fell further and further behind academically.

CARLOS

Carlos is an additional case study who is a good example of a *vaivén* student. He lives near the border between Mexico and Texas. He grew up in Mexico. His mother is a single parent. Carlos began school in Matamoros, Mexico. When he was eight, his mother met a Mexican-origin man who had legal residency in the United States and lived across the border in Brownsville, Texas. When she got pregnant with his baby, he wanted to get married and have the baby born and educated in the United States. Carlos and his mother moved to Brownsville, and Carlos started second grade in Texas.

Since then Carlos has moved back to Matamoros twice to live with relatives. Once he attended school, but the other time he did not. He says he hates schools in the United States and doesn't like his stepfather. Although he tries to impress Mexican friends and relatives with his fluent oral English, he struggles academically in English. At sixteen Carlos is back in Mexico for the third time. He isn't attending school there, and his relatives can't support him in hard economic times. He will probably return to Brownsville soon, but one wonders if he will attend school there or not.

Potential Long-Term English Learners

A fourth group of English language learners are students who are either new arrivals in grades K–1 or elementary-age students who come to school with a home language other than English and who have lived most or all of their lives in the United States. They are best seen as potential long-term English learners who need a great deal of support to achieve academically.

For these students, the kind of support they receive in school is extremely important. For example, if they are placed in a bilingual program, they can build on their home language skills as they learn English. Support from their families is also crucial. If their parents are well educated and financially successful, their chances of adjusting quickly to school in the United States improve.

Both Tou and Ler Moo were potential long-term English learners when they entered school. Neither was provided with strong home-language support because it was not available. A newcomer ESL program where students are taught basic communicative English was not helpful since they already spoke conversational English. Some strong thematically organized programs that provided ELD support in the content areas taught by teachers with ESL or bilingual certification would have provided the education these students needed. In schools where teachers use standards-based curriculum and have both content and language objectives, potential LTELs can become fully English proficient.

Academically Successful Emergent Bilinguals

Emergent bilinguals can succeed when schools provide the kinds of support we listed for Tou and Ler Moo. Well-implemented ESL and bilingual programs are essential for English learners to succeed. Mentors are also important, as are community organizations that support families and their children.

Elena, the DACA student we discussed earlier, was an academically successful emergent bilingual. When Elena entered school in kindergarten, she spoke Spanish and some conversational English. She was provided with bilingual education in a dual language program in her early grades and did well. In middle and high school she thrived. The support of her parents throughout her schooling and her counselor in high school helped her to succeed.

REFLECT OR TURN AND TALK

We have discussed five different kinds of emergent bilinguals and their characteristics: newly arrived students with adequate schooling, limited formal schooling students, long-term English learners, potential long-term English learners, and academically successful emergent bilinguals. Consider examples of these types of English learners that you teach. How would you classify your English learners?

Conclusion

Emergent bilinguals' success or failure results from complex interactions of factors in different contexts. The case study stories here certainly show this. No single factor can explain success or failure, but change in any one area may alter the dynamics of the whole system in such a way that success is more likely.

The contextual interaction model is dynamic, and the perspective on failure affects student outcomes. Educators need to understand their students' needs. Societal and educational contexts constantly change as new families enter the community and the school. For example, when we visited the Midwest, educators were talking about the impact large numbers of refugees from Somalia and Myanmar were having on their classrooms. These educators had adjusted for their immigrants from Mexico, but immigrants from another part of the world brought new challenges. Teachers in the Southeast had questions about the growing numbers of Hmong students in their schools. There had been some Central and South American Latinx in the past, but now Southeast Asians brought new cultural and educational considerations.

There are other examples of the constant change in contexts for English learners. The influx of unaccompanied minors in schools has brought new challenges to some areas. In addition, the largest numbers of emergent bilinguals in this country now are students actually born in this country and coming from homes where the home language is not English. The changes in school contexts require educators to be flexible, especially as new factors, such as the need to incorporate new technologies through distance learning, make language teaching an added challenge.

REFLECT OR TURN AND TALK

Having read about the contextual interaction model, perspectives on failure, and types of learners, what do you see as your greatest challenges as a teacher of emergent bilinguals?

3

How Do People Learn and How Do They Acquire Language?

Key Points

- Learning and language acquisition occur during social interaction in different contexts.

- Vygotsky claims that students learn when instruction is targeted to their zone of proximal development.

- Goodman and Goodman argue that teachers should encourage personal invention in the context of social conventions to promote learning.

- Vygotsky distinguishes between spontaneous concepts acquired through everyday experience and scientific concepts developed in school.

- Cummins distinguishes between academic and conversational language as emergent bilinguals learn a new language.

- Two types of linguistic competence are communicative competence and grammatical competence.

- Krashen's monitor model for language acquisition consists of five hypotheses: the acquisition versus learning, natural order, monitor, input, and affective filter hypotheses.

- Swain has proposed that output plays a key role in second language acquisition.

- Van Lier's model of language acquisition includes both input and output.

Before examining research and theories of language acquisition, in this chapter we consider how people learn generally. The model of learning we present holds that all learning, including language learning, must always be regarded as a social process. This is the view Halliday (1982) developed. He argued that we learn language, we learn through language, and we learn about language. As Halliday explained, children learn language through social interactions. As they learn language, they learn about the world around them by using language. In schools children learn about language as they study language as a subject.

Faltis and Hudelson point out, "Learning and language acquisition overlap to a great extent in the sense that both are social, contextual, and goal-oriented. That is, individuals learn both content and language as they engage with others in a variety of settings to accomplish specific purposes" (1998, 85). While it is generally accepted that children go through a process of creative construction as they form and test hypotheses about academic content subjects and language, the learning they do is always social. According to Faltis and Hudelson, "learning does not happen exclusively inside the heads of learners; it results from social interactions with others that enable learners to participate by drawing on past and present experiences and relating them to the specific context at hand in some meaningful way" (87).

A recent comprehensive review of research on learning by the National Academies of Science, Engineering, and Medicine states, "The committee has taken a sociocultural view of learning" (2018, 22). The authors (the Committee on How People Learn II) draw on the work of Cole and Wertsch, who explain the importance of the work of three theorists, Vygotsky, Luria, and Leontiev, also known as the troika of pioneers in sociocultural, social-historical, or cultural-historical theories of development (Cole 1998; Wertsch 1991). The review of research also relies on the work of John-Steiner and Mahn (1996), who show that social, cultural, and historical contexts define and shape children and their experiences. They explain,

> *The underlying principle in this body of work is that cognitive growth happens because of social interactions in which children and their more advanced peers or adults work jointly to solve problems.* (26)

The research the committee reviews in detail confirms the view that learning occurs in social interaction. This finding is particularly important for teaching and learning languages and should influence how teachers teach language in schools.

REFLECT OR TURN AND TALK

In this section we have described a social view of learning. In what ways does your teaching reflect this view? Share one specific example.

Vygotsky's Social View of Learning

The report of the Committee on How People Learn II is built on the work of Vygotsky and his colleagues. Vygotsky (1962) developed a social theory of learning that included two important concepts: the zone of proximal development (ZPD) and the distinction between spontaneous and scientific concepts.

Zone of Proximal Development

Based on his research, Vygotsky argued that for learning to take place, instruction must occur in a student's zone of proximal development, which he defined as "the distance between the actual developmental level as determined by independent problem solving and the level of potential development as determined through problem solving under adult guidance or in collaboration with more capable peers" (1978, 86). According to Vygotsky, learning results as we interact with someone else, an adult or a more capable peer, in the process of trying to solve a problem. This applies to both learning about the world and acquiring fuller proficiency in one or more languages.

Vygotsky explains that the learner has a certain zone in which the next learning can take place. For example, a student might use the *-ing* forms of verbs to express progressive tense, as in "I studying English." The next area of learning for this student might be to add the auxiliary verb *am* to produce a more conventional sentence: "I am studying English." The teacher, recognizing a teachable moment, could point out the correct form, and this could help the student begin to use the auxiliary. However, until the student begins to use the *-ing* form, attempts to have them add the auxiliary are usually not effective. Students might also notice auxiliaries as they interact with more proficient English speakers and then incorporate them into their speech and writing. A student who already uses auxiliaries would not benefit from instruction on this topic, and a student who is just beginning to study English and uses only simple present tense, such as, "I study English," would not be ready to add the auxiliary because it would be beyond the student's learning zone. The ZPD refers to the area that is just beyond what the student can currently do. Good teachers try to aim instruction at this zone by building background and scaffolding instruction. They also plan regular pair and small-group work so students can learn from one another.

Another way to think about the ZPD is to consider two students who both score 60 percent on a math test. This score would represent their independent level. A teacher might work with both students and then retest them. One student's score might rise to 70 percent while the other student might get an 80 on the second test. This would suggest that the two students had different zones of proximal development. One was ready to take a big leap with a little help, while the other could make only a modest gain.

Yvonne remembers her statistics class as a graduate student. She had a math phobia and a weak background in math in general. The textbook was way beyond her zone of proximal development. The instructor was good and helped her understand through class lectures, but it was when she was part of a study group that she was able to understand enough to pass the statistics exams. She did not excel, but that social interaction with her peers moved her into her zone, which was enough to allow her to understand the basics and pass the course.

REFLECT OR TURN AND TALK

Vygotsky's concept of a zone of proximal development is widely accepted and forms the basis for scaffolded instruction. Sometimes students already know what is being taught and are not pushed into that zone of new learning and sometimes the instruction even with scaffolding is far beyond someone's zone of proximal development. Think of a specific example of a time when your own learning occurred in your ZPD because of the support you received and one example of when the instruction you received was either in your zone of independent learning (you could do it on your own and the instruction was not useful) or was beyond your zone. Share your examples and try to observe how the ZPD works in your class or in your life more generally.

Personal Invention and Social Convention

Central to the concept of the zone of proximal development is the view of learning as a process of internalizing social experience. Vygotsky emphasized the role of social forces working on the individual. Goodman and Goodman, however, argue that "language [and other aspects of learning are] as much personal invention as social convention" (1990, 231). The Goodmans present a view of learning that recognizes both the effects of social forces and the efforts of individual learners: "Human learners are not passively manipulated by their social experiences; they are actively seeking sense in the world" (231). Social interaction is crucial. Individuals present their personal inventions to others, who provide feedback the learners can use to make their inventions conform, to a greater or lesser degree, with social conventions.

We see this process occur when young children begin to write and invent spellings for the words they use. Over time, if teachers and peers respond to the messages they are attempting to express and if children are exposed to lots of print, their spellings change, moving steadily toward conventional usage. The key is to achieve a balance between the two forces of invention and convention. The Goodmans compare invention and convention with the centripetal and centrifugal forces that keep a satellite revolving around Earth. Both forces are needed to keep the satellite in orbit. In the same way, in classrooms, if students are allowed to write any way they wish, they may produce spellings no one can read. On the other hand, if teachers insist on correct spelling, some students may choose not to write at all.

Helen was able to help her student Magdalena shape her personal inventions to move toward social conventions by engaging her in a writing workshop and being sure she was exposed to lots of reading. Helen wrote:

> *At the beginning of the year, Magdalena was not concerned if her work was readable or followed any of the conventions of standard English. She knew she was putting down her thoughts and ideas, and that was what I emphasized to her. I felt confident that her spelling and grammar would come along if she felt more comfortable in class, was allowed to write in a writer's workshop environment, and was exposed to more texts during reading times. I decided to follow my instincts and only focus on one area with Magdalena. I wanted her to understand that writing is a process and that her misspellings were normal for a child who knew two languages. Recently, she started asking more questions about sentence structures and about the "right way" to spell. During a conference time with her group, she and I worked together to pick out the types of words she seemed to misspell or misuse most often. Then we problem solved the reasons why these words might cause her grief when writing. Most of the words we found were words she could spell correctly when she reread her writing.*

Helen encouraged Magdalena to invent spellings to get her ideas down on paper. At first, Magdalena was not concerned with correct spellings. However, in the context of a writing workshop and rich reading experiences, Magdalena wanted her teacher and other students to be able to read what she had written, so she started to ask her teacher how to spell words. Helen helped Magdalena develop strategies that allowed this English learner to make her writing more conventional. If Helen had insisted on correct spelling from the beginning, Magdalena probably would not have developed the confidence to write. Helen took her cue from her student and helped her focus on spelling once Magdalena had produced writing she wanted others to read. By taking this approach, Helen provided instruction in Magdalena's ZPD.

When emergent bilinguals first try to communicate in their new language, they often invent structures or words based on what they know about the language. For example, many students learning Spanish use *Yo gusto* instead of the irregular, conventional form, *Me gusta*, for "I like." Since other verbs add *o* to form the first-person singular, they invent forms like *Yo gusto*. As they interact with more proficient speakers, they begin to notice the conventional form, *Me gusta*, and then they modify their personal invention to conform to the conventional Spanish form.

Selinker (1972) explains that in the process of acquiring a language, learners go through several gradual approximations that move them from their home language to their new language through a series of what he calls interlanguages. These interlanguages are their personal inventions. Over time, these inventions come closer to the conventional forms of the language they are acquiring.

REFLECT OR TURN AND TALK

Think of an example in your own language learning or your students' oral or written language development in which the personal inventions gradually approximated the social convention. Share your example.

Spontaneous and Scientific Concepts

A second important theoretical construct that Vygotsky developed was the distinction between spontaneous and scientific concepts. Spontaneous concepts are ideas we develop fairly directly from everyday experience. For example, we know what *car* means if we live in a society in which people drive cars. We develop the concept for *car* by riding in cars and seeing cars. The word *car* becomes a label we can use to talk about this concept. We acquire spontaneous concepts without any special help. They are simply part of our daily lives.

Scientific concepts, on the other hand, are abstract ideas that societies use to organize and categorize experiences. The concept of *transportation*, for example, is a scientific concept. We use this term to categorize a number of different means of conveyance, whether the mode be a car, a bus, a boat, or an airplane. Children do not acquire scientific concepts from exposure to everyday events. Most often, they learn them in school.

The ideas of spontaneous and scientific concepts are important in two ways when we apply them to language learning. Krashen (1982) makes an important distinction between acquiring a language and learning one. He argues that we acquire a language in the course of daily living and without much conscious awareness of the process itself. We acquire both spontaneous concepts and the language we need to communicate them. On the other hand, if we study a language in school, we usually learn scientific concepts, such as *verb* and *present tense*, which we can use to categorize aspects of the language. As Krashen points out, acquisition allows us to use language to communicate, while learning gives us abstract terms, the scientific language and concepts to talk about language.

Similarly, Cummins (2000) makes a distinction between conversational language and academic language. Conversational language is what we use to communicate spontaneous concepts and talk about daily events. In contrast, academic language involves the use of terms and language forms we use to communicate scientific concepts that we study in school. This distinction is important for teachers working with emergent bilinguals. As Cummins points out, students may appear to have developed a high level of basic English communicative proficiency but still struggle with grade-level academic work. This is because they have not yet acquired the scientific concepts and language needed in school even though they can communicate in English with teachers and other students. What they need is greater exposure to the academic register, both oral and written, that occurs as students read, write, and discuss school subjects. They can acquire the concepts and the vocabulary used in academic language in school in the same way they acquire conversational language outside school settings.

Suárez-Orozco and Marks explain that less-developed academic English proficiency "can mask the actual knowledge and skills of immigrant second language learners (SLLs), which they are unable to express and demonstrate" (2016, 114). They go on to explain that even when they seem to be able to participate, students whose English is just developing often read more slowly and struggle with the "language and cultural knowledge native-born middle-class students" have (114). Emergent bilinguals who lack academic language have lower standardized test scores, get lower GPAs, repeat grades more often, and generally have lower graduation rates. Suárez-Orozco reports: "Scholarly research has shown a high correlation between proficiency in academic language skills and academic achievement" (2018, 6).

Language Acquisition

As students develop their first and additional languages, they develop different types and levels of language. It is helpful to consider the main types of competence needed to communicate in settings in and out of schools.

Grammatical Competence

Grammatical competence is knowledge of a language that allows us to get and give information about the world. Linguists use the term *grammatical* to refer to an ability to use the grammatical forms and structures of a language to communicate. It does not refer to consciously knowing the scientific language of forms and structures or to what most educators mean when they teach grammar in English classes. We can communicate in a language without knowing that the word is a noun or whether a sentence is declarative or interrogative.

Instead, grammatical competence allows us to say, "Today is Monday," or "The man chased the dog." Linguists such as Chomsky have described grammatical competence. They include the following areas when they discuss grammatical competence: (1) phonology, (2) morphology, (3) syntax, and (4) semantics.

Phonology refers to the sound system of a language. Each language consists of a set of sounds (phonemes) that speakers use to indicate differences in meaning among words. Developing grammatical competence involves learning which sounds in a language make a difference in meaning and being able to distinguish and produce those sounds. So, for example, native speakers of English can recognize the difference in meaning between *cat* and *hat* because of the difference in the phonemes represented by the letters *c* and *h*. Phonology also includes other areas, such as intonation and stress.

Morphology is our knowledge of the structure of words. It involves knowing which prefixes or suffixes can be added to a root or base form. We add *-ed* to some verbs to make them past tense, for example. English morphology is fairly simple compared with that of other languages. English relies more on the order of the words (the syntax) than on prefixes and suffixes. Languages such as Turkish, on the other hand, have complex morphology, but there are fewer restrictions on the order of the words.

Syntax is the area most linguists working in English have focused on, since English relies heavily on the order of words to convey meanings. We know that there is a big difference between "The man chased the dog" and "The dog chased the man." This difference in meaning depends on the order of the words. Syntax is a study of the acquired rules that native speakers use to combine words into sentences.

Semantics is a fourth aspect of grammatical competence. Semantics has to do with word meanings. If we know English, we know that *dog* refers to a particular kind of animal, and *cat* refers to a different kind of animal. Meanings can be complex. Both *dog* and *cat* can have secondary meanings. You can dog it at work, and someone can be catty.

Semantics also has to do with the knowledge of words that commonly go together or collocate. Words like *dog* and *cat* are usually associated with other words referring to animals that are pets. Words like *boat* might be connected with *water* and *lake*. We organize concepts into categories and use different terms to refer to more general or more specific ideas within the categories. *Cook* is a general term and *bake* and *roast* are more specific. The three words are in the same semantic field. Grammatical competence involves a knowledge of how such fields are organized.

This is a very brief overview of some of the aspects of grammatical competence. We simply want to give you some idea of the kinds of knowledge speakers acquire as they develop proficiency in a language. In order to get and give basic information, speakers need phonological, morphological, syntactic, and semantic knowledge. That's what we all acquire as we develop our home language, and it's what English learners need to develop as they acquire English. Grammatical competence allows us to talk about the world, but we need more than grammatical competence to function effectively in a new language.

Communicative Competence

A second kind of competence that language learners need to function in a new language and culture is communicative competence. Hymes (1970) defines communicative competence as knowing what to say to whom, when, and in what circumstances. Linguists often refer to this as pragmatics. Acquiring a language, then, involves more than developing grammatical competence. Learners must also develop the knowledge of how to use the language appropriately in different contexts. The norms for communicative competence vary from one linguistic and sociocultural group to another and from one context to another, and part of what we acquire when we acquire a language is the ability to function effectively in different settings. Often, second language learners have developed grammatical competence but still lack communicative competence.

We became more aware of the importance of helping students develop communicative competence while living in Venezuela. Both of us speak Spanish well enough to communicate (we have grammatical competence), but at times we found ourselves lacking in communicative competence. For example, in Mérida there is a very popular bakery where many people go to get fresh breads, rolls, and pastries. At certain times of the day, the long counter of the bakery is crowded with people two or three rows deep. We found ourselves avoiding these busy times because we had trouble getting the attention of the clerks. The orderly rules for taking turns that apply in the United States didn't apply at this bakery.

On one occasion Yvonne waited helplessly for twenty minutes as people came, called out their orders to the clerks, and left with their purchases. Finally, a man noticed how long she had been standing there, and he called to the clerk to help the *señora*. Yvonne knew what words to use—she could understand the Spanish—but she simply could not call out her order like all the Venezuelans who preceded her. She didn't want to appear rude, but what is interpreted as overly aggressive behavior in one country may be the norm in another. Yvonne lacked the communicative competence needed to buy bread in that situation.

Communicative competence is the ability to say the right thing in different social situations. This is hard enough in one's home language and developing communicative competence in a new language is even more difficult. A professor friend of ours from Venezuela came to study with us in California. We took trips with her along the coast and to Yosemite with the dean of our graduate school and his wife. Both the dean and his wife are very religious people and also very proper. Even though the car trips were contexts for casual conversation, we maintained a fairly formal style of speech.

Our Venezuelan friend spoke excellent English, but she had not yet acquired some of the nuances needed for effective communication. As we drove into Yosemite National Park, she was very impressed with the views and continually exclaimed, "Oh, my God! That's so beautiful!" In Spanish, *Dios mío* (my God) is a very common expression that carries little emotional impact, but in English it is a much stronger expression and one we would not have used with the dean and his wife. Coming from this sophisticated professor in that company, the words sounded completely inappropriate. In other settings with other people, there would be nothing unusual about her words. One of the problems for second language learners is that teachers will seldom explain sociolinguistic gaffes. Instead, they respond to the inappropriate behavior as a discipline problem or ignore it because they do not know how to explain it. However, students benefit when teachers recognize their actual intent and help them develop the communicative competence they lack instead of disciplining them for poor behavior or ignoring these gaffes.

Johnson (1995) points out that one specific social context in which our students need to function is the classroom. Classrooms have very clear (if typically unstated) rules that govern topics for conversation and writing and roles for participants in communicative exchanges. What students need, according to Johnson, is classroom communicative competence, which she defines as "the knowledge and competencies that second language students need in order to participate in, learn from, and acquire a second language in the classroom" (160). Teachers can help students acquire a new language by making the rules for classroom interactions explicit.

For example, communicative competence involves learning how to enter a conversation or to end one. In our home language, we have acquired the rules for contributing to an ongoing discussion. However, English language learners often have trouble knowing when to add to a classroom discussion. They may jump in at what seems to be an inappropriate time, or they may remain silent, even when called on. Classroom discussions may be particularly difficult if students have had previous schooling in other countries where the unwritten rules for discussion were quite different from the rules in their new country. Teachers can help students by setting some guidelines for classroom conversations and small-group discussions. We have seen teachers do this effectively when they organize literature studies or guided reading or writing instruction. The point is that teachers need to teach communicative competence explicitly by explaining the norms for classroom communication.

Communicative competence is often thought of as the knowledge to use oral language in ways that are appropriate to different social settings. However, communicative competence includes the ability to use language effectively in any mode. School content areas have both oral and written language norms. In general, the spoken (or signed) and written language have properties of academic language (Schleppegrell 2004). This register is more formal and abstract. In addition, academic language varies from one subject to another. A book report in language arts and a science report are organized differently and use a different style and vocabulary (Freeman and Freeman 2009).

REFLECT OR TURN AND TALK

Think of a time you or one of your emergent bilingual student's communicative competence did not match their grammatical competence. In other words, a time when they said or wrote something using conventional language in the wrong context. Share your example.

Competence and Performance

Another distinction that is important for determining an emergent bilingual's language proficiency in school is the difference between competence and performance. As Chomsky (1975) explains, competence in a language is how well a person can communicate in that language under the best conditions. Our competence represents a kind of idealized best ability. In contrast, our performance represents how well we use language in a particular situation. As we all know, our performance seldom matches our competence. In most situations, we don't perform up to our full ability. We may be nervous, tired, bored, or simply careless.

The concept of competence is important for teachers trying to determine how proficient a student is. We should remember that a student's actual performance may not fully show their underlying competence. For example, ten-year-old Alfredo, educated in both Mexico and the United States, understands, speaks, reads, and writes English well despite having an accent. When he arrived at a new school, his teacher first tried to engage him in friendly conversation and then called on him to answer questions. He responded haltingly because he was nervous and was unaccustomed to the informal classroom atmosphere. Based on his performance, his teacher assumed Alfredo understood and spoke very little English. Actually, Alfredo's competence in English was much greater than his performance suggested.

Competence and Correctness

People acquire competence in one or more languages, but their ability to produce and comprehend a language or languages is not the same as their ability to use conventional or standard forms of the languages. The competence we are describing is not the kind of conscious knowledge usually associated with school grammar lessons. It is not the ability to put commas in the right places or to use *different from* rather than *different than*. Those are matters of usage and are typically associated with standard written language and are generally acquired when students receive feedback on their language use during class discussions and in the editing stage of process writing. The feedback is most effective when it is presented as a way to communicate important ideas more effectively. Many teachers do this through minilessons on particular points that several students may be having trouble with, such as writing complete sentences or avoiding run-on sentences.

Competence and Learner Strategies

Teachers can also encourage individual language learners to use some specific strategies to communicate in their new language. In order to acquire a language, students need to use it, so these strategies are designed to engage language learners who might otherwise remain passive and unengaged. Canale and Swain refer to this as helping students develop strategic competence, which they define as "the verbal and nonverbal communication strategies that may be called into action to compensate for breakdowns in communication due to performance variables or due to insufficient competence" (1980, 30). Teachers can help English learners acquire English by making them aware of these strategies and encouraging their use. As long as English learners are active participants in classroom discussions and small-group activities, they will continue to acquire grammatical and communicative competence.

There are several learner strategies students can use. One is to use nonverbal strategies, a kind of charade, such as spreading your hands apart to indicate "big." Students can also use different verbal strategies to express meanings. One strategy is to make up (coin) a word to describe something in hopes that the person they are talking to will supply the target-language word. Wells and Chang-Wells (1992) recorded a conversation in which Marilda employed this strategy by coining the word *windfinder* for *weather vane*. A teacher we work with reported that one of her English language learners asked if she could use the "pencil fixer." The teacher realized her student needed to use the pencil sharpener.

Language learners may also paraphrase, using a word or phrase that they hope is equivalent to the word they lack. When Christa, a student teacher, interviewed Moua for her case study, the Hmong student explained that his dad "puts in wind makers . . . cold wind makers" for a living. After a bit of probing, Christa figured out that Moua's father installs air conditioners. By using paraphrase, Moua was able to get his message across. Another teacher wrote about how her student used paraphrase. A small group of students was reading a book about what some children gave their mother for her birthday. The text did not name the gift, but the last page contained a colorful picture of a flower vase. One of the boys in the reading group asked, "What is that thing that you use to put flowers into?" This paraphrase allowed the teacher to help him find the word he wanted.

In addition to using paraphrase for specific words, an English learner may use a literal translation and apply the structure of their home language to their new language. For example, in Spanish adjectives usually follow nouns while in English adjectives generally precede nouns. As a result, a Spanish speaker may use a structure such as "a car red" rather than the standard English form, "a red car." However, over time with exposure to English, most emergent bilinguals acquire the conventional English syntax.

If a person is studying a language related to their native language, a good strategy is to use cognates. English and Spanish, for example, have many words in common derived from Latin roots. For instance, the Spanish noun *parque* is a cognate for *park* in English. Emergent bilinguals can access cognates when they come across an unknown word during reading, if they stop to think whether it looks or sounds like a word they know in their native language. This is especially helpful in science, since for many scientific terms, such as *ecology* and *photosynthesis*, the English and Spanish are spelled almost the same. However, cognates also exist in other content areas, like social studies, where words like *government* and *contract* are very similar in the two languages.

Teachers can find an extensive list of cognates at the Colorín Colorado website, www.colorincolorado.org.

A very common strategy that many second language learners use is to assume that the language they are learning is completely regular. Children use this strategy naturally as they acquire their home language. They overgeneralize a rule and apply it to a word that does not follow the pattern. For example, English-speaking children at a certain stage will often use a past-tense form like *goed* because they assume that all verbs form the past tense the same way. English learners use the same strategy. Moua used the word *becomed* as he talked with Christa. He also used *golds* for the plural of gold, overgeneralizing the rule for forming plurals. Even though the forms may not be correct, they enable the English learner to communicate.

A more direct strategy many students develop is to simply ask, "How do you say . . . ?" In fact, this is a handy phrase that most teachers give their students early in a language course. This strategy works very well in a language class in which the teacher is bilingual. It doesn't work as well in a setting in which the teacher and the other students don't speak both languages. If a Spanish speaker asks, "How do you say *pensar* in English?" someone needs to be able to translate *pensar* from Spanish to English in order to answer the question. This is more difficult with less common languages, such as Basque. The other problem with using this strategy too much is that it interrupts the flow of conversation more than the other strategies we have described, and students may come to rely too heavily on this one strategy rather than use a variety of strategies.

One strategy language learners often adopt, avoidance, is not productive. When specific strategies fail, language learners may simply avoid using a word, structure, or topic. For example, they may avoid a topic because they don't feel competent to talk about it in the target language, or they may stop in the middle of an explanation or story because the linguistic demands are simply too great. For this reason, the key is for teachers to scaffold language instruction to ensure students stay engaged. Students cannot acquire a language if they avoid communicating in that language.

Fillmore (1991, as cited in Grosjean 2010) reports that the successful second language learners she studied relied on three strategies in using their new language:

> *(1) Join a group and act as if you know what is going on, even if you don't; (2) give the impression, with a few well-chosen words, that you can speak the language; and, (3) count on your friends for help.* (187)

By using these three general strategies, the good language learners were more fully involved in using the new language, and, in the process, they acquired the language.

REFLECT OR TURN AND TALK

What strategies have you used to communicate in a language you were acquiring? What strategies do your emergent bilinguals use?

First and Second Language Acquisition: Becoming Bilingual

Nearly all humans develop a home language, and many develop additional languages. This raises the question of whether second language acquisition is different in some fundamental way from first language acquisition. For example, some researchers have argued that a first language is *acquired*, that is, it is picked up naturally without instruction, but second languages must be learned in the same way we learn history or biology. However, other researchers claim that humans can acquire multiple languages, and the number of bi- and multilingual people in the world suggests that people can acquire more than one language. Baker writes, "Children are born ready to become bilinguals, trilinguals, multilinguals" (2006, 116).

Simultaneous and Sequential Bilingualism

Baker (2006) distinguishes between two types of childhood bilingualism. When a child acquires two languages at the same time from birth or early childhood, this is referred to as simultaneous childhood bilingualism or infant bilingualism. Wang and other researchers have come to refer to this process as multilingual first language acquisition (Wang 2015).

Researchers have noticed differences between language acquisition in young children up to about age five and acquisition in older learners. Studies have shown that brain lateralization occurs at about age five (Brown 2007). These first five years are seen as the optimal period for the acquisition of one or more languages. Wang states: "It seems that the peak of language acquisition begins shortly before the age of 2 years, and the gradual decline sets in before the age of 5" (2015, 115). This period, which other researchers often extend to about age twelve, is often referred to as a critical or sensitive period for language acquisition.

A more common scenario is sequential bilingualism, when children learn one language at home and then another language in preschool or elementary school. Studies of individual bilinguals show that the process of second language acquisition is like first language acquisition. The keys to acquiring a second language are regular contact with people who speak another language and a need to communicate with them. When those conditions are met, people acquire additional languages.

Older language learners can attain high levels of proficiency in one or more languages, so the idea of a biological period may be less important than the quality and quantity of input in an additional language. There is no clear evidence that the process of acquiring additional languages is different from the process of the initial language acquisition. The factors that help account for acquisition are both social and biological. Language develops in response to a need to communicate, and humans seem to have an ability to acquire additional languages when they have a need and interact with users of the other language or languages, including oral or signed and written.

As emergent bilinguals begin school, the kind of input they receive changes. They continue to interact with parents, community members, and peers at school in their home language(s). However, at the same time, they interact with teachers and other adults who may use not only a different language, English, but also different registers of language including the academic registers of the various subject areas. In this process, they also develop the scientific language of the disciplines.

As English learners get older, they may suffer some attrition of their home language. These students who enter school speaking a language other than English may leave school speaking primarily English. The long-term English learners we described in Chapter 2 fall into this category. This occurs as students spend more time communicating in the new language and less time communicating in the home language. In addition, if society values English more than the home language, LTELs often avoid using the home language.

Some older students may reach a stage at which they have developed enough proficiency in English that they hit a sort of plateau as their English stabilizes, and they do not seem to acquire more complex English or they maintain some accent. Previously, scholars referred to this as *fossilization*, but *stabilization* better describes this phenomenon. As this shows, language develops to meet communicative needs, and when a certain language is not needed, it stops developing.

Unfortunately, this process of natural language acquisition does not usually occur in most foreign language classes. Students studying another language in a foreign language class are not in regular contact with native speakers of the target language except for their teacher, and they do not have a need to communicate in that language other than to pass the class. That is why in many classes foreign languages are learned the same way other school subjects are learned instead of being acquired the way languages are naturally acquired. This is also because the focus is often on the forms of the language, that is, aspects of language such as verb tenses and sentence structures.

Theory and Research

Research in second language acquisition can contribute to a theory of SLA. Examples of research would be a study of the natural order of acquisition of morphemes or a study of the relationship between intelligence and language aptitude. A theoretical researcher, for example, might develop a theory that the effects of reading in the second language will be reflected in students' second language writing. The researcher might then look at the writing of second language learners for evidence of the effects of reading.

Research always supports credible theories. However, attempts to apply research directly to practice have not been productive. In his own research into the acquisition of morphemes by second language students, Krashen found that certain morphemes were acquired earlier than others. Morphemes are the smallest parts of words that carry meaning. So, for example, in the word *unties* there are three morphemes: the prefix *un*, the base *tie*, and the suffix *s*.

In English the morpheme *s* that indicates the plural in a word like *toys* is acquired at an earlier age than the third-person *s* in a word like *unties* (He unties his shoes). Krashen maintains that research findings such as these cannot be directly applied to practice. As he himself says, "I made this error several years ago when I suggested that the natural order of acquisition become the new grammatical syllabus" (1985, 47). He realized that he could not use the research to design a grammar textbook with a lesson on the plural *s* before a lesson on the third-person *s*.

In the first place, different students would acquire the morphemes at different times. The whole class would not be ready to acquire a certain morpheme on a certain day any more than a whole class would be ready to write a complete sentence on the same day. In the second place, while linguists know something about the natural order of morpheme acquisition, there is much more to English grammar than morphemes, and linguists have not charted the acquisition of all the complex structures of English or any other language.

Krashen's research helped him develop a theory of SLA that downplays the direct teaching of grammar. Krashen points out that SLA theory acts to mediate between research and practice. Teachers can benefit from their understanding of theory in their daily teaching practice. Krashen asserts, "Methodologists are missing a rich source of information . . . if they neglect theory" (48), and "without theory, there is no way to distinguish effective teaching procedures from ritual, no way to determine which aspects of a method are and are not helpful" (1985, 52). A knowledge of SLA theory, then, allows a teacher to reflect on and to refine day-to-day practice. A teacher with an understanding of language acquisition can better evaluate different curriculum options or specific strategies and programs. With that view in mind, we describe Krashen's theory of second language acquisition.

Krashen's Theory of Second Language Acquisition

We have looked generally at how learning takes place, and we have also considered the kinds of competence emergent bilinguals acquire when they acquire an additional language. We now examine Krashen's theory of second language acquisition. Krashen's monitor model consists of five interrelated hypotheses: (1) the acquisition versus learning hypothesis, (2) the natural order hypothesis, (3) the monitor hypothesis, (4) the input hypothesis, and (5) the affective filter hypothesis. In the following sections, we explain each hypothesis and provide examples. The monitor model emphasizes the role of comprehensible input in language acquisition, and it is based on Chomsky's theory of linguistics.

The Acquisition Versus Learning Hypothesis

Krashen begins by making an important distinction between two ways of developing a new language. The first of these is acquisition. According to Krashen we acquire a new language subconsciously as we receive messages we understand. For example, if we are living in a foreign country and go to the store to buy food, we may acquire new vocabulary or syntactic structures in the process of trying to understand what the clerk is saying. We are not focused on the language. Rather, we are using the language for real purposes, and acquisition occurs naturally as we attempt to conduct our business.

Yvonne remembers learning the names of fruits in the market in Venezuela. She would point to the type of fruit she wanted and then discuss whether a specific fruit was at the perfect point of maturation with the vendor. She learned to insist that her papayas were ripe but not spoiled and tell the vendor she wouldn't buy from him next time if he didn't pick out a perfect one for her.

Acquisition can also occur in classrooms in which teachers engage students in authentic communicative experiences. For example, if students work in pairs to read and solve a math word problem, in the process of discussing a solution both students begin to acquire the academic language related to math, such as *greater than* and *less than*, *subtract*, and *add*. They also may acquire syntactic structures including questions beginning with subordinate clauses, such as "If Juan has twenty-five marbles and gives ten to Bill, how many marbles does Juan have left?"

Krashen (2004, 2013) has also shown that we can acquire language as we read. In fact, since people are able to read more rapidly than they speak, written language is a better source for acquisition than oral language. In addition, reading provides the input students need to acquire academic language since written language has more of the characteristics of academic language than does spoken language (Biber 1986; Halliday 1989).

Krashen contrasts acquisition with learning. Learning is a conscious process in which we focus on various aspects of the language itself. It is what generally occurs in classrooms when teachers divide language up into chunks, present one chunk at a time, and provide students with feedback to indicate how well they have mastered the various aspects of language that have been taught. A teacher might present a lesson on regular verbs in the past tense, for example, giving attention to the *ed* that we add to the verb in sentences, such as "He played chess yesterday." It is this structure that students are expected to learn. Learning is associated with classroom instruction and is usually tested.

Although Krashen's theory focuses on individual psychological factors involved in second language acquisition, Gee offers a definition of acquisition that expands on Krashen's by including a social component:

> *Acquisition is a process of acquiring something subconsciously by exposure to*
> *models, a process of trial and error, and practice within social groups, without*
> *formal teaching. It happens in natural settings that are meaningful and functional*

in the sense that acquirers know that they need to acquire the thing they are
exposed to in order to function and that they in fact want to so function.
(1992, 113)

For example, teenagers pay close attention to how their peers dress. They acquire a knowledge of current clothing styles that are appropriate in different settings. In the 1950s girls wore "poodle skirts" and currently they may wear jeans with rips and tears. No one teaches them how to choose the clothing.

This expanded definition of acquisition brings an important social element into the distinction between acquisition and learning. Acquisition occurs in social contexts as people attempt to communicate with others. When the context of learning is a social studies class, students acquire this register of academic language as they acquire knowledge of social studies.

It appears that acquisition and learning lead to different kinds of abilities. As Gee puts it, "we are better at performing what we acquire, but we consciously know more about what we have learned" (1992, 114). In the case of second languages, acquisition allows us to speak and understand, read and write the language. Learning allows us to talk about (or pass exams on) the language. Many adults who have studied a foreign language in high school or college and received high grades never developed the ability to speak or understand the language they studied. Their performance on grammar and vocabulary tests determined their grades.

Yvonne's experience with studying French in college certainly demonstrates this. She took four years of French, could translate French into English quite well, and knew French grammar. Her grades were always very high in the courses she took. However, her ability to communicate in French is severely limited. Recently, when Yvonne and David were in Costa Rica staying at a remote inn, the only other guests were from Paris. Although Yvonne had studied French extensively, she struggled to understand simple conversation and communicate basic ideas.

A good example of the acquisition versus learning distinction comes from the experiences of José Luis, Guillermo, and Patricia, whom we discussed in Chapter 2. The teens studied English in El Salvador. This was a case of learning the rules and structures of the language. When they came to the United States, they did know some English, but it was very limited. In their new home in Tucson, they were immersed in English and began to acquire the language as they used it daily.

Krashen argues that children acquire (they don't learn) their first language(s) as they use language to communicate and to make sense of the world. Krashen claims that both children and adults have the capacity to acquire additional languages because they possess what Chomsky (1975) calls a universal grammar, a mental ability to acquire language. Krashen claims that acquisition accounts for almost all of our language development and that learning plays a minimal role. Second language classrooms should be places for acquisition, but more often second and foreign language teachers focus on learning.

When teaching Spanish, Yvonne, like many foreign language teachers, worried that students needed to learn the grammar, because that is what the department tested. At the beginning of the course, she explained the difference between acquisition and learning to her students in Spanish 1 and Spanish 2. She suggested students study the grammar in the books at home and take advantage of classroom time for language acquisition.

She organized activities to help her students develop Spanish proficiency by talking, reading, and writing about current events and topics related to their lives. Discussions of music and television programs involved her students in using language for authentic purposes, and they acquired language as they used it. Yvonne ensured that the conversations included the grammar points and structures in the textbook grammar lessons but were put into an engaging context. So, for example, students used the past tense to describe what had happened in a movie or in a current event. Yvonne had departed from traditional approaches to engage her students and to change her classroom from a place for learning to a setting for acquisition. This required careful planning and a search for materials in Spanish that included current events and trends in society. At the end of the semester, students were able to pass the level exams despite the limited time spent in class on the teaching of grammar.

REFLECT OR TURN AND TALK

If you studied a foreign language in high school or college, did your teacher use a method that emphasized acquisition or learning? Did you develop proficiency in the language? If you are bilingual or multilingual, how did you develop your additional language or languages? Was it through learning or acquisition? Discuss this with others and consider how your experiences affect your teaching of emergent bilinguals.

The Natural Order Hypothesis

Krashen's second hypothesis is that language is acquired in a natural order. Some aspects of a language are developed earlier than others. For example, the *ing* morpheme added to a word like *run* to form *running* comes earlier than the possessive *s* added to the word *John* in "John's book." Most parents are aware that phonemes like /p/ and /m/ are acquired earlier than others, like /r/. That's why English-speaking parents are often called *Papa* or *Mama* by babies, not *Roro*. In the area of syntax, statements generally precede questions. Children do not acquire the structure of questions early, so they often use statement structures such as "I go store, too?" or "You like teddy?" to pose questions. Krashen points out that all learners of a particular language, such as English, seem to acquire the language in the same order no matter what their home language may be.

Krashen bases this hypothesis on studies carried out by Dulay and Burt (1974). These researchers collected samples of speech from Chinese- and Spanish-speaking students acquiring English. They found that both groups acquired English morphemes in about the same order. They found, for example, that students acquired the articles such as *a* and *the* before they acquired the regular past tense *ed*. These early studies were subsequently confirmed by the work of a number of other researchers.

The natural order applies to language that is acquired, not language that is learned. In fact, students may be asked to learn aspects of language before they are ready to acquire them. The result may be good performance of the items on a test but inability to use the same items in a natural setting. During grammar tests, students' performance may exceed their competence.

In teaching Spanish, Yvonne found that the expression for *like* in Spanish was a late-acquired item. In Spanish, "I like" is *Me gusta* (It is pleasing to me). If the things I like are plural, I say *Me gustan* (They are pleasing to me). This structure caused no end of confusion for Yvonne's beginning students. She worked with them diligently, explaining how the structure worked and giving examples. Even those who did well on the department test had not acquired the structure. When Yvonne asked her students to evaluate the course in their daily diary at the end of the semester, almost all the students incorrectly wrote *Yo gusto* for "I like." They knew that *yo* meant "I" and knew the verb *gustar* was "to like." So they simply conjugated the verb as a regular verb despite the emphasis on learning the expression *Me gusta*.

Most books used in language courses present grammar in a certain order, but since linguists have only a rudimentary understanding of the complete order of acquisition of phonemes, morphemes, syntax, and so on, no book can be written that can claim to mirror the natural order. Even if such a book were written, students would invariably be at different stages, and in a class of thirty students, no grammar lesson would be appropriate for everyone. Krashen, however, points out that if a teacher focuses on acquisition activities, rather than trying to get students to learn certain grammatical points, all students will acquire the aspects of a language that they are developmentally ready to acquire in a natural order. The rate of acquisition of morphemes and structures will vary for different students, but the order will be the same.

The Monitor Hypothesis

The monitor hypothesis helps explain the different functions that acquisition and learning play. Acquisition results in developing the phonology, vocabulary, and syntax that we can draw on to produce and comprehend a new language. Without acquisition, we could not understand or produce anything other than limited aspects of the language we have learned. Learning, on the other hand, provides us with rules we can use to monitor our output as we speak or write. The monitor is like an editor, checking what we produce. The monitor can operate when we have time, when we focus on grammatical form, and when we know the rules.

Yvonne applied her monitor during her oral exams for her doctorate. Her committee of five had asked her several questions in English about language acquisition and bilingual education that she had answered fairly comfortably. Then, one of her committee members asked a question in Spanish, a clear suggestion that Yvonne should also answer in Spanish. Her most vivid memory of the incident was how much she was checking to be sure her Spanish was correct—how much she was applying her monitor. In particular, she was careful to watch for the correct use of the subjunctive mood, verb endings, and adjective agreement, all aspects of Spanish that she had learned and had not fully acquired. In this situation, Yvonne was focusing on form, and she had studied the rules. She did not want members of her doctoral committee to judge her Spanish as nonstandard. It seemed especially important in this setting to speak standard Spanish. Of course, the content of what she actually said was secondary, and to this day she cannot even remember what the question was.

The problem with using the monitor during speaking is that one must sacrifice meaning and speed for accuracy. A person can't concentrate on the form and the meaning at the same time, and overmonitoring slows down natural communication. On the other hand, the monitor is useful in the editing stage of writing. At that point, a writer has time to focus on form rather than meaning. In contrast, at the rough-draft stage, writers who slow down and think about correct form may forget what they were going to write. Monitoring is helpful if the monitor is not over- or underused, but even then, the monitor can only check the output.

The teens from El Salvador differed in their use of the monitor. Guillermo in particular focused on communication. He seldom monitored his output and was at times difficult to understand. Nevertheless, he was enthusiastic and personable and used a number of strategies (gestures, tone of voice, and so on) to be sure his listener understood. Guillermo underused his monitor even though he had studied English grammar and knew many of the rules.

His brother, José Luis, on the other hand, was quiet and shy. He did not like to speak English unless he could produce language that was grammatically correct. He too knew the rules, and he applied them carefully. His focus on form kept him from expressing his ideas freely. He overused the monitor. Since acquisition requires engagement in language use, overmonitoring slows acquisition down.

Patricia seemed less self-conscious than José Luis. She generally concentrated on what she wanted to say rather than how she would say it. At the same time, she did check her output to be sure she was producing understandable English. She also knew the rules and seemed to have found an optimal use of the monitor.

REFLECT OR TURN AND TALK

Think of a time you were speaking or writing in a second language. How would you characterize your monitor use? Was there a difference between your monitor use when speaking and writing? Now think of an emergent bilingual you know. How would you characterize that person's monitor use? How would you help someone become a more effective monitor user?

Teachers can help students become optimal monitor users. It does help to know the rules, but it's essential to know when to apply them and when to concentrate more on the meaning of a message. Sometimes teachers hope that by correcting their students' errors, they will increase students' proficiency. However, Krashen (1985) claims that while error correction in learning situations allows students to modify their knowledge of learned rules, it has no effect on their acquired language. "According to the theory, the practice of error correction affects learning, not acquisition. When our errors are corrected, we rethink and adjust our conscious rules" (8). Since the monitor can be accessed only under certain conditions, error correction has limited value. Learning, according to Krashen, has no effect on basic language competence.

The Input Hypothesis

In Krashen's theory of language acquisition the key is comprehensible input. He claims that people acquire language in only one way—when they receive oral or written messages they understand. Krashen asserts that these messages provide comprehensible input. In order for acquisition to take place, learners must receive input that is slightly beyond their current ability level. Krashen calls this $i + 1$ (input plus one). If the input contains no structures beyond current competence ($i + 0$), no acquisition takes place. There is nothing new to acquire. On the other hand, if the input is too far beyond a person's current competence ($i + 10$), it becomes incomprehensible noise, and again no acquisition can take place.

Krashen's explanation of comprehensible input as $i + 1$ is consistent with Vygotsky's concept of the ZPD. According to Vygotsky, we learn when we receive help (or scaffolded instruction) from a teacher or a more competent peer. For many of us, a YouTube how to video can provide this help. If the instruction is at our current level, we cannot develop new understanding or skills, and if it is too far beyond our ZPD, it does not help us.

According to Krashen, comprehensible input is the source of all acquired language. Students do not have to produce language in order to acquire it. Only input leads to acquisition, and so output—speaking or writing—does not contribute to acquisition, although it may result in cognitive development. As Krashen notes, output can help people learn academic content; or, as he puts it, output can make you smarter. In addition, through output, a person can engage others in conversation with the result that the person receives more input. Thus, output can lead to comprehensible input needed for acquisition.

Since comprehensible input is the key to language acquisition, the teacher's job is to find ways to make academic content comprehensible. This is why the theory is so important for teachers. Most current language methods for teaching students who are developing a new language are designed to help teachers develop techniques for turning academic content matter into comprehensible input (Freeman and Freeman 2009; Freeman et al. 2016).

SIMPLIFIED INPUT

Studies by Hatch (1983) suggest that the kind of input that leads to language development is simplified input. According to Hatch, simplified input includes caregiver talk, teacher talk, and talk to nonnative speakers. Hatch identified some characteristics of simplified talk. The phonology includes fewer reduced vowels and contractions, and the rate of speech is slower, with longer pauses. The vocabulary is characterized by more high-frequency items, fewer idioms, and less slang. There are fewer pronouns, and speakers often use gestures and pictures. At the level of syntax, sentences are shorter, with more repetitions and restatements. Discourse includes more requests for clarification and fewer interruptions.

During our year in Venezuela, one thing we noticed in early interactions with colleagues was that they often tried to provide us with simplified input. When speaking directly to us in a meeting, for example, they obviously slowed their speech. In fact, if someone in the meeting used slang, the meeting would usually stop, and everyone would try to explain the expression to us. Our landlord spoke no English at all and was nervous about talking to us. In our first meeting, she used very slow speech and lots of gestures in an effort to make herself understood. She used all the techniques of an excellent language teacher, even though she is a lawyer by profession.

One problem with claiming that simplified input leads to acquisition is that simplified input may not contain new language structures or items. In other words, the input may not be $i + 1$ but may include language the learner has previously acquired.

REFLECT OR TURN AND TALK

What techniques or strategies have you used to make academic content comprehensible? When talking to students, do you consciously change the way you speak when you are talking with emergent bilinguals? Idioms are difficult for emergent bilinguals to understand. Do you monitor your own use of idioms as you teach?

A second problem with simplified input is that it may result in unnatural language with short sentences and short, everyday words. Language that is not natural is more difficult to acquire because it doesn't follow predictable language patterns. In addition, texts with short sentences and words do not prepare students for the academic language in school textbooks (Goodman and Freeman 1993). Further, while it is helpful for teachers to pause and to write things down as they speak, a slow rate of speech is not natural. Parents don't slow their speech down as they interact with babies, but they do use other ways to make messages understandable.

The Affective Filter Hypothesis

The affective filter hypothesis explains the role of affective factors in the process of language acquisition. Even if a teacher provides comprehensible input, acquisition may not take place. Affective factors such as anxiety and boredom may serve as filters that block input. When a filter is up, input can't reach those parts of the brain where acquisition occurs. Many language learners realize that the reason they have trouble is because they are nervous or embarrassed and simply can't concentrate. Lack of desire to learn can also clog the affective filter. In addition, students who are suffering culture shock as they adjust to a new culture and students who have had traumatic experiences may not be able to process the input they receive.

Suárez-Orozco states:

> It is well established that a safe environment is vital for learning for all students, but findings from our case studies pointed to ways to address safety and belonging that specifically support immigrant students and their families. One of the impediments to learning in a new country is entering a context where students feel unsafe or that they don't belong. These feelings can lead to low motivation, low self-esteem, and debilitating anxiety that can combine to create an "affective filter" that can shut down the language learning process. While not sufficient by itself, a positive affect facilitates language acquisition to take place. (2018, 6)

Yvonne's intern experience teaching high school Spanish to get her credential provides an example of the affective filter. Her class consisted of twenty-four boys, all on the junior varsity football team, and three girls. Most of the students had signed up for the "new intern" teacher mainly because they had failed Spanish 1 the year before, taking it with an experienced teacher who had taught in the school for years. Positive affective factors such as high interest or motivation can help keep the filter down, but those students had neither. Yvonne's major job was to try to lower the students' filter by getting them interested and convincing them that they wanted to learn Spanish.

Since Krashen's theory of language acquisition is based on input, in his discussion of the affective filter he refers only to language that is coming in, not to language the person is attempting to produce. In other words, the affective filter can prevent a person from getting more comprehensible input. This hypothesis does not apply to a person's output, only to the ability to acquire language. At times, students who have developed high levels of language proficiency may not perform up to their capacity. As we explained earlier, there are times when students are nervous, bored, or unmotivated, and their performance does not match their competence. Students may also not perform well in a new language if they overuse their monitor.

> ## REFLECT OR TURN AND TALK
> Think of a time when you were studying a new language. Were you motivated to learn, or were you either nervous or bored? How did affective factors impact your ability to develop the language? What do you do as you teach or what do effective teachers you know do to increase students' motivation and lower their affective filters?

Summary

The five interrelated hypotheses constitute Krashen's monitor model of SLA. Krashen sums up his theory by stating, "We acquire when we obtain comprehensible input in a low-anxiety situation, when we are presented with interesting messages, and when we understand these messages" (1985, 10).

Kristene, a graduate student and a bilingual teacher, wrote the following reflection on her own acquisition of Spanish as a second language after studying Krashen's theory.

> *Perhaps my success in Spanish language classes in high school came about because my first exposure to Spanish was through communicative practice in real situations as Krashen suggests. I lived in Spain at the age of ten for six months. My parents*

hired a tutor who spoke only Spanish. She took us to the beach, to town on the bus, shopping at la plaza, to church, to the movies, to the park, to buy bread at the bread shop. (I can still remember the fabulous aroma and taste of freshly baked Spanish bread some thirty years later!) The input was comprehensible.

Krashen would take this example from Kristene to support his theory. Kristene acquired Spanish in a natural order because she was in a setting in which the input was comprehensible and her affective filter was low. Later, in high school, she drew on her acquired knowledge of Spanish. The result is that Kristene has developed a high level of proficiency in Spanish.

Krashen's Suggestions for Teaching Language Online

Krashen has responded to the teaching conditions caused by the COVID-19 pandemic. He offers the following seven tips (Soika 2020):

1. *Less traditional instruction may be a good thing.* Krashen notes that online teaching can provide a great deal of the comprehensible input needed for acquisition while traditional teaching often includes practicing rules and grammar, which are ineffective practices.

2. *Remote learning can support language acquisition.* Two useful practices for online learning are listening to stories available at online sites and reading for pleasure.

3. *Parents should share heritage language at home.* Through talking with parents and listening to stories, emergent bilinguals can strengthen their home language.

4. *Teachers should encourage students to read fiction.* According to Krashen, fiction is the most beneficial form of input for acquisition.

5. *Students should avoid self-instruction language learning texts.* Krashen and a colleague conducted research that showed people who checked out self-instruction language learning texts from the library only read about 5 percent of the pages in the book. This showed that these books were not useful for language acquisition.

6. *Students should find out if the library is open online.* Many public libraries have continued to offer electronic versions of books online. These can be an excellent source of comprehensible input.

7. *Language scholars should increase access to publications.* Krashen encourages scholars to publish short educational research articles in forms that are open to the scholars to increase knowledge of the field.

What About Output?

Krashen argues that acquisition occurs when learners receive comprehensible input, messages that they understand. Other researchers have given importance to output as well as input. Ellis (2005) refers to theories such as Krashen's as reception-based. He classifies theories that include attention to output as production-based. According to Johnson, "Reception-based theories contend that interaction contributes to second language acquisition via learners' reception and comprehension of the second language, whereas production-based theories credit this process to learners' attempts at actually producing the language" (1995, 82).

Long developed the interaction hypothesis, a reception-based theory of SLA. Long claims that learners make conversational adjustments as they interact with others and that these adjustments help make the input comprehensible (Doughty and Long 2003). Johnson points out, "Like Krashen, Long stresses the importance of comprehensible input but places more emphasis on the interaction that takes place in two-way communication and the adjustments that are made as a result of the negotiation of meaning" (1995, 83).

Swain (1985) argues that language learners need the opportunity for output. She noted that students in French immersion classes did not reach nativelike proficiency in French. These French immersion classes in Canada were not the same as dual language immersion programs in the United States. The students in the French classes were all native English speakers while dual language classes include home-language speakers of two languages. In the French immersion classes, teachers were the only source of native-sounding input in French in early grades. Peer interaction was limited, and when interaction occurred, students spoke only with others acquiring French, not with native speakers of French.

Based on her observations of these students, Swain proposed that second language acquisition depends on output as well as input. She observed that when teachers prompted students to explain their ideas more clearly, the students became more aware of their language and were forced into what she referred to as a syntactic processing mode that is different from the process of comprehending input. Swain wrote:

> *Negotiating meaning needs to incorporate the notion of being pushed toward the delivery of a message that is not only conveyed, but that is conveyed precisely, coherently, and appropriately. Being "pushed" in output . . . is a concept parallel to that of the i + 1 of comprehensible input. Indeed, one might call this the "comprehensible output" hypothesis.* (1985, 248–49)

For Swain output is a process students go through that gets them to notice their language and modify it to communicate more effectively. She argues that this process is a necessary part of language development. Many people have noticed that it is easier to understand a new language than to produce it. However, as we produce the new language, we become aware of times when we are not communicating well. As we work for more effective communication, we develop our language proficiency. The key for teachers is to respond to students in a way that motivates them to communicate more clearly instead of simply correcting them and asking them to repeat the correct form. Correction, by itself, seems to have little effect on improving students' language. Teacher responses that are aimed at helping students convey a message more clearly, on the other hand, do seem to increase students' language proficiency.

Problems with Forcing Output

Traditional approaches to language teaching often require students to produce language before they have received enough comprehensible input. While SLA theories point out the importance of output as well as input, requiring emergent bilinguals in early stages of acquisition to produce language too soon can have negative consequences.

This became clear to us as we worked with student teachers in Venezuela. Because of their own experiences as students in English classes, the new teachers at first asked their beginning students to say everything on their lesson plans in complete sentences and even asked them to stand and recite what they were learning. Use of visuals was minimal, and chalkboards were filled with vocabulary lists and language structures. Although the topics of the lessons were personally interesting—explaining likes and dislikes or discussing similarities and differences among classmates—the insistence on output raised the students' affective filters. These beginning-level English students expended so much energy trying to pronounce words, learn vocabulary, get verb endings right, and put sentences together that little real language acquisition took place.

After we explained the importance of making the input comprehensible and not forcing early production, the student teachers began to use a variety of visuals and other strategies to ensure that the input they were providing was comprehensible. They allowed students to show comprehension through gestures and one-word answers. The emphasis in the classroom moved from correct pronunciation, vocabulary, and sentence structures to comprehension and interaction. What was most exciting was that the teachers saw how much more English their students were acquiring and how much more positive they were about the class.

Stages of Language Acquisition

Krashen and Terrel (1983) identified several stages that emergent bilinguals go through as they acquire a new language. The first is preproduction, or a silent period when students can understand the language but haven't begun to produce it. They can still show they understand by using gestures, such as pointing or following instructions by standing or sitting. During this period, teachers often use methods like total physical response, which requires students to respond to verbal commands, such as "stand up" or "raise your right hand" (Asher 1977).

The second stage, which often occurs after about a month, is early production. At this stage, students can answer yes-or-no questions and produce short phrases to answer questions. For example, if someone asks, "Who has a blue shirt?" they might respond, "I do." As students continue to expand their vocabulary and command of syntactic structure, they move into the third stage, speech emergence. Students can now produce short, simple sentences, such as "The shirt is green" or "I play baseball." In the fourth stage, intermediate fluency, students expand their vocabulary further and produce more complex sentences. As these stages of oral language develop, students also begin to be able to read and write increasingly complex material.

Over time, different organizations such as TESOL (Teachers of English to Speakers of Other Languages) have developed more elaborated descriptions of stages of acquisition. The TESOL stages are labeled starting, emerging, developing, and bridging. The final stage explains what ELs should be able to do to bridge to mainstream classes. Similarly, states have developed a set of standards to describe the levels of language proficiency that ELs go through as they move from being labeled as limited English proficient to fully English proficient or fluently English proficient (FEP), at which point they can be placed in mainstream classes.

Van Lier's Model of Language Acquisition

One model of SLA that includes both input and output has been developed by van Lier (1988) and is shown in Figure 3–1. Van Lier claims that certain conditions are necessary for certain outcomes. According to this model, if learners are receptive during exposure to a new language, their attention will be focused. If attention is focused, the language becomes input. If learners invest some mental energy in the input, they will begin to comprehend it. Language that is comprehended changes from input to intake.

C	EXPOSURE		O
O	receptivity	focused attention	U
N	**INPUT**		T
D	investment	comprehension	C
I	**INTAKE**		O
T	practice	retention and access	M
I	**UPTAKE**		E
O	authentic use	extension and creativity	S
N	PROFICIENCY		

Figure 3–1 • Van Lier's Model of SLA

If learners practice with intake (if they use the language in meaningful interactions), they can retain the language and access it later. Language that can be accessed is considered uptake. Finally, with continued authentic use, learners can extend their language and use it creatively. It is the ability to use language creatively that is a measure of proficiency. By saying that a learner can use language creatively, linguists mean that an emergent bilingual can create new sentences rather than repeat something they have heard before. For example, an English learner might make a statement such as, "I like swimming and hiking as well as riding on a bike." This is a new sentence the speaker has created, not one the student heard someone else say.

Van Lier's model includes both Krashen's idea of comprehensible input and Swain's concept of comprehensible output. It provides a good explanation of the steps involved in second language acquisition.

Two of our grandchildren, Christiana and Alexander, are examples of van Lier's model of SLA. When they moved to Mexico City from New York City with their parents at ages five and seven, they did not know any Spanish beyond *hola* (hi) and *gracias* (thank you). Their parents put them in the American school, where most instruction was in English. However, almost all the other students in the school were Mexican and used Spanish almost exclusively outside of class time and during class discussions.

At first, Christiana and Alexander suffered culture shock and seemed to pay attention only to basic needs, like foods they wanted or directions teachers and classmates gave in Spanish. Their exposure, however, was extensive on the playground and with other children in their apartment complex. Little by little they became more receptive and began to focus their attention on the language, as they needed it to interact more fully. At this stage, the language became what van Lier labels as input.

As they invested more mental energy into the input, they developed a greater understanding and comprehended more of the language. As their comprehension increased, the input became intake. They started to use Spanish to take part in games and even in simple conversations, and with this increased use they retained more Spanish and could access their knowledge. At this point, the intake became uptake. As they continued to use the language each day, they extended their ability. By their third year in Mexico, their Spanish was uptake as they used it authentically in almost all settings, including most academic school activities, and drew on the knowledge they had to creatively use the language. When they left Mexico after four years, they were quite proficient and could move easily back and forth between Spanish and English.

REFLECT OR TURN AND TALK

Both Swain and van Lier argue that comprehensible output is important in the development of language proficiency. What is your view of output? If you are currently teaching, how do you balance the need for both input and output as you work with emergent bilinguals? Share your reflections.

Conclusion

There was a time when teachers would say that silence is golden. However, our review of both learning theory and second language acquisition theory strongly suggests that, especially in classes with emergent bilinguals, silence is deadly. Since all learning, including acquiring a new language, requires both oral and written comprehensible input, teachers and students should be engaged in lively classroom discussions as well as in extensive reading and writing. Teachers should use techniques to make input comprehensible and to extend students' talk by asking them to clarify and extend their responses.

With increased use of distance learning, teachers face the challenge of mastering new technologies that allow them to communicate effectively with students, using platforms like Google Classroom or Zoom and using features like chat rooms so that students can talk with one another. While it is relatively easy to assign reading and writing for students, it is important to also find ways to facilitate oral communication with students and between students during distance learning.

To help students learn language using technology, teachers need to be creative. An often-used approach is to send packets home with worksheets and discrete skills practice. However, this approach does not help emergent bilinguals because they are aimed at learning, not language acquisition. With a good understanding of what their students already know and what they are interested in, teachers can provide readings and videos on these topics that help the students deepen and expand their background knowledge (Major 2020). For example, our grandson is studying a unit on animals, so his teacher gave him a choice of doing his research on the animal that most interested him. Then students can make short videos with oral reports on their research. This could be followed up by chat room discussions among students about what they learned from the report and what questions they have.

This allows for culturally responsive, or what Paris (2012) has called culturally sustaining, teaching for emergent bilinguals. For example, students can interview family members about their jobs and how they found them. They can interview family about their backgrounds and how their families immigrated to this country. They can cook favorite dishes with family members, write down recipes, and find out where recipes came from. They can talk to family about celebrations and why they celebrate them when others do not. They can then research those customs and compare and contrast their research with what their family does. If these are carried out in the home language, students can build their English by reporting both in writing and orally about what they learned during class online meetings or in chat rooms. Students may return to classrooms after the pandemic, but teaching and learning will be forever modified, and the modifications will include some online learning. Teachers of students from different languages and cultures need to find creative ways to help students acquire language in meaningful ways both in the classroom and during distance learning.

4

What Influences How Teachers Teach?

Key Points

- A variety of factors influence how teachers teach.

- Changes in legislative requirements such as the change from NCLB to ESSA have had a great impact on teachers of emergent bilinguals.

- Over time people's orientations toward English learners have changed, from viewing their home language as a handicap to seeing it as a civil right to more recently viewing it as a resource, and these shifts in orientation have resulted in different programs for teaching emergent bilinguals.

- Teachers' attitudes toward teaching emergent bilinguals have a strong influence on student success.

- Coping with the changes in student population and changes in legal requirements for teaching and testing is stressful for teachers.

- Coping with change during the COVID-19 pandemic will result in a new normal, and teaching online will become something that most teachers will need to adjust to in some form.

- Yvonne's story shows how teachers can become principled by reflecting on their teaching and increasing their understanding of current research and theory.

Factors That Affect How Teachers Teach

When we visit classes, we see teachers using a variety of techniques and methods to help their students learn English and academic content. This variation is not surprising. In fact, even within the same school and at the same grade level with a similar student population, teachers differ considerably in how they teach. Why is this?

In this chapter the basic question we wish to explore is, What influences how teachers teach? A number of factors seem to be at work, and these help to account for the variation in classroom practices we have observed. For one thing, teachers have been students themselves, and often the way they teach reflects the way that they were taught. If they were taught a second or foreign language using drills and dialogues based on the grammatical structure of the language, then they would naturally adopt a similar method in their own practice. Since most teachers were good students themselves, they assume that the way they were taught should work for their own students. They follow the adage "Experience is the best teacher."

On the other hand, teachers study teaching methods in their education classes, and they are expected to apply them during a student teaching experience or an internship. As a result, they plan to apply these methods when they have their own classes to teach. In many cases this may lead them to introduce new methods and materials at the school where they begin their teaching careers. However, school practices do not change quickly, and methods introduced by new, inexperienced teachers usually gain little traction within their school.

In part, this lack of implementation of new practices is the result of another strong factor that affects how teachers teach. Teachers, and especially new teachers, are influenced by the other teachers at their school and by their administrators. If the more experienced teachers follow different practices from the ones the new teachers have studied in teacher education classes, most new teachers decide that what their university professors taught does not apply in the real world, and they adopt the practices the other teachers use. Further, since administrators in most schools expect new teachers to follow the status quo established at the school, they evaluate new teachers by whether or not they use the standard practices of the other teachers. New teachers realize that they need good evaluations to keep their jobs and therefore adopt the established methods.

If teachers change schools or grade levels, or if they are asked to teach a new subject, they may change their practices to conform with the established practices used at the new school or grade level. They may also change their teaching to meet the demands of teaching a new subject. David taught high school English for several years. One year, the French teacher resigned, and David was the only teacher qualified to teach French based on his university coursework. Students who had taken French 1 the previous year had been scheduled to take French 2, and David had to change from teaching English to native English speakers to teaching a foreign language using a very different set of methods.

Sometimes teachers use new techniques in their classrooms because they have learned about them in a professional learning community, a book study, during a conference, or during a professional development session or series of sessions. Progressive schools are always trying to improve and to follow what are deemed best practices. Even so, new practices are only slowly assimilated into established teaching methods, and not all teachers implement new ideas consistently.

Another factor that plays a role in how teachers teach is the curriculum materials that are available (or required) for them to use. School administrators generally expect all teachers to use the materials that the school or district has adopted and purchased. Teachers may adapt the curriculum materials, but it is difficult to create new materials without any support from the school, and most teachers use the adopted curriculum materials. In fact, if they do not use the adopted materials, they may receive low evaluations.

An additional factor that has been increasingly important is the availability of technological resources. Both new and experienced teachers have been affected by the need to include these resources in their teaching. For some teachers, this means learning how to negotiate technologies they have not used before. For example, in teaching university classes, we had to learn how to operate Blackboard Collaborate, which meant learning how to do video chats, put students into chat rooms, and other features. In K–12 schools there is a variety of technology available. In many schools, homework is submitted online. In some cases, schools adopt a specific online program like Lexia and require all teachers to have their students use the program for a certain amount of time each week. Teachers have to adjust their teaching and include time to use the program. And with the coronavirus pandemic many teachers had to conduct some or all instruction online. We will discuss this in further detail later in this chapter.

Teachers also adjust their teaching in response to the needs of their students. With the increase in the English language learner population, many teachers have adopted new methods to meet these students' needs. Many mainstream teachers now have emergent bilinguals in their classes, and they develop scaffolding techniques to ensure that all their students learn academic English and academic content taught in English.

At the same time, many schools adopt specific models for language teaching to be applied to emergent bilinguals at lower levels of English proficiency or to all the students. Some schools use pull-out or push-in ESL support for emergent bilinguals. In other schools an early-exit bilingual program is in place. Increasingly, schools have implemented dual language bilingual programs. Clearly, the model used will be a factor that influences how teachers teach.

In addition to these factors, legal mandates have always influenced how teachers teach. For example, as we discussed in Chapter 1, several initiatives—Proposition 227 in California, Proposition 202 in Arizona, and Question 2 in Massachusetts—severely limited the use of instruction in the home language when educating English language learners. Now the adoption of new laws has opened up the possibility of greater use of students' home languages during teaching. In California, after the passage of Proposition 58, the Multilingual Education Act of 2016, there was an increased demand for dual language schools. This has resulted in a huge need for more bilingual teachers, a resource that is lacking because students had not been taught in the home language under Proposition 227.

One of the best examples of the effects of legislation on teaching was the passage of the Elementary and Secondary Education No Child Left Behind Act and the implementation of the Reading First initiative, which radically changed the way reading was taught. More recently, the passage of the Every Student Succeeds Act and the accompanying testing have again shifted the way teachers are teaching.

As this brief review shows, a number of factors influence how teachers teach. A combination of these factors accounts for the approach and methods teachers use. Effective teachers evolve their methods to meet the challenges of new students, new legislation, and new technologies. These changes have been especially prevalent since the COVID-19 pandemic, as we address later in our discussion on coping with change. Figure 4–1 lists the factors we have discussed.

Factor	Results
past academic experiences	We teach as we were taught.
educational training	We teach as we were taught to teach.
colleagues/ administrators	We teach as others teach or as we are required to teach.
changes in teaching situation	We adjust teaching to meet demands of a new grade level, subject, or school.
professional development	We teach using strategies learned through professional development.
curriculum materials	We teach using required curriculum materials.
technology resources	We teach using new technology resources.

(continues)

(continued)

Factor	Results
students	We teach in response to our students' needs.
legislation	We teach to ensure that students meet the requirements.

Figure 4–1 • Factors That Influence How Teachers Teach

Orientations Toward Language

Legal mandates, such as the shift from NCLB to ESSA that we described earlier, reflect the ways people view effective educational practices. These changing views strongly affect how teachers teach, especially the way they teach emergent bilinguals. The programs and materials that are developed reflect current views. The shifting attitudes toward speakers of non-English languages are reflected in the kinds of programs for English language learners that have been offered in US schools during the last half of the twentieth century and now in the twenty-first century.

Ruíz (1984) has described these changes by tracing the historical development of three different orientations toward students' home languages: language as a handicap, language as a right, and language as a resource. He defines an orientation as a "complex of dispositions toward language and its role, and toward languages and their role in society" (16).

During the fifties and sixties, language as a handicap was the prevalent orientation. Ruíz points out that at this time, educators saw English language learners as having a problem, so that "teaching English, even at the expense of the first language, became the objective of school programs" (19). In other words, educators with this orientation believed that to overcome the handicap they had, English learners had to transition to English as quickly as possible. This orientation resulted in the establishment of ESL and transitional bilingual programs. These programs were designed to compensate for the language handicap these students were thought to have had.

Ruíz explains that in the seventies, the language-as-a-right orientation emerged. As a part of the civil rights movement, bilingual educators called for the rights of nonnative English speakers (NNES) to bilingual education. In many districts instruction given in English excluded some students from access to a meaningful education.

This began to change in 1974 when Chinese parents in San Francisco sued the school district for violation of the civil rights of their children.

The school district claimed that the Chinese students were given an equal education because they were provided the same materials and taught the same content as native English speakers. The Chinese parents argued that by teaching non-English speakers in English, a language they did not understand, the district was denying them an equal opportunity to learn and discriminating against them under Title VI of the Civil Rights Act of 1964.

The Supreme Court sided with the parents in the *Lau v. Nichols* case. Although it did not require a specific program for English learners, the Supreme Court did issue guidelines for districts to follow. These guidelines called for schools to identify students with limited English proficiency and to provide special services that would give them access to the core curriculum. According to the Lau decision, schools could meet these requirements in different ways, including providing bilingual instruction or ESL. Students could be given some instruction in their home language or be placed in ESL classes. ESL teachers could pull out groups of students or work with mainstream teachers by providing extra support in the classes.

In 1981 a second civil rights case provided clearer guidelines for the kinds of programs that schools are required to implement in educating emergent bilinguals. In the case of *Castañeda v. Pickard*, the Fifth Circuit Court ruled that a school district in Texas had not provided an appropriate program for their English learners. Because of their low proficiency in English, the students could not participate equally in the school's instructional program.

This case was important because the court established three criteria for any program serving English learners. The program must (1) be based on a sound educational theory, (2) be implemented effectively with adequate resources and personnel, and (3) after a trial period, be evaluated as effective in overcoming "language handicaps." Although the ruling still used the negative terminology of a language-as-a-handicap orientation, it established guidelines for programs for which English learners had a legal right. These three criteria have often been used by states and districts in evaluating programs for English learners.

Ruíz (1984) also identifies a third orientation: language as a resource. He sees this orientation as a better approach to language planning for several reasons:

> It can have a direct impact on enhancing the language status of subordinate
> languages; it can help to ease tensions between majority and minority
> communities; it can serve as a more consistent way of viewing the role of

non-English languages in U.S. society; and it highlights the importance of cooperative language planning. (25–26)

Dual language bilingual programs are all based on the language-as-a-resource orientation. These programs have raised the status and importance of languages other than English in many communities across the United States. They raise the status of non-English languages, in part, because as native English-speaking children become bilingual, parents and students alike see the value of knowing more than one language. In some communities dual language programs have eased tensions between groups who speak different languages. The programs have helped build cross-cultural communities and cross-cultural friendships among students and parents, relationships that probably would not have developed without the programs.

Dual language programs benefit both native speakers of English and native speakers of languages other than English (LOTE). These programs serve English language learners in a unique way because the English learners become proficient in English and, at the same time, develop and preserve their home language. Because their peers are also learning their language, they maintain pride in their home language and culture. Native English speakers add proficiency in an additional language and increase their cross-cultural understanding. These benefits are the direct result of viewing all languages as valuable community resources.

Another important trend in working with emergent bilinguals is the use of translanguaging in ESL, bilingual, and dual language classrooms. Although we will discuss translanguaging in detail in Chapter 5, it is important to point out that when teachers use well-planned translanguaging strategies, they are drawing on their students' rich linguistic repertoires, which include home-language knowledge. They are using the linguistic repertoire as a resource.

REFLECT OR TURN AND TALK

Think about your own teaching. What factors have influenced your methods? How has your teaching changed over time? Share your reflections. Consider your own orientations toward students' home languages. Have you seen their home languages as a handicap, right, or resource?

Teacher Attitudes

All the factors listed in Figure 4–1 may influence how a teacher teaches. In addition, teachers are also influenced by specific experiences they have. Loretta, a Mexican American who was teaching high school classes when we worked with her, reflected on her student teaching experience:

> During my student teaching experience, I had the opportunity to work with ESL classes in math, history, and English. In one of these classes the teacher was trying to give me some of her educational insight. She told me that the Asian students (Lao, Hmong, etc.) were much better students than the Mexican students. She went on to say that these [Asian] children wanted to learn and were not a behavioral problem like the others. I do not think she knew that I was Mexican. Needless to say, I was extremely bothered by her remarks, and I immediately went home and shared this experience with my parents. They were both angered by her false statements. They felt that this new wave of immigrants is being treated much better than they were when they were in school.

The teacher Loretta worked with during her student teaching reflected an attitude that teachers working in schools with large numbers of immigrant students sometimes develop. As we mentioned earlier, teachers' opinions about students have an important influence on how they teach. We believe that some teachers may need to develop new attitudes toward the new students in their schools (Freeman and Freeman 1990).

Based on their research in a number of schools, Suárez-Orozco and Marks state, "In schools that serve immigrant students we commonly find cultures of low teacher expectations; what is sought and valued by teachers is student compliance rather than curiosity or cognitive engagement" (2016, 116). They found that the teacher expectations were often based on teachers' stereotypical impressions of groups of students. This was the case for the teacher that Loretta worked with. Low expectations generally result in teachers holding students to less challenging standards when what the students need is to be both challenged and supported.

Almost every state now has a significant number of emergent bilinguals in schools at every grade level. Working with these students is both challenging and rewarding. Teachers have responded to changes in the school population in different ways. We have seen four common responses from teachers in schools with high populations of English learners. In describing these responses we will use hypothetical situations that represent what we have observed. In each scenario, teacher attitudes and perceptions, developed in response to the influences listed in Figure 4–1, play an important role in how teachers teach. We briefly analyze each scenario and then offer some possible positive responses. The scenarios we describe represent only a small proportion of the teachers we have worked with. The vast majority of teachers adjust to working with new student populations and report that they enjoy working with them.

"Teaching Isn't Like It Used to Be"

Mrs. Brown has taught kindergarten at Baker School in the south end of town for fifteen years. When she first began teaching there, the neighborhood was made up mostly of middle-class whites, but over the years large numbers of Blacks, Latinx, and Southeast Asians have moved into the area, causing a "white flight" to the north. The majority of her present students arrive with limited English proficiency.

Mrs. Brown complains that these new students cannot do what her students in the past could. She remembers the past fondly. On the first day of school, children arrived eager to learn, holding the hands of parents who offered support. Now, she complains, the students, especially the Southeast Asian children, enter the classroom reluctantly. They are either alone or with parents who don't speak English and seem eager to escape as quickly as possible. Though she has an English-only rule for the classroom, she constantly has to remind students not to speak their native languages. Her biggest complaints are that the children don't seem motivated and the parents don't care.

ANALYSIS

There are several reasons that Mrs. Brown may be responding as she is. In the earlier days, most of her students spoke English and came from a background similar to hers. She now finds herself trying to teach students who not only do not speak the same language literally but also do not understand her customs and values any more than she does theirs. Previously, Mrs. Brown had strong parent support, but now she is not sure how to communicate with the parents. Mrs. Brown does not know how to change her teaching to help students, and she responds by blaming them and their families.

POSITIVE RESPONSES

Many teachers who suddenly find themselves with large numbers of English language learners make it a point to inform themselves about their new students. They read and discuss books and articles about other teachers working with emergent bilinguals. They talk with their fellow teachers and share materials and ideas that have been successful. They attend workshops offered by school districts and local universities. They join professional organizations for teachers of bilingual and second language learners.

Once they learn more about emergent bilinguals, they become advocates for them. They seek people and materials that can provide home-language support, and they promote school events that highlight different cultural traditions. In addition, they make an effort to include the parents of their new students, not only at special events but in the regular classroom day. Even if parents do not speak English, teachers invite them to class to read a book in their first language, cook, or do crafts. Though all of these things require extra effort, they make these teachers' classrooms exciting places where all their students learn.

"English Learners Make Me Look Like a Failure"

Ms. Franklin is a second-year, second-grade teacher. Like most nontenured teachers in the district, she has been assigned to a classroom of diverse students, mostly Latinx, but also including a Somali refugee, two students from Iraq, and one student from China. Many of her students are classified as LEP. Ms. Franklin's teacher education program included some coursework in second language acquisition, ESL methodology, and diversity. As soon as she began to work with her emergent bilinguals last year, she fell in love with them. She read with the children, encouraged them to write often, and, in general, created activities that drew on their interests and background knowledge. The children responded well to this type of program, and she could see tremendous growth in their English.

Despite this success, Ms. Franklin has encountered problems. She teaches in a school that has not met the state goals for annual yearly progress. The test scores for her students have remained low, and the principal has talked about this with Ms. Franklin. Even though he did not threaten her directly, Ms. Franklin now feels her job is on the line. From the coursework she has taken and her own experiences, she realizes that standardized tests do not chart the progress of her bilingual students fairly. Still, she is tempted to try this year to teach to the test, despite the fact that she does not feel that worksheets and drills are meaningful to her students, especially to her second language learners. She is beginning to view her students as having deficits—deficits that could have direct consequences for her career. She is also beginning to wish that she could transfer to a school in another part of town with fewer English learners.

ANALYSIS

Ms. Franklin began her teaching with enthusiasm and caring. Her college coursework prepared her to work effectively with English learners. However, Ms. Franklin is a new teacher and not really experienced enough to defend her curriculum. The emphasis on test scores has begun to erode her confidence in doing what is best for her students. She is beginning to view the students she once was trying to help as the source of her problems. Her solution is to try to get away from her present teaching situation.

POSITIVE RESPONSES

Many of the teachers who take our graduate courses are like Ms. Franklin. They are new teachers who want to help their students and are studying second language acquisition. However, they are concerned because they feel pressure from standardized testing and do not want to be judged by the poor performance of emergent bilinguals. After taking further graduate coursework, these teachers begin to understand how long it takes to speak, read, and write a second language with near-native proficiency and how critical home-language support is for content learning.

Even when teachers use effective practices, emergent bilinguals need about five years to meet state norms on standardized tests (Collier 1989; Cummins 1981; Hakuta, Butler, and Whitt 2000). It is important for administrators to understand this research. In addition, schools should use formative assessments (MacDonald et al. 2015) to monitor and document their emergent bilinguals' progress. If the emergent bilinguals can be shown to be making consistent progress, then state agencies should not penalize schools, and this is happening in many states. The key is for schools to adjust their programs to ensure that all their student populations are succeeding. In many districts schools have instituted dual language bilingual programs, since these programs have been shown to be the most effective programs for emergent bilinguals, and native English speakers also improve (Freeman, Freeman, and Mercuri 2018).

"It's Not Fair to the Rest of My Class to Give Those Students Special Attention"

Mr. Martin teaches in a farming community where he has lived since he was a child. At the beginning of the year, his sixth-grade class included a group of Latinx children who were all fairly proficient in English and all reasonably successful learners. At the end of the first month of school, the principal called Mr. Martin in to explain that five sixth-grade migrant children had just arrived from Mexico and that they would be placed in Mr. Martin's class.

Mr. Martin wasn't sure what to do with these new students, whose English was extremely limited. The district paid him to take training to learn new techniques, but he resented the idea that he had to attend extra classes and learn new ways to teach, especially when he had been successful for a number of years. Why should he be the one to change? If these students couldn't meet the expectations for his class, maybe they weren't ready for it.

Nevertheless, the students were in his class, and the principal was not about to transfer them out. Since he was a good teacher, Mr. Martin knew he should be doing something for them, and he felt guilty that they just sat quietly in the back of his classroom. On the other hand, it seemed to him that giving those students special attention wasn't fair to the rest of the students, who were doing just fine with his traditional instruction. At the same time, the extra training he was receiving made him feel guilty because it stressed that teachers should not simply give students busywork; they should engage students in meaningful activities with other students in the classroom. However, Mr. Martin's teaching style did not include much student interaction. He became doubly frustrated, as he felt that he was being asked not only to deal with new students but also to change his way of teaching.

ANALYSIS

Mr. Martin, like Mrs. Brown, is a conscientious teacher in a school system that is changing. He has succeeded in the past and resents the fact that he has been designated to deal with the new students. It is probable that the principal chose Mr. Martin because he was an experienced teacher, and she believed he could handle the new challenge. However, Mr. Martin feels singled out and resentful of the extra time and training necessary to work with emergent bilinguals. In addition, he believes that giving them special instruction is actually going to be detrimental to his other students. At this point, Mr. Martin does not understand that what is good instruction for emergent bilinguals is beneficial for all students.

POSITIVE RESPONSES

Teachers we have worked with have come to realize that it is impossible to use a traditional teacher-centered model of teaching to reach a very diverse student body. In addition, as they try interactive activities in which heterogeneous groups of students work on projects together, they see that all their students, including their native English-speaking students, learn more. Several teachers who entered our graduate classes determined never to change their teaching styles later gave enthusiastic testimonials of how exciting teaching can be when it is organized around units of inquiry and includes literature studies, creative writing, and projects involving art, science, music, and drama.

At the same time, it is important for schools to provide appropriate education for all their students. Placement for older students with limited formal schooling is difficult unless the school has developed specific programs to educate its students with limited formal education who also have low levels of English proficiency. More resources are now available to guide schools in working with this group of students, such as texts by Custodio and O'Loughlin (2017) and Samway, Pease-Alvarez, and Alvarez (2020); see also the CUNY-NYSIEB website (Carpenter, Espinet, and Pratt n.d.).

"Who Wants to Be the Bilingual Teacher?"

Mr. González went into bilingual education because he himself had come to the United States as a non-English-speaking child, and he knew how difficult it was to succeed in school as an emergent bilingual. His education classes had taught him that instruction in the home language helps children academically and actually speeds their success in English. He is a certified bilingual teacher. During his first two years of teaching, he enthusiastically worked with his fourth graders, supporting their home language and helping them succeed in their new language.

By the end of the third year, when he was tenured, his enthusiasm began to wane. Mr. González was troubled by the subtle way his fellow teachers treated him. The bilingual program was considered remedial, and constant remarks in the teachers' lounge showed him that fellow teachers did not really believe emergent bilinguals were capable of the kind of success other students could achieve. In addition, he had not been given good-quality materials for teaching in Spanish, and he had to spend extra time creating or finding resources. Further, the principal asked him to translate school documents going out to parents, and even for someone with high levels of proficiency in a language, translation takes considerable time.

In addition, Mr. González soon discovered that Latinx children who were discipline problems were being transferred into his class throughout the year even though they were not English learners. When he objected, the principal explained that since he was Latinx, he could understand those children better. Mr. González's attempts to explain that his program was geared to work with Spanish speakers to help them succeed academically, not with discipline problems, fell on deaf ears. He began to feel that his expertise was not respected and that his classroom was becoming a dumping ground. He put in a request to be taken out of the bilingual program.

ANALYSIS

Mr. González's situation is one that has repeated itself many times in different school districts. When there is little understanding of what bilingual education really is and why it is important, bilingual teachers feel isolated and misunderstood. Often, uninformed teachers make assumptions about emergent bilinguals and do not hesitate to express their opinions about the limited potential of that group of students.

Some administrators who have heard about the importance of ethnic and cultural role models but do not really know the theory behind bilingual education try to find quick and easy solutions to problems of students from diverse backgrounds. In this case all Latinx were lumped together, and Mr. González was asked to solve all the problems of the Latinx students at the school. Given these factors, it is no wonder that some bilingual teachers ask to be placed in nonbilingual classes.

POSITIVE RESPONSES

A bright spot in the area of bilingual education is the changing attitudes toward bilingual education and the continued increase in the number of dual language bilingual programs. These programs have had positive results for native English speakers and those learning English, as both groups become bilingual and biliterate.

Nevertheless, dual language is difficult in contexts where not enough bilingual teachers are available, or where the emergent bilinguals speak multiple languages. For many languages there are not enough students speaking one language in a school to justify dual language programs. In schools that have a mix of emergent bilinguals with different home languages, teachers have experienced success using translanguaging when given instruction and guidance in using translanguaging effectively (Freeman, Soto, and Freeman 2016; Fu, Hadjioannou, and Zhou 2019; García, Ibarra Johnson, and Seltzer 2017; García and Kleyn 2016).

REFLECT OR TURN AND TALK

Looking back at the scenarios of different teachers, which one(s) have you observed? Think of one or two specific examples of teachers whose attitudes affect their teaching, positively or negatively. Jot down some notes and share your example (without identifying the teacher).

Coping with Changes in Student Populations

Despite the positive changes that are taking place in some schools, there is still much to be done to improve the education of emergent bilinguals. Although many teachers and administrators are learning about English learners and are implementing effective programs in their schools, some schools have not adjusted to the changes in the school population. In their extensive study of immigrant youth in high schools, Suárez-Orozco, Suárez-Orozco, and Todorova (2008) found that only 10 percent of the students named a teacher as someone they would go to for help, 21 percent named a teacher as someone who respected them, and only 3 percent named a teacher as someone who was proud of them.

When the researchers talked to the teachers and administrators about the students, they responded that they were happy to have new immigrants who had "a desire to learn, [were] more disciplined, and value[d] education" (Suárez-Orozco, Suárez-Orozco, and Todorova 2008, 134), but for long-term English learners there was less enthusiasm. In a teachers' lounge in a largely Dominican and Puerto Rican high school, the researchers heard a teacher ask her colleagues, who nodded as she spoke, "What do you expect me to do with these kids? Within the next few years, most of the girls will be pregnant and the boys are going to be in jail" (Suárez-Orozco, Suárez-Orozco, and Todorova 2008, 137). In an interview with a superintendent of a highly diverse district with a large number of immigrants, the researchers asked, "What is the hardest thing about your job?" He responded, "To get the teachers to believe these children can learn" (137). With the growing number of second language students, the process of developing the skills, knowledge, and positive attitudes for teaching the changing school population effectively becomes more critical daily. Change is stressful, but a number of teachers are not only coping with it but learning how to celebrate the growing diversity in their classrooms.

Coping with Change During and After the COVID-19 Pandemic

In 2019 in Wuhan, China, a novel coronavirus, COVID-19, spread rapidly. Unfortunately, it wasn't contained in China, and because of international travel, the virus spread throughout the world. By February 2021, there were almost 28 million cases reported in the US and more than 500 thousand deaths. The figures grow daily and the pandemic has caused havoc around the world to not only health but also economies. The data available online changes daily as cases and deaths increase (www .worldometers.info/coronavirus). Even with vaccines, it will take some time for enough people to be vaccinated for the spread to be reduced.

As a result of this pandemic, countries have gone into lockdown, and businesses, houses of worship, and schools have been shut down. In the United States, as in most places, education changed overnight. Teachers at every level of education suddenly had the responsibility of doing all or some of their teaching remotely. Many students were confined to their homes and had to adjust to learning through technology and also having to manage their learning on their own. Even when schools have opened to in-person learning, many parents and teachers have been concerned since outbreaks continue to occur.

In a policy brief from the Migration Policy Institute (Sugarman and Lazarín 2020) the authors state that "The COVID-19 pandemic has brought into sharp relief the inequities that English Learners (ELs) and children from immigrant families experience in U.S. schools and in their communities." They explain that despite great efforts by educators, in the spring of 2020 the school systems with the largest number of ELs reported that less than half the ELs were logging in to online instruction. They point out that "Among the most significant barriers to ELs' participation were: a lack of access to digital devices and broadband; parents' limited capacity to support home learning; inadequate remote learning resources and training for teachers; and school–family language barriers." The report concludes that if schools continue distance learning through the fall, many students will lose 7 to 11 months of learning. In addition, "for many families of ELs, the pandemic and accompanied school building closures have compromised their access to food and income security as well as social and mental-health supports" (1).

For the many emergent bilingual students, there have been additional challenges. Even when districts have provided students with Chromebooks and students have access to internet services, crowded home conditions have kept students from concentrating. Many families have several family members sharing one device. Some teachers find they can communicate only via a cell phone needed by all family members. As a result of these conditions, students have had trouble completing work effectively.

Psychological and emotional issues are also at play. Families of English learners are affected in both cities and rural areas. Many of the adults in these groups are considered essential workers in grocery stores, making deliveries and food packing, and as a result, they are exposed to the virus daily. Members of EL communities have above-average infection and death rates. Other immigrants have lost jobs because they worked in service industries that closed, like restaurants and hotels. Hunger has become an issue too, because children are no longer fed at school and parents sometimes have no money for food to feed families. The stress on students and the families is immense.

In all of this change, teachers have tried to use the resources they have to teach their students. Some teachers are more comfortable than others using online platforms that allow them to interact with students remotely, but all have noticed problems with students' attention spans and the stress students are experiencing. While many online resources have become available, the sudden inundation of possibilities is overwhelming to many teachers trying to simply teach some key ideas each day. Students and teachers all want things to go back to normal.

Schools have tried different ways to get students back into classrooms. That has meant creating smaller classes to provide physical distancing and having students wear masks. Some schools have had to remodel their ventilation systems. By making these changes, many schools have been able to offer a blend of teaching in person and online.

All of these changes in settings where teachers had emergent bilingual students only made teaching more complex. Teachers ask themselves how they need to teach emergent bilinguals content using proven techniques and strategies in limited time frames. At this point, teachers are being creative and trying to find new ways to support their English learners in person and remotely.

Yvonne's Story

A teacher's practice changes over time in response to new experiences and challenges, new studies, new materials, new types of students, new legal mandates, a new emphasis on standards and accountability, and new environmental conditions. While teachers can learn from all their experiences, effective teachers develop a set of principles that guide their teaching. These principles are based on their understanding of research and theory in second language acquisition and second language teaching. They help teachers choose methods and techniques for working with their second language students. Yvonne's story provides a good example of a teacher who has developed principles that guide her teaching. As she has read theory and research and as she has experienced new teaching situations, she has continually refined her teaching to provide the best education she can for her students.

Yvonne has moved through different stages of understanding about how language is learned and how language and content might best be taught to emergent bilinguals. Her teaching has been influenced by several of the factors listed in Figure 4–1. We hope that Yvonne's story will help you reflect on your beliefs and practices. Greater awareness of why we teach the way we do can help us refine our principles and make the changes necessary for providing the best education for all our students.

Yvonne studied several different languages in high school and college. Her four years of high school Latin were taught through a grammar translation method in which students memorized grammar rules and vocabulary and carefully translated great works such as *The Odyssey* and *The Iliad* from Latin to English. The study of Latin was considered a good scholarly exercise that would provide a base for English vocabulary development, but there was never any consideration that knowledge of the Latin language might be useful outside the Latin class.

As a high school junior, Yvonne, who at the time had no intention of ever becoming a teacher, decided to study Spanish. Students in her Spanish class studied less grammar and vocabulary than in the Latin class. Instead, they memorized dialogues that they practiced and recited. The most memorable and enjoyable activities in the Spanish class were learning and performing the Mexican hat dance and singing songs in Spanish. Yvonne continued her study of Spanish at community college. The advanced class was tedious, with grammar tests and long hours spent repeating drills in the language laboratory.

It wasn't until she went to a university as a junior majoring in Spanish that it dawned on Yvonne that there was more to language learning than memorizing rules and taking tests. Her Spanish grammar class was going well, but she was put into a Spanish literature class with an instructor who lectured only in Spanish. For the first three weeks of class, she took limited and inadequate notes, because the language seemed to fly by her unintelligibly. She knew something had to be done, so she made plans to go to Mexico that summer.

The Mexican summer experience was a turning point in her Spanish proficiency. Yvonne's train trip to Guadalajara gave her the opportunity to put the language she had learned to real use. She was amazed when her carefully formed sentences were understood, and somewhat shaken when rapid answers came shooting back. She and three fellow students stayed with a family while she studied in Guadalajara, and because she had the strongest Spanish language background of the three, she soon found herself in the role of language negotiator. Her success with the family, a brief romantic interlude, and exciting weekend travel excursions convinced Yvonne that she had found her niche. Her interest in the Spanish language and the Latinx culture led naturally to her decision to become a Spanish teacher.

Back in the United States, Yvonne enrolled in a cutting-edge teacher education program. In just one year, students in this program got both a teaching credential and a master's degree in education. Teacher training included videotaped micro teaching sessions that allowed student teachers to view their performance and critique their own lessons. Methodology classes presented the latest techniques of leading different kinds of audiolingual drills. These techniques were based on a behaviorist view of learning. In fact, one of her education-methods professors was considered an international expert on teaching language. Yvonne accepted the idea that learning, and especially language learning, consisted of forming habits. All her own language instruction had assumed that kind of a model. In her classes, students had memorized dialogues, and teachers had corrected errors quickly. Yvonne and her classmates had repeated their lines as their cheerleading teachers led them rapidly through carefully selected language-pattern exercises. Yvonne's teacher education classes prepared her to teach as she had been taught.

She received her credential and took a job in an inner-city high school. Despite all her preparation, her first teaching position was a real eye-opener. She was teaching five classes a day of Spanish 1. Her audiolingual method (ALM) Spanish 1 book included lesson after lesson of dialogues and drills. Her students hated what they called the "boring repetition" and "stupid dialogues." Yvonne was devastated. She wanted her students to love speaking Spanish as much as she did. She remembered her positive experiences in Mexico but had forgotten how bored she had been when forced through similar drills.

Faced with 150 resisting and restless high school students each day, Yvonne began to look closely at the lines from the dialogues that the students were repeating. Instinctively, without really knowing what she was doing, she began to change the dialogues to make them more relevant. *A mi no me gustan las albóndigas* (I don't like meatballs) became *A mi no me gustan las hamburguesas con cebolla* (I don't like hamburgers with onion), and she encouraged the students to expand the talk to include other things they did not like. She even gave them choice in the dialogues they practiced. Yvonne wanted her students to realize that Spanish is a language that real people use for real purposes. She invited some friends visiting from Mexico to her class.

The students prepared and asked questions they wanted to know about teenagers in Mexico. That class period was one of the best of the year.

The classroom context for learning was improving. However, contexts interact, and what goes on outside the classroom has a great impact on curriculum. Yvonne soon found herself in trouble on two very different fronts. In the first place, the department chair discovered that Yvonne was giving students vocabulary lists with words that were not part of the department curriculum and was encouraging students to create their own dialogues. The problem, of course, was that the students were not always saying things correctly and were undoubtedly learning some incorrect Spanish. The department chair, a strong advocate of ALM, did not want students to develop bad language habits. In the second place, as she attempted to use more authentic Spanish with her students, Yvonne realized that she had not learned enough "real" Spanish to truly help her students say everything they wanted to say.

Yvonne decided to find an opportunity to improve her Spanish proficiency. She and her adventurous husband, a high school English teacher, decided that they should live abroad, so they both took teaching jobs at an American school in Colombia, South America. Yvonne found herself with absolutely no background for her teaching job. Educated as a high school Spanish teacher, she was assigned to teach fifth grade in Colombia using curriculum from the United States. Some of her students spoke English as a foreign language and would never visit the United States. Others were native speakers of English whose parents expected them to attend college in the United States.

Like many teachers faced with a difficult assignment for which they are not prepared, Yvonne relied heavily at first on the textbooks the school provided. Basal readers from the United States as well as social studies and science textbooks were the center of her curriculum. Again, however, she found herself responding to her students. Many of the basal reading stories were boring or completely unrelated to the students' interests and needs. The social studies and science texts were almost impossible for the students to read and understand. Though other materials were not easy to find, Yvonne centered much of what she and the students did on projects, stories, and discussions. Since most of the teachers in the school were experiencing the same problems, they shared ideas about what was working in their classrooms.

The teaching couple returned to the United States after a year, more fluent in Spanish. Yvonne's husband found a job teaching high school English in a small city, but there were no high school Spanish jobs. When a local government assistance agency in their new town called to ask if she would volunteer to teach English to Spanish-speaking adults, Yvonne decided to try it. Her first class of students included two Mexican women with no previous schooling and a college-educated couple from Bolivia. With no materials, not even paper or pencils, and diverse students, Yvonne, in desperation, asked the students what English they wanted and needed to learn. Starting with any materials she could get, including props, maps, pamphlets, and resource guides, Yvonne soon found herself teaching a class that had grown to forty adults on a variety of topics including nutrition, shopping, community services, childcare, and geography.

Yvonne's class became a part of the public school's adult education program, and Yvonne began teaming with another teacher who also loved teaching adult ESL. The two collaborated daily, making up skits, writing songs, organizing around themes, and creating a community with students who came from Mexico, Central America, South America, Northern and Eastern Europe, the Middle East, Japan, Korea, and Southeast Asia.

Though Yvonne had come a long way from having students memorize dialogues and do drills, she was still uncomfortable about what she should be doing to teach language. She and her team teacher, a former high school English teacher, often would pull out traditional grammar sheets and do a part of their daily lesson with some of those exercises to be sure the students understood the structure of the language. When those lessons seemed to go nowhere, especially with adults who had had little previous schooling, the teachers dropped the grammar books in favor of books with stories and discussion questions. However, the readings were seldom related to student needs and experiences, so the two teachers kept returning to skits, songs, and projects created around relevant themes.

Yvonne and her partner had an additional experience that stretched them in new directions and strengthened their conviction that language learning was more than memorizing grammatical rules and repeating pattern drills. The two were asked to teach as adjunct instructors in an intensive English program at the local university. A large group of Japanese college students had arrived, and although these students had extensive background in English grammar and vocabulary, they understood and spoke little English. Initially, the Japanese students resisted classroom activities that were not carefully organized around grammar exercises, but Yvonne and her partner worked hard to get the students to take the risk to speak English in class and in the community. Several of the Japanese students came to appreciate the emphasis on using English for real purposes and began to attend the adult ESL classes as well as the university classes.

After she had taught the Japanese students for two years and the adults for nine, Yvonne and her husband decided that they would like to teach abroad again, taking their children along. They moved to Mexico City, where new learning and teaching experiences awaited them. They first taught professional adults English in a large language institute. The institute was moving away from using a textbook based on audiolingual methodology to a new series using the notional-functional approach, so both Yvonne and her husband learned about teaching language communicatively around functions such as apologizing, giving directions, and making introductions, and around notions such as time and space.

Since their teaching schedule did not fit the school schedule for their young children, Yvonne left her job with adults and began teaching fifth grade at the bilingual school her daughters attended. The school was typical of most private schools in Mexico City. The student body for kindergarten through sixth grade had about five thousand students. The playground was a huge expanse of cement with no trees or play equipment of any kind. Classrooms had one chalkboard in the front of the room, with a raised platform for the teacher's desk. There was one bulletin board, decorated monthly by the teacher and checked by the supervising administrator. Desks were bolted in rows filling up the entire room.

The school where Yvonne taught had classes of only forty students. This school was popular because of the small class size. Other schools had sixty or more in a class. Yvonne soon learned that most parents in Mexico City, if they could scrape together any money, sent their children to a private school such as this because public schools had larger classes and fewer materials.

At this bilingual school, half of the day was taught in Spanish and the other half in English. The English curriculum was centered on basal readers and textbooks from the United States, as it had been in Colombia, and the Spanish curriculum used Mexican government texts. The school required teachers to follow the textbook-based curriculum carefully. All assignments involved copying and memorizing. Students' needs were viewed only in terms of passing the textbook or government tests that were administered by the school monthly. Discipline was strict. Students stood up to answer questions and were not to speak otherwise.

Fortunately, the administration of this school discovered that Yvonne had a master's degree in education, a very high degree among Mexican teachers at schools like this. Many elementary teachers in Mexico have little training beyond high school.

After teaching a month of the regimented fifth-grade curriculum, Yvonne found herself the administrator in charge of the English curriculum for twenty-three teachers. She began to reflect on how many times she had found herself in positions she was unprepared for and yet how similar her conclusions were each time. Again, she wondered how meaningful the curriculum was for the students. If the Mexican students were studying at a bilingual school so that they could learn to read, write, and speak English, were the US textbooks appropriate? Should they be reading in basal readers about blond, blue-eyed Americans going to an American birthday party or going ice-skating in snowy weather? Would they really learn English when their teachers rarely allowed them to speak English, or any language, in class, and when the teachers rarely spoke to them in either English or Spanish?

Yvonne encouraged the teachers to center their curriculum on themes of interest to children of various ages. She collected stories and information related to celebrations, science topics, and biographies of famous people that seemed to lend themselves to language use and content learning. She encouraged teachers to involve students in drama and music using English songs and plays. She helped teachers write plays for their students and tried to encourage conversation activities. However, all of this was done on a limited basis, as the school requirements were stringent, and any activities beyond preparing students for tests were considered frills.

After two years of teaching in Mexico City, Yvonne and her husband moved back to the United States, where her husband began graduate study and she took a position teaching senior composition and freshman English at a private high school. The composition class was organized around a packet of materials that students were to follow carefully, completing assignments at their own pace with no class discussion. The freshman English class curriculum included short stories, a library unit, the play *Romeo and Juliet*, and study of a grammar book written in England.

Again, Yvonne looked at her students, this time all native speakers of English, and wondered about teaching to their interests and needs. In this situation, unlike the Mexico and the high school Spanish experiences, the English department chairperson was flexible and sympathetic to deviations from the set curriculum. Before the year was over, Yvonne had students in the composition class meeting in groups, having whole-class discussions, writing joint compositions, and sharing their writing. She largely ignored the grammar book for the freshmen, had them write and edit their own compositions, and encouraged discussion of their reading. Before teaching *Romeo and Juliet*, Yvonne planned with another freshman English teacher to have their students view the movie *West Side Story*, which provided them with valuable background for the Shakespeare play.

However, Yvonne did not feel that her previous experiences were best utilized by teaching English to high school students, so the following year, she went back to graduate school and worked as a graduate teaching assistant in the Spanish department. Her graduate work included both a second master's degree, this time in English as a second language, and doctoral work in education. In her ESL program she studied SLA theory and second language teaching methods. Many of the writers advocated a communicative approach to teaching language. She was especially impressed by the work of Krashen (1982), who differentiated between acquisition and learning, a distinction that made sense to Yvonne because of her own language learning and teaching experiences.

While her ESL classes were interesting, it was her doctoral studies that really challenged Yvonne to think seriously about learning and teaching and the relationship between the two. She majored in language and literacy and minored in bilingual education. This combination seemed to fit her interests and her experiences. She began studying about language learning with a focus on the development of second language literacy. As she read the work of Ferreiro and Teberosky (1982), Goodman (1986), Goodman et al. (1987), Halliday (1975), Halliday and Hasan (1989), Graves (1983), Heath (1983), Lindfors (1987), Piaget (1955), Smith (1988), and Vygotsky (1962, 1978), Yvonne began to make connections among her language learning and teaching experiences and the theories she was studying. She realized two things: First, what she was learning about made sense because of what she had experienced in her own language learning and her many teaching jobs. Second, much classroom practice was not consistent with current theory.

As she studied, Yvonne made her beginning college Spanish classes her laboratory. With her first-year Spanish classes, she talked about how children learn language, how language is acquired naturally in a risk-free environment, and how language must have meaning and purpose for learners. Students wrote in Spanish daily in their journals, and she responded in writing. Students read current articles of interest to them, working in groups to interpret the Spanish. Students learned Spanish in the course of investigating themes such as friendship, professions, and dating customs. One of the most successful projects was a pen pal exchange between students in different college classes. Yvonne realized that students would devote more energy to writing a nongraded assignment, a letter to a peer, than to writing a composition in Spanish for the instructor to grade.

After graduation, Yvonne and her husband found teacher education positions at a small, private university in California that was known for innovative literacy practices but needed to expand its program offerings for teachers to include teaching English language learners. Yvonne was hired to teach language acquisition and bilingual education courses for students working on a master's degree in ESL or bilingual education.

A teacher always learns more than the students, and for Yvonne this seemed to be especially true. She did a great deal of reading to be sure that her students were reading the latest theory and research, and at the same time, she worked hard to be certain that her practices as a college professor reflected what she had learned about how people learn best. Her assignments for her students always combined theory and practice as students applied what they were learning to their own emergent bilingual students and then shared with other teachers what had been successful. An outgrowth of the reading she was doing, and of the projects and work with the practicing teachers at the university, was the coauthoring with her husband of teacher education books on the topics of ESL methodology, language acquisition, reading for English learners, and linguistics.

After ten years of teaching at this university, Yvonne and her husband were awarded Fulbright Scholarships to teach at the University of the Andes in Venezuela. Here again, Yvonne experienced lessons in second language acquisition. She had become more proficient in Spanish. However, since she had developed a high level of grammatical competence in Spanish and could converse with her colleagues at the university fluently in Spanish, she worked to become more communicatively competent in this social setting. Was she saying the right thing to the right person at the right time? Yvonne now had to be careful not to be rude unintentionally. She could not apply her US English communicative norms to her colleagues at the university. For example, she soon learned that trying to communicate with people efficiently and quickly was frowned upon. It was much better to stop by someone's office several times and miss them than to leave a note. The note was perceived as an emergency that had to be taken care of immediately. While discussing the details of a surgery and displaying scars with a casual acquaintance was acceptable, blowing one's nose in public was not! All these types of lessons helped Yvonne understand language learning at new levels.

After returning to California, Yvonne had another important experience with language learning. She wrote and directed two Title VII bilingual dual language grants. They were to prepare preservice teachers to teach in Spanish or Hmong dual language classrooms. Through this experience with schools and preservice Mexican and

Hmong bilingual teachers, Yvonne grew to understand more deeply the challenges involved in learning how to teach and learn bilingually.

The passing of Proposition 227, banning bilingual education in California, made it difficult to attract students into the graduate programs in bilingual education. Colleagues in Texas encouraged Yvonne and her husband to move to Texas, a bilingual-friendly state with a growing number of dual language bilingual schools. They spent three years at one university. During this time she had the opportunity to work in several of the Texas-border one-way dual language schools where Spanish-speaking students learned in both Spanish and English and both languages and cultures were valued. This work, the experience with the dual language grants in California, and research in different kinds of dual language schools led her to write a book with her husband and a California colleague on dual language education.

Yvonne then worked at a different Texas university that had a doctoral program in curriculum and instruction with a specialization in bilingual studies. She taught teachers and administrators who worked in schools with emergent bilinguals. Most of these teachers and administrators began school speaking a language other than English. They were English learners at one time in their lives. However, as professionals and doctoral students, many of them found they still struggled with reading and writing academic English. Yvonne worked with these students to help them develop the academic language they needed to succeed as future professors themselves.

With every teaching experience she had, Yvonne's beliefs were confirmed that teaching must be geared to student needs and that learning occurs when students are engaged in the topic they are studying. Yvonne learned many lessons through her experiences, but perhaps the most important of these is one she came to gradually throughout her teaching career: that theory and research inform practice, and reflection on practice can shape a teacher's working theory. Yvonne, like most teachers, began with an eclectic view. She used whatever seemed to work. She also used the language teaching methods being advocated at the time. However, with more experience and study, she found that by reflecting on her practice and basing it on current research and theory, she was able to move away from eclecticism and develop a principled approach to her teaching, which she now shares with other educators through her writing and speaking.

Now retired but continuing to be active professionally with writing and speaking, Yvonne has discovered a new challenge. How can bilingual and ESL teachers and teacher educators meet the needs of their students and help them develop language in the new normal of teaching virtually and, when possible, also in person? What is the best way to support dual language teachers teaching content in two languages and helping students develop biliteracy? What are the best supports for teachers with multilingual students in ESL and content classes? How can translanguaging be implemented online to draw on students' linguistic repertoires? Presently, Yvonne and her husband are talking to dual language teachers, teachers with multilingual learners, and teacher educators to work with them to solve these issues. As always, teachers need to draw on their students' needs and interests and develop curriculum that engages them in learning what they need to know. Yvonne is convinced that a principled approach drawing on the latest research, theory, and successful practices is key.

REFLECT OR TURN AND TALK

In what ways does Yvonne's teaching story parallel your own experiences? How have you adjusted your teaching in response to your teaching experiences and the theory and research you have read? Share your reflections with a colleague.

What have your virtual and in-class teaching experiences been like? What has helped you juggle both teaching experiences?

Principled Teaching

Principled teaching involves implementing practices consistent with our knowledge of theory and research as well as our reflection on our practice. These beliefs are what we refer to as our *orientation*. A principled orientation is one in which beliefs are based on theory tested in practice.

When a teacher works in a school with a prescribed curriculum, the teacher's options are limited. While it is possible to make adaptations in implementing a fixed curriculum, there are limits on what a teacher can do. Schools that adopt programs for teaching reading, math, or other subjects to all their students—including their emergent bilinguals—rely on the expertise of the team that created the program rather than the needs of the students and the knowledge of individual teachers. Prescribed programs are applied to all students equally despite the great differences among them.

Teachers in many schools are expected to use the district's curriculum, textbooks, and other materials. Even though these prescribed materials include suggestions for working with emergent bilinguals, we have found the suggestions very limited. In her teacher education classes, Mary engaged the student teachers in a variety of activities based on a principled orientation. They were designed to make the curriculum more comprehensible for English learners. The students loved the strategies, but teachers found it difficult to implement them in school settings where they were expected to use the district-prescribed curriculum. Mary's future teachers realized that what was being required did not fit the needs of all their students, especially their emergent bilinguals.

Since many teachers across the country face the problem of teaching mandated curriculum to English learners, Yvonne, David, and Mary worked together to write a book (Soto, Freeman, and Freeman 2020) that included a discussion of strategies that would give emergent bilinguals equitable access to curriculum designed for native English speakers. We described how these strategies could be applied in teaching language arts units on seeds and plants, habitats, oceans, and natural disasters. Each of the chapters begins with a discussion of one of the principles that guides our writing and our work with teachers. These principles are explained in detail in *ESL Teaching: Principles of Success* (Freeman et al. 2016). We list these principles in Figure 4–2.

Principles for Effective Teaching

1. Teaching should be learner centered.
2. Teaching should go from whole to part.
3. Teaching should develop academic language and content.
4. Teaching should be meaningful and purposeful to engage students.
5. Teaching should include carefully planned interactions to develop both oral and written language.
6. Teaching should support students' languages and cultures.
7. Teaching and assessment should reflect faith in the learner to expand student potential.

Figure 4–2 • Principles for Effective Teaching

REFLECT OR TURN AND TALK

Reflect on your own practices and beliefs about best ways to teach emergent bilinguals. List the principles you follow. Share them with a colleague.

How have you adapted mandated curriculum to meet the needs of emergent bilinguals?

5

How Have Views of Bilinguals Changed and What Models Have Been Used to Teach Them?

Research in several fields, including neurolinguistics, sociolinguistics, and education, have contributed to a better understanding of emergent bilingual students. At the same time, the number of English learners in US schools has steadily increased, and the education of these students is no longer the sole responsibility of an ESL teacher or a bilingual teacher. Rather, all teachers must be prepared to educate emergent bilinguals. Research on programs for English learners has shown the effectiveness of well-implemented dual language bilingual models, and schools have responded to the changes in the school population

Key Points

- In the United States the number of bilinguals has steadily increased but monolingualism is still the norm.

- Bilinguals have greater cross-cultural competence than monolinguals.

- Bilingualism has linguistic, academic, economic, and cognitive benefits.

- Studies in neurolinguistics and sociolinguistics have led to changing views of bilinguals.

- Researchers have found that bilinguals are not balanced (equally competent in two languages).

- Two views of bilingualism are monoglossic and heteroglossic.

- A monoglossic view is that bilinguals are essentially two monolinguals in one person with two separate languages.

- A heteroglossic view is that bilinguals have one complex linguistic repertoire that has features of two or more languages.

- It is a misconception that the two languages of a bilingual should be kept separate for instruction.

- Cummins conducted research showing that the languages of a bilingual have a common underlying proficiency and that the languages are interdependent.

- Teachers can use translanguaging strategies to affirm students' bilingual identities, build metalinguistic awareness, and scaffold instruction.

- Translanguaging is not code-switching.

- Schooling models for emergent bilinguals include ESL programs (pull-out, push-in, and stand-alone programs) and bilingual programs (early-exit, late-exit, and dual language programs).

- Long-term dual language bilingual programs lead to more academic success for emergent bilinguals than other models.

- The use of effective practices may be more important than the program model.

by implementing more dual language bilingual programs designed to make all their students bilingual and biliterate.

Bilingualism Around the World and in the United States

Although estimates vary, there are around seven thousand languages found in the 192 countries in the world. Most of these countries are bilingual or multilingual. Grosjean (2010), looking at the numbers of countries and the numbers of languages in the world, estimates that at least half the world's population must be bilingual. In fact, with the exception of Iceland and possibly North Korea, the world's countries have almost always been inhabited by people who have spoken two or more languages (Grosjean 2010). Many of these bilinguals are really multilingual, especially if we accept Grosjean's definition of bilinguals as "those who use two or more languages (or dialects) in their everyday lives" (2010, 4).

Baker and Wright have come to a similar conclusion:

> Bilinguals are present in every country in the world, in every social class, and in all age groups. Numerically, bilinguals and multilinguals are in the majority in the world: it is estimated that they constitute between half and two thirds of the world's population. (2017, 60)

Although bilinguals are in the majority worldwide, for many people living in the United States, monolingualism is still considered the norm. While 56 percent of those polled in the European countries reported that they were fluent in at least one other language, Grosjean (2012) estimates that only around 20 percent of people living in the United States are bilingual and those include people who pair "English with Native American languages, older colonial languages, recent immigrant languages, American Sign Language, and so on."

Reports show that the number of bilingual and multilingual people in the United States has steadily increased. According to a Migration Policy Institute report on language diversity in the United States by Batalova and Zong (2016), 60 percent of those who do speak a language other than English at home reported that they are also fully English proficient; that is, they are bilingual. The number of immigrants and US natives speaking a language other than English at home represents one in five US residents. Grosjean (2020) in a recent blog and using a different database concluded that the number of bilinguals in the US is about 63 million people.

As the US population becomes more diverse, schools reflect this increasing linguistic and ethnic diversity. The changes in school populations bring a challenge because many more students at all grade levels have limited English proficiency. For that reason, all teachers need to develop a better understanding of how best to educate classes that include many emergent bilinguals.

Linguistic and Cultural Capital

Many different languages are spoken in the United States but until recently schools have privileged English and have not promoted the development of English learners' home languages. One reason for this is that in much of the world, English is associated with prestige. Certainly, in the United States those who speak English well have *linguistic capital* (Bourdieu and Passeron 1977), a kind of power that those who do not speak the language well do not have. There are other kinds of capital. Students from the dominant culture who understand how things are done within a culture have *cultural capital*.

Students coming to school with a home language other than English have neither linguistic nor cultural capital when they begin school. As they are learning English, they lack this power because they are not yet proficient in either the language or the cultural practices. Even people who speak two or three languages other than English daily may lack linguistic capital because the languages they are using are not valued, and their skills at using their home languages are not appreciated. English and other major languages are so predominant that speakers of other languages come to see the dominant languages as more important than their own. Many speakers shift from their native tongues to the power language, giving up not only their language but also their culture in the process.

However, education in the twenty-first century is beginning to change to reflect the realities of our rapidly changing world. Not only are science, math, and technology important, but so is the ability to read, write, and speak two or more languages. Policy makers and educators have recognized the critical need for Americans to become multilingual in the growing global economy. When former Secretary of Education Riley highlighted the dual language approach as the most effective way to teach English and encourage biliteracy, he pointed out that "language is at the core of the Latino experience in this country, and it must be at the center of future opportunities. It is high time we begin to treat language skills as the asset they are" (Riley 2000).

Benefits of Bilingualism

When emergent bilinguals develop high levels of linguistic proficiency in English and in an additional language, their linguistic and cultural capital greatly increase. The linguistic advantages are obvious. Bilinguals can communicate in more contexts with more people than monolinguals can. This proves beneficial when people travel to other countries as well as when they communicate with people living in the United States who do not speak English or do not speak it well. The linguistic benefits of bilingualism also result in academic, economic, and cognitive benefits. In addition, bilingual programs help all students develop cross-cultural competence and global awareness, one of the interdisciplinary themes listed in the Partnership for 21st Century Learning (2019) framework. The framework lists several skills as part of global awareness. They include

- using twenty-first-century skills to understand and address global issues
- learning from and working collaboratively with individuals representing diverse cultures, religions, and lifestyles in a spirit of mutual respect and open dialogue in personal, work, and community contexts
- understanding other nations and cultures, including the use of non-English languages. (2)

Copyright © 2020, Battelle for Kids. All rights reserved. www.bfk.org.

Academic Benefits of Becoming Bilingual

In a review of research on dual language, Lindholm-Leary (2020) found that emergent bilinguals "achieve at or above grade-level norms in English reading and writing by grades 5–7" and native English speakers "acquire the same or higher levels of English competence as their peers in mainstream programs" (2).

In a longitudinal study of a large district, Valentino and Reardon (2014) analyzed the standardized test scores of 13,750 bilinguals in English language arts each year from second through eighth grade and in math from second to sixth grade. They compared results for students in the different programs that the district offered: English immersion, transitional bilingual, developmental bilingual, and dual language bilingual programs. The longitudinal data for tests of English language arts showed that while the scores of English learners in English immersion, transitional bilingual, and developmental bilingual programs all increase at about the same rate as the state average for all students, scores for students in dual language bilingual classes increase more rapidly than the state average. Valentino and Reardon comment, "This rate is so fast, that by fifth grade their test scores in ELA catch up to the state average, and on average by seventh grade ELs in DI are scoring above their EL counterparts in all of the other programs" (21).

Collier and Thomas (2009) conducted a series of large-scale long-term studies on dual language programs in different parts of the United States. They consistently found that by sixth grade students in dual language bilingual programs score higher than native English speakers in national norms on standardized tests of reading and math in English.

In addition, several meta-analyses have shown that bilinguals in well-implemented, long-term bilingual education programs succeed academically at higher rates than students in transitional bilingual programs or ESL programs (Greene 1998; Rolstad, Mahoney, and Glass 2005; Slavin and Cheung 2003). As these studies all show, emergent bilinguals in programs that develop high levels of proficiency in both their home language and English succeed academically at higher levels than other English learners and, when the programs are long-term, they also succeed academically at higher levels than monolingual English speakers.

Economic and Cognitive Benefits of Becoming Bilingual

In addition to the linguistic and academic advantage, programs that develop students' bilingualism provide economic and cognitive advantages for all students. Callahan and Gándara, in *The Bilingual Advantage: Language, Literacy, and the US Labor Market* (2014), provide evidence of the economic benefits of bilingualism. The chapters present empirical studies from researchers in education, economics, sociology, anthropology, and linguistics showing the economic and employment benefits of bilingualism in the US labor market. Unlike previous studies, this book focuses on individuals who have developed high levels of bilingualism and biliteracy. Such people have greater employment potential than monolinguals.

Our own daughters, Ann and Mary, have both benefited from developing high levels of bilingualism and biliteracy. They started their education in a bilingual school in Mexico City and returned after two years to the United States, where they continued to develop their bilingualism in a dual language school in Tucson, Arizona. In Tucson they became friends with three teens from El Salvador who had been given asylum in the United States and spoke Spanish with them. Later, Ann attended a semester of high school in Mexico City, and Mary married a man from El Salvador.

More recently, Ann's husband was assigned to work for his company in Mexico City, and the family lived there for four years.

Their bilingualism has helped them in their teaching. Ann taught in Spanish and English in an elementary school, and Mary taught drama in Spanish at a high school and later taught classes for secondary English learners. Both completed their doctorates and have taught in bilingual programs at the university level. Their bilingualism and biliteracy enabled them to find employment at both the K–12 and university levels.

Being bilingual has cognitive advantages as well. Bialystok (2007, 2011) has conducted a series of studies showing that bilinguals have better problem-solving ability than monolinguals. In addition, her studies have shown that bilinguals have lower rates of dementia and Alzheimer's disease than monolinguals. She reports, "The main empirical finding for the effect of bilingualism on cognition is in the evidence for enhanced executive control in bilingual speakers" (2011, 1).

Hamayan, Genesee, and Cloud explain the concept of executive control functions:

> The advantages of bilingualism have been demonstrated in cognitive domains related to attention, inhibition, monitoring, and switching focus of attention. These processes are required during problem solving, for example, when students must focus their attention if potentially conflicting information needs to be considered; in order to select relevant information and inhibit processing of irrelevant information; and when they must switch attention to consider alternative information when a solution is not forthcoming. Collectively, these cognitive skills comprise what are referred to as executive control functions. (2013, 8)

As Bialystok points out, considerable research has shown that both languages of a bilingual speaker are constantly active, even in contexts where only one language is being used. As a result, bilinguals must use the executive control functions during linguistic processing. She comments, "A likely explanation for how this difficult selection is made in constant online linguistic processing by bilinguals is that the general-purpose executive control system is recruited into linguistic processing, a configuration not found in monolinguals" (2011, 2). She argues that the result of constantly using the executive control system in linguistic processing changes bilinguals' brains in ways that improve the ability to solve problems and resist diseases like dementia and Alzheimer's.

Hamayan, Genesee, and Cloud point out that "the bilingual advantage found by Bialystok is most evident in bilingual people who acquire relatively advanced levels of proficiency in two languages and use their two languages actively on a regular basis" (2013, 7). Well-implemented dual language bilingual programs are long-term and help students develop the high levels of bilingualism and biliteracy needed for the cognitive benefits of bilingualism.

As these studies show, when students develop high levels of bilingualism and biliteracy, they derive a number of benefits. While English learners in ESL programs and in short-term bilingual programs generally score below native English speakers in standardized tests of reading and math in English, emergent bilinguals in long-term bilingual programs where they become bilingual and biliterate succeed academically at higher levels than monolingual students and also gain linguistic, economic, and cognitive benefits.

REFLECT OR TURN AND TALK

Can you think of specific examples of the benefits of bilingualism that you have, your students have, or bilinguals you know have? Share with a partner or small group.

Changing Views of Bilinguals and Bilingualism

Changes in our understanding of bilingualism can help educators develop effective programs for teaching emergent bilinguals. In addition to research in cognitive science (Bialystok 2011), studies in sociolinguistics and education have provided a better understanding of bilingualism (Cummins 1979, 2000; García and Wei 2014; Grosjean 2010). This research has implications for language use in programs for emergent bilinguals. However, a misconception about bilingualism has led to pedagogical practices that make learning more difficult for bilinguals.

Misconception of Balanced Bilinguals

One commonly held misconception has been that the goal of bilingual education should be to produce balanced bilinguals. A balanced bilingual is someone who is equally competent in two languages. This would mean that students in a bilingual

Mandarin-English program should develop the ability to understand, speak, read, and write both English and Mandarin equally well in all settings.

An image used to represent the two languages of a balanced bilingual is a bicycle with two wheels that are the same size and do the same work. In contrast, a monolingual is represented by a unicycle (Cummins 2001). The concept of a balanced bilingual comes from the perspective of a monolingual person. From this view, a student in a dual language program would start as a monolingual in one language and then add a second language to become two monolinguals in one person.

However, studies in cognition have found that bilinguals are not simply two monolinguals. Over time, the neural structures in the brain of a bilingual change as the result of using two languages. Bialystok observed that the lives of bilinguals "included two languages, and their cognitive systems therefore evolved differently than did those of monolingual counterparts" (2011, 8). As Bialystok's studies in neurolinguistics have shown, the neural networks of bilinguals are modified to accommodate their development and use of two languages. In very fundamental ways, bilinguals are different from monolinguals because of their experience of living with two languages.

Studies in sociolinguistics give further evidence that bilinguals should not be viewed as two monolinguals in one person. Rather than picturing a bilingual as two monolinguals, Grosjean (2010), a sociolinguist, takes a holistic view. He argues that "the bilingual is an integrated whole who cannot easily be decomposed into two separate parts . . . he has a unique and specific linguistic configuration" (75).

Grosjean compares a bilingual to a high hurdler in track and field. The hurdler has to have the skills of a high jumper and the skills of a sprinter and combines both jumping high and running fast into a new and different skill. High hurdlers don't have to jump as high as high jumpers or run as fast as sprinters. High hurdlers have unique skills combining the two. Bilinguals seldom speak both languages perfectly in all settings, but they should be valued for the skills they have as bilinguals.

The Complementarity Principle

Research by sociolinguists into how bilingual people use their languages concludes that bilinguals don't develop their two languages equally. During communicative interactions bilinguals do not use their two languages in a balanced way. Instead, as Grosjean states:

> *bilinguals usually acquire and use their languages for different purposes, in different domains of life, with different people. Different aspects of life often require different languages.* (2010, 29)

Grosjean refers to this phenomenon as the *complementarity principle*. Rather than developing equal abilities in each language, bilinguals develop the language they need to communicate with different people in different settings when discussing different subjects. Each language complements the other.

David's proficiency in Spanish and English provides a good example of the complementarity principle. When he spent a year at a university in Mérida, Venezuela, David could carry on a conversation in Spanish with colleagues at the university, go shopping, and read articles on topics for which he had some background. He felt as though his Spanish was improving until he took his car to a shop for a mechanical problem. Mérida is in the Andes, and most driving involves going to higher or lower elevations. From David's house to the university across town, there was a change in elevation of two thousand feet. Friends had advised David to have his car's brake pads changed every six months and to have the shock absorbers checked as well since some of the roads were rough.

David does not have a strong background in car mechanics, but he felt confident that he could communicate what he needed at a local garage. However, when he got there, the mechanic was confused about what David wanted, and David realized he did not have the vocabulary or syntax to explain what he needed to have done. His Spanish proficiency was not as good as his English in this context, and although he finally communicated what he wanted done, he had to use gestures and point to parts of the car. Fortunately, this worked, but it helped David see that he was certainly not a balanced bilingual.

Grosjean concludes his discussion of the complementarity principle by stating that most bilinguals "simply do not need to be equally competent in all their languages. The level of fluency they attain in a language . . . will depend on their need for that language and will be domain specific" (2010, 21). Because bilinguals develop their two languages for use in different domains, very few are completely balanced.

REFLECT OR TURN AND TALK

Consider how language is used for teaching and assessing emergent bilinguals. Is the goal of your school's programs for emergent bilinguals that they become balanced? Share with a partner.

Monoglossic and Heteroglossic Views of Bilingualism

Current research has shown that proficient bilingual and biliterate people are not balanced. The misconception of balanced bilinguals comes from what García (2009) refers to as a monoglossic view of bilingualism. *Monoglossic* comes from the prefix *mono*, meaning "one," and the root *glossic*, meaning "tongue" or "voice." Monoglossic views of bilinguals and bilingual education consider that each language is one separate entity. García considers programs such as early-exit bilingual and ESL programs to be monoglossic because students often enter school speaking their home language, but in the process of acquiring English, many fail to develop, or even lose, that language. As a result, English learners may begin and end their programs as monolinguals.

Even in effective bilingual programs, language instruction is often organized in a way that keeps the two languages separate. This approach is based on the monoglossic view because the goal of these programs is to develop a person who is the equivalent of two monolinguals. During instruction and assessment, the two languages are kept separate. As García observes, "bilinguals are expected to be and do with each of their languages the same thing as monolinguals" (2009, 52). Students are expected to perform like English monolinguals during English time and like Spanish monolinguals during Spanish time. Monoglossic views of bilinguals and of programs for emergent bilinguals have predominated in schools.

The twentieth-century views that bilinguals are two monolinguals in one person and that the goal of bilingual education is to produce balanced bilinguals have led to practices that Cummins (2007) argues are based on misconceptions. One of these misconceptions applies specifically to dual language bilingual programs. Cummins refers to this as the *two solitudes assumption*. The misconception is that in bilingual programs the two languages should be kept rigidly separated. Cummins points out:

> *This assumption was initially articulated by Lambert and Tucker (1972) in the context of the St. Lambert French immersion program evaluation and since that time has become axiomatic in the implementation of second language immersion and most dual language programs.* (233)

The practice of keeping the two languages strictly separated is based on assumptions rather than on empirical research. In dual language bilingual programs where the two languages are strictly separated, students are treated like two monolinguals. For example, in a Spanish-English dual language program during English time, all students are taught like monolingual English speakers and during Spanish time they are treated like monolingual Spanish speakers. Although the teachers make the input in English or Spanish comprehensible, there is no recourse to using students' home languages as a resource.

The practice of separating the two languages developed to ensure that enough time was allocated to each language for students to acquire the language. Without sufficient exposure to a language, it is not possible to develop proficiency in the language. In some cases, even when bilingual programs allocated a specific time for each language, some teachers translated each thing they said to help students understand a lesson. This practice, called concurrent translation, is not effective because when students know that the teacher will translate, they ignore the input given in the target language. So a Hmong speaker in a Hmong-English program might ignore the English, and an English speaker might ignore the Hmong. Strict separation of languages in many programs developed to avoid concurrent translation and to ensure that administrators could monitor language use since they would know what language to expect during an in-class evaluation.

An example of how concurrent translation works comes from driving a car. The speedometer shows both miles and kilometers, and drivers simply ignore the system that they are not familiar with. Drivers in Mexico would gauge their speed in kilometers per hour and most drivers in the United States would focus on miles per hour. In the same way, some banks show the temperature in both centigrade and Fahrenheit, and again people pay attention to the system they are familiar with. If teachers translate everything into emergent bilinguals' home languages, the students may not try to make sense of the new language they are trying to acquire.

In many dual language bilingual programs there is one teacher for each language; in others, different subjects are taught in each of the languages. For example, math might be in English and science in Spanish. In other programs the languages are distributed by time—mornings in English and afternoons in Spanish. Still other programs alternate languages on a daily or weekly basis. In all cases, there are specific times, subjects, or teachers for each language with no overlap.

Many effective practices are excluded when instruction is limited to one language at a time. For example, having students access cognates depends on using both languages simultaneously. When the languages are not separated, students can carry out linguistic investigations and build metalinguistic awareness by comparing and contrasting languages. For example, students could compare and contrast the structure of possessives in English and Spanish sentences.

Cummins explains his support of these types of activities as he writes,

> *It does seem reasonable to create largely separate spaces for each language within a bilingual or immersion program. However, there are also compelling arguments to be made for creating a shared or interdependent space for the promotion of language awareness and cross-language cognitive processing. The reality is that students are making cross-linguistic connections throughout the course of their learning in a bilingual or immersion program, so why not nurture this learning strategy and help students to apply it more efficiently?* (2007, 229)

Cummins points out that there is theoretical support for using both languages for instruction. Research has shown that new knowledge is built on existing knowledge, and if that knowledge was developed in the home language, it can best be accessed through the home language (National Academies of Sciences, Engineering, and Medicine 2018). In addition, literacy skills are interdependent, so teaching should facilitate cross-language transfer. Cummins concludes his discussion of the two solitudes misconception by stating, "the empirical evidence is consistent both with an emphasis on extensive communicative interaction in the TL [target language] (ideally in both oral and written modes) and the utility of students' home language as a cognitive tool in learning the TL" (2007, 226–27).

Instead of operating from a monoglossic perspective, García argues, educators should take a heteroglossic perspective. The prefix *hetero* comes from the Greek meaning "other." The term *heteroglossic* comes from the writing of the Russian literary critic Bakhtin (1981). He used the term to refer to the multiple or other voices that coexist within a novel, the voices of the characters and of the narrator. García uses the term to refer to the two or more languages that exist in the mind of a bilingual speaker. As Bialystok points out, the two or more languages are always active in the mind of a bilingual. These languages cannot be strictly separated because they are always present.

This view is a better reflection of how bilinguals really use their languages. García argues that strict separation of languages is not natural. It does not reflect the customary use of language by bilinguals. Instead of keeping languages apart, bilingual programs in schools should draw on all the linguistic resources of emergent bilinguals.

García refers to bilingual programs based on a heteroglossic view of emergent bilinguals as dynamic. For García and her colleagues (García, Ibarra Johnson, and Seltzer 2017), *dynamic bilingualism* better describes bilingualism in a globalized society. From a perspective of dynamic bilingualism, bilinguals and multilinguals use their languages for a variety of purposes and in a variety of settings. They are more or less proficient in the different contexts where they use the languages and are more or less proficient in different modalities (visual, print, and sound). García explains that dynamic bilingualism is consistent with the definition of *plurilingualism* given by the Language Policy Division of the Council of Europe: "the ability to use several languages to varying degrees and for distinct purposes" (García 2009, 54). She challenges educators to look at bilingual education in a new way, taking a heteroglossic view of dynamic bilingualism. She argues that this new view of bilinguals and of bilingual education is needed because bilingual education in the United States has been built on the misguided monoglossic view.

REFLECT OR TURN AND TALK

Do the programs for emergent bilinguals at your school have a monoglossic view or a heteroglossic view of bilingualism? Consider how the home language is used in ESL or bilingual classes for emergent bilinguals. Share with others at your school.

Research on Bilingualism

Two hypotheses based on research Cummins (1979) conducted provide support for viewing bilingual students holistically and as learners drawing on both of their languages: the interdependence hypothesis and the common underlying proficiency (CUP) hypothesis.

A seemingly commonsense assumption that is made in teaching emergent bilinguals in many places is that more English equals more English. This idea seems logical. It is a variation of the time-on-task assumption that claims the more time spent on a task, the greater the proficiency a student develops. In this case, the assumption is that the more time students spend being instructed in English, the more proficient they will become in English. However, Cummins explains that this seemingly logical assumption fails to recognize that languages are interdependent, and the development of the home language has a positive effect on the development of an additional language. He states:

> To the extent that instruction in L_X is effective in promoting proficiency in L_X, transfer of this proficiency to L_Y will occur provided there is adequate exposure to L_Y (either in school or the environment) and adequate motivation to learn L_Y. (1979, 29)

In other words, when students are taught in and develop proficiency in their home language, L_X, that proficiency will transfer to an additional language, L_Y, assuming they are given enough exposure to the second language and are motivated to learn it.

Cummins explains that the reason proficiency transfers from one language to another is that a common proficiency underlies an emergent bilingual's languages. Because of this common underlying proficiency there is an "interdependence of concepts, skills, and linguistic knowledge that makes transfer possible" (1979, 191).

According to Cummins, the common underlying proficiency can be thought of as "a central processing system comprising (1) attributes of the individuals such as cognitive and linguistic abilities (memory, auditory discrimination, abstract reasoning, etc.) and (2) specific conceptual and linguistic knowledge derived from experience and learning (vocabulary knowledge)" (2000, 191). As a result of this interdependence, an emergent bilingual can draw on cognitive and linguistic abilities and skills acquired in the home language to develop literacy and content knowledge in an additional language. For example, if the home language shares features, such as cognates or syntactic structures, with English, those components of the home language can transfer to English when teachers use strategies to bridge between the two languages.

Spanish and English share many cognates since the two languages both include many Latinate words. Linguists estimate that 30 to 40 percent of English words have Spanish cognates. Teachers can create cognate word walls to help students become more aware of the cognates. In addition, a good strategy for Spanish speakers reading in English is to check to see if an unknown English word looks and sounds like a word in Spanish.

There are many ways that teachers can use cognates in teaching in either bilingual or ESL classes. They can put students in pairs where both students are at least somewhat proficient in Spanish. Students can look at key vocabulary in English around a topic and try to identify cognates that exist in Spanish. So students studying zoo animals might identify *giraffe* and *jirafa*, *hippopotamus* and *hipopótomo*, and *tiger* and *tigre*.

Students working virtually could help each other either though an online conversation or through texts as they look for cognates. If students are reading a text in math, science, or social studies, there are many opportunities to work together to find Spanish–English cognates as they read. Once they find cognates, they can add them to a classroom cognate wall or contribute to a shared Google document if working online. Alternatively, the teacher can pick out scientific terms or complex social studies vocabulary from English textbooks and challenge students who speak Spanish or who are learning Spanish to identify the Spanish equivalents.

Cummins' CUP hypothesis can help account for the difference in academic performance of students with similar levels of English proficiency. Because content knowledge and literacy skills transfer, a fourth-grade emergent bilingual who can read and write at grade level in his home language and who has developed grade-level content knowledge in that language will succeed academically in English much more quickly than another fourth grader who has developed only a low level of home language literacy and lacks academic content knowledge, even if they are both classified as low intermediates in English proficiency.

Cummins (2000) contrasts the idea of a common underlying proficiency with that of a separate underlying proficiency (SUP). Those who hold to the SUP theory must believe that what we learn in one language goes to one part of our brain and cannot be accessed when we are learning and speaking another language. This must be what opponents of bilingual education believe when they say that students learning in their home language are wasting time. They should be learning only in English. However, students in programs that build their home language as they acquire English develop higher levels of academic proficiency than students schooled only in English.

Cummins uses the image of an iceberg with two peaks to illustrate his CUP hypothesis. The two peaks of the iceberg that are above the waterline represent the surface features (the sounds or writing) of the two languages. The part of the iceberg below the surface of the water where the languages overlap represents the knowledge and skills that are common to the two languages and can transfer from one language to the other. Figure 5–1 is a representation of the iceberg with two peaks.

Students who have more schooling in their home language can draw upon that knowledge as they are acquiring an additional language. Over time students with greater total underlying proficiency can do well academically in English. Students without the underlying academic proficiency in their home language, however, struggle because they have less to draw upon as they are learning academic content and literacy in a new language.

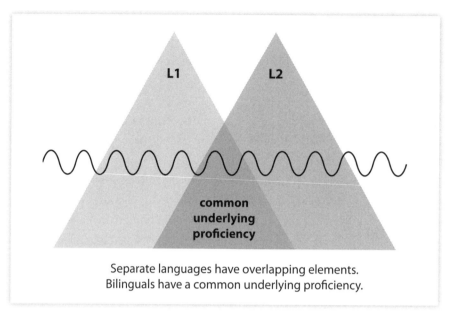

Separate languages have overlapping elements.
Bilinguals have a common underlying proficiency.

Figure 5–1 • Dual Iceberg Model

In Chapter 2 we discussed Tou, a long-term English learner. Although he entered school a dominant Hmong speaker, he never developed literacy in his home language. He had conversational English but struggled academically. Long-term ELs studying in this country do not develop academic language or grade-level proficiency in literacy in their home language. They struggle with understanding the curriculum taught all in English and get farther and farther behind.

Schooling in the home country helps immigrants when they come to live in this country. Mary's husband, Francisco, came to the United States at age fourteen with no English, but he liked school in El Salvador and read every book he could get his hands on. His schooling in this country was all in English. Although it took him time to do well in school, his eventual success can be linked to the transfer of literacy skills and his knowledge of math, science, and history in Spanish, which supported his understanding of instruction in English.

Translanguaging

García, Ibarra Johnson, and Seltzer (2017) take Cummins' concept of a common underlying proficiency a step further. Instead of viewing the bilingual as having two separate languages with a common underlying proficiency, they argue that bilinguals have one complex linguistic system that has features of two or more languages, which they refer to as a linguistic repertoire. (See Figure 5–2.)

García and her colleagues (2017) explain that the linguistic repertoire is a set of linguistic features that people draw on to communicate. Bilinguals and multilinguals have linguistic repertoires with features that are used in more than one language. Linguistic features include phonemes, morphemes, syntactic structures, and so on, that constitute a language. Some features, such as the order of words in a sentence (subject, verb, object) or certain phonemes, such as /d/, might be the same in some languages and different in other languages. Emergent bilinguals can draw on the features of both languages, features that are unique to either language and features that are common to two languages as they communicate.

In the process of making meaning, bilinguals draw on their full linguistic repertoire in a process García and Wei (2014) refer to as translanguaging. The term *translanguaging* comes from Williams (1996), a Welsh educator, who was teaching Welsh to English-speaking students in Wales as part of an effort to revitalize the language. In his teaching, Williams had students read or listen in one language and then write or speak in the other. He referred to this process as translanguaging. Students went across (*trans*) languages as they studied using Welsh and English.

García (2009) defines translanguaging as the typical way bilinguals use language as they communicate both in and out of school. She explains, "Translanguagings are

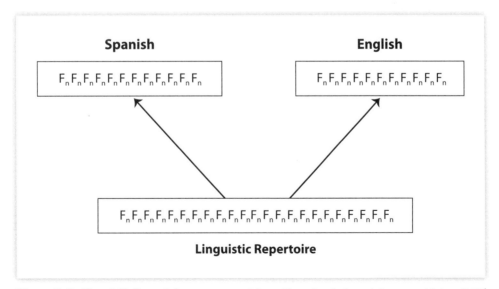

Figure 5–2 • Linguistic Repertoire   Adapted from García, Ibarra Johnson, and Seltzer (2017)

the multiple discursive practices in which bilinguals engage in order to make sense of their bilingual worlds" (45). That is, they draw on all their language resources to communicate effectively. Similarly, Baker and Wright point out that "children pragmatically use both their languages in order to maximize understanding and performance in any lesson" (2017, 280). They go on to say, "Translanguaging is the process of making meaning, shaping experiences, understandings, and knowledge through the use of two languages" (280).

In his review of the definitions of *translanguaging*, Cummins concludes:

> *Translanguaging is clearly non-problematic when viewed as a descriptive concept to refer to (a) typical patterns of interpersonal interaction among multilingual individuals where participants draw on their individual and shared linguistic repertoires to communicate without regard to conventional language boundaries, and (b) classroom interactions that draw on students' multilingual repertoires in addition to the official or dominant language of instruction.* (forthcoming, 2)

These different researchers all conclude that translanguaging is a typical way that bilinguals communicate and that it can be used in bilingual classes to affirm students' bilingual identities, build metalinguistic understanding, and scaffold instruction by strategically drawing on students' home languages while still allocating the major portion of the time for each of the languages of instruction. The key is to use the home language strategically and not simply revert to concurrent translation. An effective approach to strategic language allocation in dual language is to plan at both a macro level and a micro level. At the macro level, teachers should use the target language most of the time during a lesson. For example, in a Spanish–English dual language class that alternates the two languages each day, on an English day, English would be used most of the time. This is the macro level. However, at the micro level, teachers can use the home language strategically. For example, the teacher could use Spanish to provide a brief preview of the lesson or to compare how to form the possessive in the two languages. Figure 5–3 shows how teachers can allocate languages at the macro and micro levels during instruction (Ebe, personal communication).

Whether bilinguals have a single linguistic system, as García argues, or two overlapping systems with a common underlying component, as Cummins contends, there is an agreement that translanguaging serves an important role in educating emergent bilinguals. See Cummins (2017, forthcoming) and Otheguy, García, and Reid (2015, 2018) for further discussion of this question.

Alternation at the Macro Level	Alternation at the Micro Level
Dedicated time for each language	Translanguaging spaces within the dedicated Spanish or English time
• by day: Spanish one day, English the next • by time: Spanish in AM, English in PM • by subject matter: math in English and social studies in Spanish	• flexible language use by teachers and students • strategic, scaffolded, differentiated • preview, view, review
Program level	Classroom or online

Figure 5–3 • Language Allocation at the Macro and Micro Levels   Adapted from Ebe

REFLECT OR TURN AND TALK

What are the implications of the research on translanguaging by Cummins and García for teaching emergent bilinguals? How is this reflected in your school? Share your reflections with others at your school if possible.

Bilingualism Is Dynamic

García (2009) explains that bilinguals don't simply add a new language to an existing language. Instead, they incorporate the features of the new language into an integrated, dynamic system. As Cummins observes, García uses the term *translanguaging* to describe the "dynamic *heteroglossic* integrated linguistic practices of multilingual individuals" (forthcoming, 1). Teachers can implement translanguaging strategies that use the entire linguistic repertoire of bilingual students flexibly in order to teach both rigorous content and language for academic use.

The term *dynamic bilingualism* reflects the fact that the languages of an emergent bilingual are always active in the brain, and bilinguals draw on all their language resources as they communicate. García and Kleyn explain:

> *Dynamic bilingualism goes beyond the notion of additive bilingualism because it does not simply refer to the addition of a separate set of language features, but acknowledges that the linguistic features and practices of bilinguals form a unitary linguistic system that interacts in dynamic ways.* (2016, 16)

Dynamic bilingualism is the appropriate term for bilingualism in a globalized society. From a dynamic bilingualism perspective, bilinguals and multilinguals use their languages for a variety of purposes and in a variety of settings. They are more or less proficient in the various contexts where they use the languages and are more or less proficient in different modalities (visual, print, and sound). Their languages continually develop as they use each language in a variety of settings.

García, Ibarra Johnson, and Seltzer explain that in a classroom with emergent bilinguals there is a translanguaging *corriente* (current in a stream):

> *We use the metaphor of the translanguaging corriente to refer to the current or flow of students' dynamic bilingualism that runs through our classrooms and schools. Bilingual students make use of the translanguaging corriente either covertly or overtly to learn content and language in school and to make sense of their complex worlds and identities.* (2017, 21)

Picture this corriente as a constant stream above your students' heads or under their feet. In this corriente, the language knowledge in their linguistic repertoire is flowing all the time. So, if the teacher is reading and talking about a novel in English with the class, emergent bilinguals can draw upon their other language or languages to make sense of what the teacher is reading and discussing.

However, the teacher has to strategically invite students to access their full linguistic repertoires. The teacher might have students turn and talk about the characters in the novel or the setting or the conflict using their home languages if they wish and then report back in English. The teacher might direct students to do a quickwrite in their home language or English listing key events in the novel so far and have the whole class brainstorm together a list on the whiteboard. Each of these activities draws upon knowledge students have in their home language, that corriente, and gives them more access to the curriculum taught in English.

García, Ibarra Johnson, and Seltzer state that teachers can use the translanguaging corriente to

1. Support students as they engage with and comprehend complex content and texts
2. Provide opportunities for students to develop linguistic practices for academic contexts
3. Make space for students' bilingualism and ways of knowing
4. Support students' socioemotional development and bilingual identities. (2017, ix)

Translanguaging Is Not Code-Switching

Until García and others began using the term *translanguaging* to describe the language practices in bilingual communities, researchers referred to the process as code mixing or code-switching. *Code* here refers to a language. A language can be seen as a system for encoding meanings. Linguists used *code-switching* to describe the process of switching from one language to another, sometimes in the same sentence. For example, a Spanish-English bilingual might say, "I haven't eaten since lunch, and *ahora tengo hambre* [now I'm hungry]."

Linguists and sociolinguists have studied code-switching as a process of switching from one language to another. Grosjean writes, "Code-switching is also used as a communicative or social strategy to show speaker involvement, mark group identity, exclude someone, raise one's status, show expertise, and so on" (2010, 54–55). In South Texas along the border, bilinguals often code-switch to identify themselves as part of the Mexican American community. After reading about and discussing translanguaging, two of our graduate students studying bilingual education compiled a list of reasons people code-switch with examples from their own experiences (see Figure 5–4).

Although linguists have found that bilinguals draw on two languages as they communicate for a number of different reasons, code-switching has a negative connotation for many people. Some bilinguals we have worked with have apologized for mixing two languages or using Spanglish. Some people assume that bilinguals have to code-switch because they are deficient in one or both of their languages.

García points out that code-switching is a way to describe the language practices of bilinguals from an external point of view. Someone observing two bilinguals might

Purpose	English–Spanish Example
1. To emphasize a particular point in conversation	*Andale*, go do your homework.
2. To substitute an unknown word in another language	Voy a hacer mi trabajo en la *laptop*. La *teacher* nos dejo mucha tarea.
3. To express a concept that has no equivalent in the culture of the other language	There was a *piñata* at the party. That lunch looks good! *Bon appétit.*
4. To reinforce a request	Get to work—*pónganse a trabajar.* Come, come! *¡Córrele!*
5. To clarify a point	Animals adapt to their environment—*los animals se adaptan a su medio ambiente, es decir, se acostumbran al lugar donde viven.* For this exercise you are going to do three circles, *tres círculos.*
6. To express identity or communicate friendship or family bonding	Come here, *mijito.* *Así es, amor,* good job!
7. To report a conversation held previously	Holding a conversation in English, but retelling it to someone else in Spanish: When he came into the room, we all yelled, *¡Feliz cumpleaños!*
8. To interject into a conversation	If two people are having a conversation in Spanish, and you interject by saying, "*Excuse me.*"
9. To indicate a change of attitude or relationship	People code-switch when there is less social distance, more solidarity, and growing rapport: Angela told me, "*Dra. Freeman, Ud. Me conoce. No soy así.*"
10. To exclude people from a conversation	Grandparents speak in a language their grandson does not understand.
11. To refer to certain topics, such as money	*Fui al dealership y el car costaba* five thousand dollars.

Figure 5–4 · Reasons for Code-Switching

conclude that they were switching between languages. However, from the bilingual person's own viewpoint, the use of the two languages is simply a way of using all their language resources to communicate. From a holistic view of a bilingual as a person with one complex linguistic system, there is no switching between codes of separate languages. Instead, the bilingual is drawing on features of one complex linguistic system to communicate effectively. García and Wei state:

> Translanguaging differs from the notion of code-switching in that it refers not simply to a shift or shuttle between two languages, but to the speakers' construction and use of original and complex interrelated discursive practices that cannot be easily assigned to one or another traditional definition of a language, but that make up the speakers' complete language repertoire. (2014, 22)

From this perspective, drawing on words and phrases from both languages allows a bilingual to communicate more effectively in the same way that having a large vocabulary in one language allows a person to express themselves more fully.

Bilinguals translanguage in certain contexts. They would draw on features of two languages only when communicating with another bilingual. In the same way that speakers shift from formal to informal registers depending on whom they are talking with and the context, bilinguals shift languages to communicate effectively in different situations with different people. They do this automatically in order to use their language resources effectively.

Translanguaging Strategies in Schools and During Remote Teaching

In bilingual and ESL (or ELD) programs that take a view of dynamic bilingualism, teachers use translanguaging strategies to affirm students' bilingual identities, to help them build metalinguistic awareness, and to promote the development of their academic language proficiency and their academic content knowledge. Teachers do this by using students' home languages strategically during both in-classroom and remote teaching. As a result of the coronavirus pandemic, many schools have adopted ways to combine face-to-face and remote teaching. In the following sections we provide examples of translanguaging strategies teachers are using. We have written about translanguaging strategies in several publications (see Freeman, Soto, and Freeman 2016; Freeman et al. 2016; Freeman, Freeman, and Mercuri 2018; Soto, Freeman, and Freeman 2020).

Affirming Students' Bilingual Identity

When teachers use strategies that draw on all students' home languages, they tap into the translanguaging corriente and affirm students' bilingual identity. They ensure that the school's linguistic ecology reflects the languages and cultures of all the students in the school by including those languages in murals, signs, and student work in hallways and classrooms as well as in correspondence with parents. School libraries include books and other resources that reflect students' languages and cultures. Teachers also incorporate activities that draw on and showcase students' languages, such as posting bilingual and multilingual word walls. They include routines such as turn-and-talks where students can use their home language or English. All of these practices affirm students' languages and cultures and promote linguistic and cultural equity.

Mary and Elizabeth, two professors in a teacher education course, wanted to help their teacher candidates design activities to develop their own students' cultural identities. First, they organized students into groups. Each group represented as great a variety of cultures as possible so that different voices could be heard during group discussions. Some of the students were white with a variety of backgrounds, others were Hmong, and the majority were Latinx. First Mary and Elizabeth asked the groups to come up with a definition of *culture*. They asked them not to look up a definition, but to consider their own experiences and ideas. Some of the groups defined *culture* as their home language and ways they did things at holidays. Others mentioned typical cultural dishes and strict rules. Still others mentioned expectations like going to college or being married in the church. The groups shared their definitions with their classmates.

After considering the different definitions of *culture*, each group made a mandala. The groups had a template to complete, and each student in the group chose different aspects of their culture and represented it on the outside circle of the group mandala. After sharing the drawings, the group decided on what all members of the group had in common and wrote that in the middle. For example, one group with two students of Mexican background and one with Hmong background found they had a lot in common, including food, religion, sports, family, language, and celebrations (see Figure 5–5). Another group representing Hmong and Mexican cultures chose just one commonality, family (see Figure 5–6).

Figure 5–5 · Cultural Mandala 1

Figure 5–6 · Cultural Mandala 2

Then the teachers assigned a second activity to make the students think even more deeply on the topic of culture: the culture Venn diagram. They gave students the following directions:

Partner up with someone in your group.

- *Each of you should pick a shape that represents your culture.*
- *Draw your shapes overlapping (as in a traditional Venn diagram).*
- *On the outside sections, write characteristics of your culture.*
- *On the overlap, write about how your cultures are similar.*

Each pair of students used a different piece of poster paper and worked to think of something that represented their culture. In the cultural Venn diagram shown in Figure 5–7, Jessica drew a Hmong drum often used in festivals and funerals in traditional Hmong culture and Gregoria drew a nopal cactus, symbolic of both arid landscapes in Mexico and the nopal leaves and fruit, which are used for different purposes. Within each symbol the students wrote reflections of their own culture. Then they wrote what they had in common in the overlapping section.

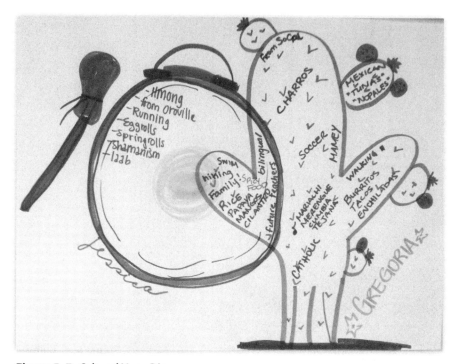

Figure 5–7 • Cultural Venn Diagram

After completing these activities, the students in this teacher education class looked again at their original definitions of *culture*, added to them, and then read articles to see how others had defined the word. The approach Mary and Elizabeth took in using these different activities helped prepare these future teachers to affirm their students' cultures and languages by modifying the activities and using them with their own students.

These activities focusing on culture and what it means to students could also become an assignment carried out at home. Students could interview family members about what they see as features of their cultures, make a list, and illustrate it. This could be posted and shared in Google Docs. Students from the same cultural background could each add to a Google doc and create and then present their finished work to the class on Zoom or another platform. Students could work in pairs or small groups in either same-language or same-culture groups or mixed groups, via a Zoom or Teams platform, and create a group poster of their culture or cultures using an online poster maker.

Building Metalinguistic Awareness

In addition to affirming students' bilingual identities, translanguaging strategies also can build students' metalinguistic awareness. When teachers compare and contrast languages, emergent bilinguals build an understanding of how their additional language is similar to and different from their home language. Marzano, Pickering, and Pollock (2001) list identifying similarities and differences as one of the most effective strategies for improving instruction.

In some cases, the home language and English may be quite similar. A good example is English and Spanish. In other instances, the languages are very different. Mandarin or Hmong and English differ in many respects. But all languages have some similarities, and even when they differ, they do so in predictable ways (Freeman and Freeman 2014; Pinker 1994). For example, all languages have a normal sentence structure even though the constituents (subject, verb, object) may differ. All languages have nouns and pronouns.

Many teachers in both ESL and bilingual classes create cognate walls. The study of cognates is especially helpful when the vocabulary is organized around the units teachers are studying. For example, a middle school biology teacher posted a list of English and Spanish cognates of science vocabulary including *cell* (*célula*), *nucleus* (*núcleo*), *mitosis* (*mitosis*), *organism* (*organismo*), and *skeletal* (*esquelético*). Cognate walls like this help students expand their vocabulary and also recognize different patterns in the two languages. For example, Spanish uses just one *l* in *célula*. Words in Spanish need accents on the antepenultimate syllable for pronunciation if they end in a vowel, *n*, or *s* (*núcleo célula, esquelético*), and words in Spanish begin with *es* when English words begin with *s* followed by a voiceless stop, as in *skeletal* (*esquelético*), *school* (*escuela*), and *Spanish* (*español*).

Another teacher in a dual language bilingual program asked her fourth-grade students to find words in their reading in Spanish that looked like English words that begin with *s* except that the Spanish words started with an *es*. She listed words pairs such as *stamp* and *estampa*, *scorpion* and *escorpión*, *special* and *especial*, and *study* and *estudio*. She explained the rule and encouraged her emergent bilinguals to remember this regular variation as they wrote in either English or Spanish.

When students are aware of cognates, they can use their knowledge of vocabulary in their home language as they study in English. One teacher teaching math in English gave her students a short reading on measurement in English and put a translation in Spanish next to it. Students read the article in English and then looked at the article in Spanish to identify words that looked similar in the two languages. They found a number of cognates and added them to their list of math cognates. Then the teacher worked with the whole class to update a math cognate wall that they had developed.

While many of the Spanish words in math are cognates (*dividir* and *divide*; *grupos iguales* and *equal groups*), some are not. Even then, posting the equivalent in students' home languages can be helpful. An upper-grade math teacher posted a word wall with key concepts in English and also wrote the Spanish translation of several key terms, including *hundreds* (*centenas*), *multiplication sentence* (*enunciado de multiplicación*), and *place value* (*valor posicional*). Figure 5–8 shows this math word wall.

Students can also learn about cognates at home. Teachers can ask students to keep a list of cognates from their reading in a journal and also try to find regular variations in the spelling of the cognates. Students can carry out their investigations working alone or in pairs using different online platforms. Teachers can also follow up a cognate assignment during a Zoom meeting with the class by creating a class cognate list. Students might also illustrate their cognate lists and include images of the words gathered through internet searches and then share their lists with the class using Google Classroom or another online platform.

In classes with students who speak several different home languages, teachers can create multilingual word walls of key words from the topic the class is studying. This can be done in the classroom or remotely. Students can post the words in their home languages and find images online where appropriate. The teacher can combine student

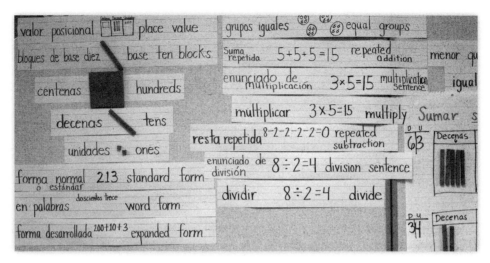

Figure 5–8 · Math Bilingual Word Wall

responses to create the multilingual word wall using Padlet or other applications. Students might also post on a Padlet wall the teacher has set up for them.

Teachers can also compare specific language structures. We observed one kindergarten teacher in a bilingual class who made a list of phrases that contained possessives. She used students' names and classroom objects, such as *Mario's notebook* and *el cuaderno de Mario*, to help her students build metalinguistic awareness of the difference in structure between Spanish and English. An equivalent activity for online teaching would be to have students choose personal objects at home, take pictures, write the possessive in English and the home language and post it on a Padlet wall the teacher has set up. So a student might post a picture of a bicycle and write under the picture *Miguel's bicycle* and *la bicicleta de Miguel*.

Another teacher chose sentences from bilingual books her class was reading to point out similarities and differences between the two languages. One book, Carmen Lomas Garza's *In My Family/En mi familia* (1996), has short readings in both Spanish and English on each page. The teacher picked out passages from the page showing people dancing outside on a restaurant patio with a small band playing. The comparison phrases she used included *This is Saturday night* and *Ésta es una noche de sabado*; *a neighborhood restaurant in my home town* and *un restaurante familiar de mi pueblo natal*; and *It is like heaven* and *Es como el cielo*. Students discussed the differences and similarities in syntax, vocabulary, and capitalization used in the two languages to express the same ideas.

They listed cognates like *restaurant* and *restaurante*. They also noted differences. While days of the week are capitalized in English, they aren't in Spanish. Adjectives precede nouns in English (neighborhood restaurant), but they follow nouns in Spanish (*restaurante familiar*). In English, *heaven* does not take an article. English speakers don't say "the heaven," but it is preceded by an article in Spanish: *el cielo*. By having her students compare and contrast these passages, the teacher increased her students' metalinguistic awareness. Students could complete a similar assignment at home, working alone or with a partner, using an online platform like Google Classroom. The teacher could also have students post their assignments on a class website and report on their findings in a whole-class Zoom meeting.

Scaffolding

Teachers also use translanguaging strategies to scaffold instruction. Krashen (1996) has reviewed research on the importance of using the home language for instruction. He argues that we acquire language when we receive comprehensible input, messages that we understand. For emergent bilinguals, use of the home language is the best way to make input comprehensible. To acquire a language, students need to have an understanding of what they hear or read. If students enter school speaking languages other than English, and if English is the only language of instruction, then the students may simply not understand enough English to acquire the language or to learn any subjects taught in English.

While bilingual education may not be possible in some schools for a variety of reasons, teachers of emergent bilinguals can find ways to use their students' home languages to promote academic success. We have observed how teachers we have worked with have used translanguaging strategies to support their students' home languages as they teach. Sánchez, García, and Solorza (2018) refer to these strategies as scaffolds that teachers can use to support individual students or groups of students. "They include the use of bilingual instructional material, technology assistance such as Google Translate, multimodal provisions including videos, collaboration with peers, and small groups that can offer translanguaging support, among others" (10).

Effective teachers group students in pairs and small groups. Teachers who use translanguaging strategies organize bilingual pairs and small groups of students who speak the same home language. Then during a turn-and-talk or a small-group discussion, they encourage students to use either their home language or the target language. In a bilingual class, Spanish speakers might use Spanish or English during time allocated for English, and English speakers could use Spanish or English during Spanish time.

In an ESL class, English learners could use their home language to clarify assignments or discuss a subject and then report back or write in English. Students could also use their home language to discuss how to do homework and to discuss homework with parents. These discussions can take place in a classroom or online using different platforms.

One teacher incorporated the students' home languages in a social studies unit on immigration. After students had read books about immigration, they interviewed a family member about their experience with immigration, using the home language. Then students translated part of the interview and basic information about the interviewee and presented it to the class. In a bilingual class, they could use both the home language and English for the presentation and then write about the experience in English.

A translanguaging strategy teachers can use in an ESL class that draws on students' home languages is preview, view, review. If the teacher, a bilingual peer, a bilingual cross-age tutor, a bilingual aide, or a parent can simply tell the English learners in their home language what the upcoming lesson is about, it provides the students with a preview. During the view, the teacher conducts the lesson in English using strategies to make the input comprehensible. With the help of the preview, the students can follow the English better and acquire both English and academic content. Finally, it is good to have a short time of review during which students can use their home language. For example, students who speak the same home language could meet in groups to review the main ideas of the lesson and then report back in English.

The preview, view, review strategy can also be used in a bilingual class. In a Spanish–English dual language class, for example, if the first part of the lesson is given in Spanish, it would be a preview for Spanish speakers of the view in English. The review would then follow in Spanish. For an English speaker, doing the first part in English provides a preview for the lesson in Spanish, and the review would be given in English. Teachers could alternate the language for the preview and review to provide all students access to lessons through the home language. Figure 5–9 outlines the preview, view, review technique.

Translanguaging with Bilingual Books

Teachers have found several ways to use translanguaging strategies to support students' biliteracy development. Bilingual books provide translanguaging supports (Freeman and Freeman 2011a, 2011b) in several ways. Following the original model that Cen Williams described, teachers in a Spanish–English dual language class could read a

Preview
home language
The teacher gives an overview of the lesson or activity (such as giving an oral summary, reading a book, showing a film, asking a key question) in the students' home language.

View
English or partner language
The teacher teaches the lesson or directs the activity in the students' second language.

Review
home language
The teacher or the students summarize key ideas and raise questions about the lesson in their home language.

Figure 5–9 • Preview, View, Review

book in English and then discuss it with the class in Spanish. The read-aloud could be done in a regular classroom or online, using a program like Audible that includes read-alouds of a large number of books in Spanish and English.

After a read-aloud, students could write a response in Spanish or English on Google Docs or Google Classroom. They could listen to a book in English and retell it to a family member in Spanish. If the read-aloud is in Spanish, students could discuss the book in English in the classroom or online, using Zoom or another platform, and then the class could write about the book in English. Students could also read a book in Spanish and retell it to a classmate in English in the class or online. In addition, students could watch a video clip in English and discuss it in Spanish with their class or during an online whole-class virtual meeting.

Both shared and guided reading can be done in the classroom or online, using Zoom or Google Classroom. If students are at home, there are several sources for free downloadable books from sites like getepic.com and Scholastic. Many publishers, like Okapi, publish bilingual book pairs and also pair fiction and nonfiction books. For emergent bilinguals, reading the nonfiction book first in the home language builds background. Nonfiction books with limited text and good text-picture matches provide background for ELs. Reading a nonfiction book paired with a fiction book around the same topic helps prepare an English learner to understand the fiction book, and this could lead to a discussion of similarities and differences between the genres.

Bilingual books are helpful because ELs can read in English and use the home-language version of the text as a resource if they have difficulty. Emergent bilinguals can also write their own bilingual books. Other activities might include writing a dialogue for bilingual characters, writing a speech for a bilingual audience, or creating bilingual poems in two voices.

Reading and Writing Texts That Include Translanguaging

Teachers can assign students to read books that contain translanguaging, such as Alma Flor Ada's *I Love Saturdays y domingos* (2002). In this book the main character visits her English-speaking grandparents on Saturdays and her Spanish-speaking grandparents on Sundays (*domingos*). The dialogue matches the grandparents' language in each case. The teacher could discuss with her students why the author used both Spanish and English in her text, and then the students could write their own story that contains translanguaging.

If the students speak several different home languages, each student can write a book including words from that language and then read an excerpt to their classmates. One teacher did this with her eighth-grade students. Her students read a book in verse form, *Inside Out and Back Again* (Lai 2011), by a Vietnamese author, written in a language none of the students spoke. After reading a passage about a New Year's celebration in Vietnam that included words in Vietnamese, the teacher asked the students to discuss in home-language groups why the author included Vietnamese words. The class discussed the reasons and talked about how students could figure out what the words in Vietnamese meant by the context.

Next the teacher assigned the students to write about New Year's celebrations in their country. They interviewed their parents and included words from their home language. Because students were not always certain of writing in their home languages, parents edited the writing to check the language and cultural information. The teacher assembled the students' writing into a whole-class book about New Year's celebrations in different countries (Ebe and Chapman-Santiago 2016).

In response to a changing view of bilinguals and bilingualism, an increasing number of ESL and bilingual teachers now use translanguaging strategies to affirm students' bilingual identities, build metalinguistic awareness, and scaffold instruction. This shift has significantly improved instruction for emergent bilinguals.

REFLECT OR TURN AND TALK

Have you or other teachers you know implemented translanguaging strategies with emergent bilinguals? Make a list of the strategies you have used or might use, and share it with a partner.

Schooling Models for Emergent Bilinguals

Almost every school in the United States now has at least some English learners. Different programs have been developed to serve these students. The choice of program depends on the student population and the staffing for the school. When a school has only a few English learners or has students who speak a variety of languages, the school usually adopts an ESL (or ELD) program. ESL is also commonly used at the secondary level, where there are fewer staff qualified to teach bilingually. In other cases, when there are a large number of emergent bilinguals who speak the same home language, a bilingual program is generally implemented as long as there is a sufficient number of bilingual teachers. In the following sections, we discuss the different ESL and bilingual models.

ESL Programs

Many schools implement ESL pull-out or push-in programs. ESL pull-out programs do what their name indicates: they pull ELs out of their mainstream classes to receive ESL support. The traditional ESL pull-out instruction usually includes basic vocabulary and grammar instruction. What students are taught in their pull-out classes is often not connected to any instruction they receive in the regular classes since it is often difficult for the ESL teacher to coordinate instruction with the mainstream teachers. In the mainstream classrooms ELs study in English only and do not develop their home-language abilities. Sometimes, they lose their home languages completely. Thomas and Collier's (2002) large-scale study of program types identified ESL pull-out as the least effective of ESL programs; yet it is the program that is often implemented in US schools, especially when there are only a few ELs or when the ELs speak a variety of languages.

ESL pull-out teachers often have to travel to several schools each day and teach groups of students who are of different ages. Many ESL pull-out teachers have to carry their supplies with them. Students in pull-out programs miss the instruction that goes on in the regular class, and they lose instructional time when they are pulled out for ESL instruction. This is also one of the most expensive programs, since an additional teacher is hired to teach the ELLs.

In some ESL programs an ESL specialist works with students in their mainstream classrooms. In the best push-in programs, the mainstream teacher and the ESL teacher plan together and give each other feedback on student progress. When these ESL push-in programs are well implemented, what the EL students study is connected to the content they are learning in their classrooms. The push-in ESL specialist teachers teach language through content and use strategies to make the regular classroom content comprehensible to ELs.

Effective push-in programs, then, include articulation between the classroom teachers and the ESL specialist. Unfortunately, few administrators facilitate this kind of planning. Because ESL teachers work with several mainstream teachers, it is difficult to coordinate with all of them. In addition, the ESL teacher is sometimes regarded by the classroom teachers as more like a paraprofessional than a regular teacher. The mainstream teacher may ask push-in teachers to work on the side of the room, helping students with homework or doing worksheets unrelated to what the other students are doing. While this program is more effective than traditional ESL pull-out, Thomas and Collier (2002) found that ELs placed in such a program usually dropped out in high school or were doing poorly when compared with their high school peers. In fact, none of the English-only models has been shown to be as effective as bilingual models for emergent bilinguals.

At the secondary level, schools often have an ESL program with designated ESL teachers. This model is generally used when there are enough ELs to form several classes, especially when the students speak a variety of languages. Students usually are placed by proficiency level. Teachers may use traditional methods with a focus on vocabulary and grammar. Many teachers now use content-based instruction. However, as Valdés (2001) points out in her book *Learning and Not Learning English*, ESL programs like these generally do not accelerate students' language and content knowledge rapidly enough for them to be reclassified as fully English proficient and placed in mainstream classes. As a result, many emergent bilinguals become long-term English learners (Olsen 2010b, 2014).

Bilingual Programs

Bilingual programs have been more successful than ESL programs in helping students achieve academic success. However, not all bilingual programs support students equally well. There are several models of bilingual education. The main difference among the models is the amount of time in which students receive home-language instruction. Students in transitional programs typically receive some home-language instruction for two or three years, while students in maintenance or dual language bilingual programs are taught in their home language for at least six years. Baker and Wright (2017) classify the short-term transitional programs as weak bilingual programs and the long-term maintenance or dual language programs as strong programs. The authors point out that students in strong bilingual programs consistently outperform students in weak programs. This claim is supported by a large body of research.

Early-Exit Bilingual Education

Early-exit or transitional programs have been widely used in the past but are the least effective of the bilingual programs (Thomas and Collier 2002). In early-exit programs ELs are prepared to transition into all-English classrooms within three years of beginning school as non-English speakers. The rationale for these programs is that they provide students with understandable instruction for part of the day in their home language until they have developed enough English proficiency to be instructed in English. The home language serves as a bridge that helps students move into English-only instruction.

Theoretically, non-English-speaking students who enter school in second grade (or later) should also receive three years of primary-language support. However, in practice older learners usually receive fewer than three years of instruction in their first language. There are fewer bilingual upper-grade teachers, and often even those teachers are encouraged to get students into English as quickly as possible.

Early-exit programs appeal to those parents and educators who want to see their children in all-English classes as soon as possible. Since most children develop conversational proficiency in about two years (Cummins 1981), teachers and administrators often use this as an indication that the children are ready for all-English instruction. In the past, tests used to determine whether students were ready to transition to the mainstream tested only oral proficiency, so students who had developed conversational English were exited out of bilingual programs before they had developed literacy in English and grade-level academic content knowledge. Current tests are more rigorous, but as Olsen showed in a large-scale study, most of the students in California who tested as fully English proficient and were exited from LEP status scored below basic on the state language arts test (Olsen 2010b).

Cummins (1981) and Collier (1989) have conducted research that shows that it takes five to seven years for EBs to develop grade-level academic language proficiency in English. Thomas and Collier (2002) found that students in early-exit programs failed to develop their home-language proficiency beyond the two to three years of instruction, and this was not sufficient to help them with academic content learning in English. As the students moved up the grades, their conversational English was not enough to help them with the academics they needed. High school students in their study who had been in early-exit programs generally scored below the fiftieth percentile in tests of reading in English.

Late-Exit or Maintenance Bilingual Programs

In late-exit programs, students receive instruction in their home language through at least sixth grade. Late-exit is a one-way model because all of the students in a class are ELs, so their language learning is going one way, toward English; but at the same time, their home language is maintained. In the early grades, late-exit students usually receive most of their instruction in their home language, but once they get into third and fourth grades, they study subject matter and do reading and writing in English as well as in their home language. Throughout their program, English is taught through academic content.

Students in late-exit programs develop proficiency in their home language and in English. Ramírez (1991) found that late-exit students scored better in math and reading in English than students in English-only or early-exit programs. Thomas and Collier (2002) conducted research that showed that these students scored above the fiftieth percentile in reading in English by sixth or seventh grade. Although late-exit programs are fairly successful, they are implemented the least often. One drawback for late-exit or maintenance bilingual programs is that the ELs are segregated from native English speakers. A second problem is that late-exit programs may be regarded and implemented as remedial programs. In most cases, schools that had late-exit programs now have dual language bilingual programs.

Dual Language Bilingual Programs

Dual language bilingual programs are the most rapidly growing program type for emergent bilinguals. Other bilingual program models, both early-exit and late-exit, were often envisioned as a form of remedial or compensatory education to serve as a bridge to English. On the other hand, dual language bilingual programs are a form of enrichment education. Hamayan, Genesee, and Cloud explain, "These are enriched forms of DL education because they aim for full competence in two (or more) languages along with high levels of academic achievement and cross-cultural understanding and achievement" (2013, 8).

Soltero also describes dual language as enrichment education. She states:

> Dual language education is a long-term additive bilingual and cross-cultural program model that consistently uses two languages for content instruction, learning, and communication, where students develop high levels of bilingual, biliterate, and cross-cultural competencies. (2016, 3)

Dual language bilingual (or dual language immersion) programs are growing rapidly in the United States. These programs can be found in schools in both cities and rural areas. For example, Utah passed a bill in 2008 to develop dual language programs in Spanish, Mandarin, and French. Then, in 2010, the governor issued a challenge to open one hundred new dual language schools in the state teaching in English and Mandarin, French, German, Portuguese, and Spanish. In New York City, the chancellor launched an expansion of dual language schools in the city. These programs are in high demand. García (2015) reported that forty dual language schools were being added there because of the demand for dual language, citing the example of one school that had 1,100 applicants for only 20 spots in the school.

It is difficult to get an accurate count of the number of dual language programs in the United States since new programs are constantly being implemented. A search of the internet shows dual language programs in many states. The Dual Language Schools website (http://duallanguageschools.org) listed that 2,229 schools were registered as of December 2020. The Office of English Language Acquisition (OELA) reported in 2016–17 that thirty-five states and the District of Columbia had dual language programs in eighteen languages.

In California the passage of Proposition 58 in 2016 not only negated Proposition 227, the English-only law, but clearly showed that Californians were aware of the need for multilingualism in the twenty-first century. The California Department of Education published *Global California 2030: Speak. Learn. Lead* (CDE 2018). The CDE's goals for expanding dual language programs, as stated in the document, were impressive: "quadrupling the number of programs from 407 in 2017 to 1,600 in 2030" (14). To do this, there will be a need for more bilingual teachers with high levels of academic language skill and authorization to teach in two languages.

The CDE document pointed out that the state Department of Education wants to have more state-approved teacher training programs preparing teachers to teach in two languages. In 2016 there were thirty programs in the state, and the goal is to have one hundred state-approved programs by 2030. While the majority of dual language programs are and will be English–Spanish programs, California presently offers programs in other languages, including English-Mandarin, English-Korean, English-Vietnamese, English-Hmong, and English-Portuguese. Dual language programs in different languages will help to reach state goals of *Global California 2030.*

> To better prepare students to succeed in the changing economy and to strengthen
> California's own rich mixture of cultures and languages, California needs to
> vastly expand opportunities for students to learn a second and possibly even a
> third language. (CDE 2018, 4)

ONE-WAY DUAL LANGUAGE BILINGUAL PROGRAMS

There are two types of dual language programs: one-way and two-way. In one-way programs most of the students begin school speaking a home language other than English. These programs have been developed in areas where there are large numbers of students who speak a language other than English. Since two-way dual language programs need to have a sufficient number of students whose home language is English, it may not be feasible to establish a two-way program in some school districts.

One-way bilingual programs can include recently arrived immigrants with little or no knowledge of English. In addition, many of the students in one-way programs have been born in the United States or have lived here for several years. They often understand some English and may use both English and their home language every day. For example, all the students in a one-way dual language program may be Latinx with varying levels of proficiency in both Spanish and English. The programs are considered one-way because English is not the home language of any of the students. These programs are similar to some developmental or late-exit bilingual programs.

Generally, instruction in a one-way program follows a 50/50 model. Half of the instructional time is in English and half in the LOTE (language other than English). The program may offer some subjects in English and some in the LOTE. In other programs half the day is in English and half in the LOTE. Schools may also use an alternate-day or alternate-week language allocation. In some schools there are two teachers, one for each language. More often, one bilingual teacher provides all the instruction.

TWO-WAY DUAL LANGUAGE BILINGUAL PROGRAMS

Generally, two-way bilingual programs require a ratio of at least one-third to two-thirds for the two language groups. Ideally, half the students would be native English speakers and half would speak the LOTE. In two-way dual language bilingual programs all students have access to native speakers of the language they are acquiring. In addition, two-way programs include students from two or more different cultural backgrounds, so there is a greater likelihood of students gaining increased cross-cultural understanding, one of the goals of enriched education. In both one-way and two-way programs there may also be students whose home language is not either of the two languages of instruction. Since teachers constantly need to use strategies to make the input comprehensible, these students also benefit from dual language programs.

Many two-way programs follow a 90/10 language allocation. In these programs, instruction is offered for 90 percent of the day in the LOTE and 10 percent in English in kindergarten or first grade. Then more instruction is offered in English each year until there is a 50/50 language allocation.

One reason to begin with more instruction in the LOTE is that schools that do this are providing a more equitable education. Several assumptions are used to support this language allocation. First, the schools exist in an all-English context, so all students hear English outside school, but not all students have access to the LOTE daily. There is also the assumption that parents of English speakers may be able to support students' literacy development better than parents of the LOTE because in many cases they have been reading to and with their students before the students started school. In addition, beginning schooling mainly in the LOTE sends the message that the culture of the partner language and the language itself are valued.

Middle School and High School Program Models

An increasing number of dual language bilingual programs have been implemented at the secondary level. At the middle and high school levels, the division for instruction in each language is usually varied by subject. Generally, language arts is offered in the language other than English along with either social studies or science. Students take either two or three subjects each day in the LOTE. The subjects offered may vary from one year to the next. The partner language might be used in science in ninth grade and in social studies in tenth grade. Decisions about the subjects taught in the LOTE are determined by the availability of teachers who have both certification in the academic subject and academic language proficiency in the LOTE.

In many schools the LOTE teachers are first hired to teach science or social studies, and then, when the school extends dual language into the middle school level, they teach their subject in Spanish, Arabic, or another language. Language arts in the LOTE is usually taught by the foreign language teachers. Often, since students have been studying in Spanish or another language in the dual language program for several years, they take an AP language arts course in that language, and they may do this as early as middle school.

There are challenges in implementing dual language bilingual programs at the secondary level. Sometimes school counselors who are unaware of the importance of continuing study in a second language give students a choice between a popular elective like band or art and the dual language class. Scheduling is more complicated at the secondary level. In addition, teachers who have been teaching their subjects in English may be reluctant to teach them in the LOTE even though they have proficiency in it. Nevertheless, in schools that continue the classes, students show high levels of academic success. In one school in a district with high poverty and a 98 percent Latinx student body, students in the dual language bilingual program had a 100 percent graduation rate and a 100 percent college acceptance rate (Ferrón 2012).

Program Model or Effective Practices?

Baker and Wright (2017) note that the notion of a program model is now being challenged and that the emphasis should be on effective practices rather than simply on effective models. From our own research (Freeman, Freeman, and Mercuri 2018), we have also concluded that the implementation of the program is more important than the model. Schools that take a bilingual or heteroglossic perspective see bilinguals as individuals who have a complex linguistic system with features of two or more languages. Effective practices include helping students make cross-language connections and drawing on all students' language resources rather than keeping languages strictly separate. As Baker and Wright comment, "such a perspective opens up space to engage in optimal classroom translanguaging practices that maximize growth and gains for individual students, as well as positive outcomes for schools in an accountability era" (2017, 198). Figure 5–10 summarizes our descriptions of different program models for English learners.

REFLECT OR TURN AND TALK

Which program model for emergent bilinguals has been implemented at your school? What factors led to the choice? Do you think this is the best model for your context? Share with a partner.

Emergent bilinguals in US schools are placed in different types of ESL or bilingual programs. As educators we hope that programs support students not only linguistically but also academically. Dual language programs are being adopted widely for English learners because they prepare them for our multicultural world. The twenty-first-century skills they will need include bilingualism or multilingualism and the ability to work with a diverse society. Programs for emergent bilinguals must give these learners equitable access to success, the topic of the final chapter of this book.

Programs for English Learners		
Type of Program	**Description**	**Academic Result**
ESL pull-out—traditional instruction	ELs are given ESL support. They are taught basic vocabulary and language structure (grammar) and are then integrated into all-English instruction.	These students show little academic progress, and once mainstreamed, they rarely catch up. Many students drop out before graduation.
ESL pull-out or push-in content instruction	ELs are given two to three years of ESL content support services and are then integrated into all-English instruction.	By the end of high school many of these students drop out or are in the lowest fourth of their class.
Early-exit or transitional bilingual education	ELs receive a portion of their content instruction in their primary language for two to three years and then are integrated into all-English instruction.	At the end of high school these students are below the fiftieth percentile in tests of reading in English.
Late-exit, maintenance, or developmental bilingual education	ELs learn content in the home language for four to six years.	ELs outperform students in English-only programs. Students achieve above the fiftieth percentile on standardized tests in English.
Dual language bilingual education (one-way and two-way)	ELs and native English speakers learn language through content in two languages.	Students from both language groups outperform students in transitional and developmental bilingual education and score above the fiftieth percentile on standardized tests in English.

Figure 5–10 • Programs for English Learners

6

How Can Schools Provide Equitable Education for Emergent Bilinguals?

Key Points

- Segregation in education still exists sixty years after *Brown v. Board of Education*.

- Equity is not the same as equality.

- During COVID-19, treating students of varying racial, ethnic, or linguistic groups equally did not provide equity.

- Cummins suggests that societal relations and students' identities affect the school success of students in different racial and ethnic groups.

- Schools can provide equity through an intercultural orientation.

- Schools should acknowledge and incorporate students' funds of knowledge.

- A transformative pedagogy supports emergent bilinguals in schools.

- Teachers should organize groupings of students and the classroom environment to promote equity.

- Educators of ethnically and racially diverse students should adopt a culturally sustaining pedagogy.

In the 1954 landmark Supreme Court decision *Brown v. Board of Education of Topeka*, segregation in schools was declared unconstitutional. The court determined that "segregated education was inherently unequal and created irreversible harm to segregated students." The reality now is that there is still segregation, both economic and racial, in US schools. According to the National Center for Educational Statistics (NCES) in 2017 white students were a numerical minority in many schools. Between 2000 and 2017 the white population of students declined by thirteen million to 24.1 million or 48 percent, while at the same time, the Latinx population grew by eleven million, to 13.6 million, and made up 27 percent of the entire US school population. The percentage of Black students decreased by 2 million to 7.7 million. The Asian population was five million and made up 5 percent of the total, and two million students in schools were considered multiracial. Since 1954 many areas of the country have remained or returned to schools that keep students separate by race through a series of Supreme Court decisions that overturned desegregation orders across the country (Frankenberg et al. 2019). This has resulted in many racially, ethnically, or linguistically diverse students attending ghettoized schools in poor communities.

Research shows that children living in poverty are more likely to show lower-than-average academic performance from kindergarten through high school and have lower-than-average school completion rates (de Brey et al. 2019a). In 2016, 15 percent of all children under the age of eighteen were living in poverty. Significantly more of these children are Black or Latinx and fewer are Asian or white.

Racial and Ethnic Diversity in US Schools

While the students in schools are much more diverse, schools are not. "White students, on average, attend a school in which 69 percent of the students are white," according to Frankenberg and colleagues (2019, 4), and 55 percent of Latinx students attend schools with other Latinx students and Black students. Asian students attend schools where the student population is 24 percent Asian. White and Asian students are least likely to attend schools with Black and Latinx students. The landscape of school diversity is continually changing. In California, for example, there are already more Latinx students than white students. White students make up only one-fourth of the students in the state. In the South a growing number of schools that in the past had few students of color now have a majority of Latinx, Black, Asian, and multiracial students. Researchers, including economists, are calling for schools to prepare students "to live and work effectively in extremely multiracial communities" (Frankenberg et al. 2019, 7), but schools in many areas remain segregated.

For example, many ELs live in poverty and attend schools with other racially, ethnically, or linguistically diverse students. According to de Brey and colleagues (2019b), in 2015 ELs in US schools made up almost 10 percent of all students, and of that 10 percent, 75 percent were Latinx, with Asian ELs making up the second largest group at 10.5 percent. Other racial groups among ELs included white students at 6.1 percent and Black ELs at 3.7 percent. Native American and Alaska Native Americans and Pacific Islanders were at a smaller percentage, less than 1 percent. These groups of students tend to attend inner-city schools with each other and do not have teachers who reflect their backgrounds, which we discuss in the next section.

Teachers, Race, and Equity

Research has shown that having a teacher of the same race or ethnicity can have a positive impact on a student's attitudes, motivation, and achievement, and racially and ethnically diverse teachers may have more positive expectations for racially, ethnically, or linguistically diverse students' achievement than white teachers (Egalite and Kisida 2018). According to de Brey and colleagues (2019c), in public schools in 2015–16, the percentage of white teachers in US schools was 80 percent while the percentage of Black teachers and Hispanic teachers was 7 and 9 percent, respectively. Only 2 percent of teachers were Asian nationwide, and teachers who were Native Americans, Pacific Islanders, and other related groups made up 1 percent or less of the total teacher population.

The percentage of diverse teachers was higher in schools with more diversity, but white teachers were the majority even in most diverse schools, except in schools with very diverse student bodies (de Brey et al. 2019c). Schools with a student body that had 90 percent racial or ethnic diversity had the highest level of diversity among teachers at 55 percent, while in schools with less than 10 percent diverse students, only 2 percent or fewer of their teachers were racially diverse. When teachers are Hispanic, Asian, or from other racial or ethnic groups, they tend to have less experience, sometimes fewer than three years, and fewer advanced degrees, according to the report by de Brey and his colleagues.

Gándara and Mordechay (2017) discuss the importance of teachers for the large number of Latinx students in US schools. The researchers found that in schools where at least a quarter of the students were Latinx, fewer than 8 percent of the teachers were Latinx. The research showed that the more Latinx teachers young Latinas have, the more likely they are to go to college, and "this was related to the comfort they felt in talking to someone who was likely to understand their circumstances and who could talk to their parents" (154).

Gándara and Mordechay also discuss the teacher shortage in areas with large numbers of Latinx students. In California, where more than half of the students are Latinx, only about 18 percent of the teachers are of the same ethnic background. While research shows that dual language programs serve many Latinx students well, there is a massive shortage of bilingual teachers for these programs. In fact, Gándara and Mordechay report that only 5 percent of the Spanish-speaking bilingual students in the state have teachers who are bilingual, largely because of Proposition 227, which made bilingual education illegal until the 2016 passage of Proposition 58 allowed schools to offer multilingual programs. Many Latinx teacher education candidates do not have the academic Spanish they need to teach beyond kindergarten because their instruction in schools in the state was all in English.

Demographic data from a 2015–16 report (Gándara and Mordechay 2017) shows school location made a difference in the diversity of teachers. For example, city schools had a higher percentage of racial, ethnic, and linguistic groups at 31 percent, compared with town schools at 12 percent and rural schools at 11 percent. Suburban schools, however, did have more diverse teachers. Reports show that 18 percent of their teachers were nonwhite. Overall, across the country, then, the racial and ethnic diversity of students is not reflected in the teaching force.

REFLECT OR TURN AND TALK

Which of the demographics related to diversity in schools surprised you? How do you think these demographics inform schools and teachers? How are the schools that you are familiar with or work in reflected in these demographics?

Equality Versus Equity

Equity is not the same as equality. The claim is that all people in the US have equal opportunities and equal access. So, for example, a company that advertises itself as an equal opportunity employer should evaluate all who apply to work based on their qualifications, not their sex, sexual orientation, age, or ethnicity. Although this is a goal, it has not yet been realized. Black and women candidates are not hired or promoted equally with white candidates. The recent Black Lives Matter movement is based on the fact that persons of color and whites are not treated equally by the police.

Taking into consideration the demographic data we shared earlier, it is clear that not all students have equal educational opportunities. When emergent bilinguals attend schools with a large number of ethnically diverse students in poor neighborhoods, and in which teachers do not reflect the ethnicity of their students and are not as experienced as teachers in schools that are less diverse, there is a lack of equal opportunity. Kozol (1991) has documented the difference in funding for schools and the difference in school facilities and resources in districts based on the wealth of people in the district and the tax base of properties there, even in districts that are not far apart geographically.

Even in schools that provide equal resources, English learners may not receive equitable education. While equality aims at providing equal opportunity, the goal of equity is equal outcomes. In the 1974 *Lau v. Nichols* case, the Chinese-speaking students had the same teachers and used the same textbooks as native English speakers. However, since they did not speak English, they could not access the curriculum or understand the teachers. As a result, they did not achieve equal outcomes. They had equal opportunities, but the instruction did not constitute equitable education. Equity often involves removing institutional barriers that prevent some students from learning even when they are given equal opportunities. In this case, changing the requirements for language of instruction provided the Chinese students an equitable education.

Gándara and Mordechay (2017) report that Latinx students are increasingly in places where there is little infrastructure to support their educational needs. The segregation of Latinx students is now the most severe of any group and typically involves a very high concentration of poverty (Frankenberg et al. 2019, 9). For these students and all students from diverse groups, there need to be more socioemotional support systems.

For example, explicitly negative statements toward immigrants and certain racial and ethnic groups beginning with Donald Trump's 2016 presidential campaign have had negative consequences (Frankenberg et al. 2019). In 2020, racial and ethnic tensions exploded after the killing of George Floyd, accompanied by the reignition of the pain and fear surrounding the many killings of people of color by the police and others.

The rise of the Black Lives Matter movement soon became the Black and Brown Lives Matter movement. In addition, Asian Americans were targeted because President Trump blamed China for the spread of COVID-19, and, thus, any Asian was fair game to be blamed and sometimes attacked because of the pandemic. These events allowed for xenophobia to become accepted and encouraged in some circles and created fear among ethnically diverse students and their families. Research studies have shown that the current atmosphere has exacerbated racial and ethnic problems in schools, including noticeable changes in school climate.

Equality Versus Equity During COVID-19

When states across the country declared that all but essential services should close, that included all schools: elementary-, secondary-, and university-level institutions. That meant that instruction was going to be given online, a decision that gave many educators only a weekend to reorganize and revisualize the curriculum. The closures were applied equally across most communities, and administrators and teachers scrambled to deliver instruction virtually. Most students in middle- and upper-class homes had computers or tablets and internet connections. For the most part, parents were available to support these students. However, although all students in a school or district were given the same curriculum, there was a lack of equity. In many homes of emergent bilinguals, there were no computers and no access to the internet.

Teachers soon discovered that some students lived in homes with a single parent and several siblings and many other homes included multigenerational family members or more than one family sharing a home. In these settings, often the only means of communication with schools was a cell phone shared by several family members. While this situation could not be remedied in some districts, schools in many parts of the country responded by supplying tablets, but then found they needed to also find ways to provide internet access. In some areas hot spots were supplied where needed.

However, even these supports did not give many emergent bilinguals access. The *LA Times* reported that over fifty thousand middle and high school students in Los Angeles did not participate on the school's main platform for virtual classrooms after schools closed in March 2020 (Esquivel and Blume 2020). Black and Latinx students participated between 10 and 20 percentage points lower than white and Asian peers. English learners, students with disabilities, students who are homeless, and students in foster care also had lower participation rates.

In a policy brief from the Migration Policy Institute (Sugarman and Lazarín 2020), the authors state "the COVID-19 pandemic has brought into sharp relief the inequities that English Learners (ELs) and children from immigrant families experience in U.S. schools and in their communities." They explain that despite great efforts by educators, in spring 2020 the school systems with the largest number of ELs reported that less than half the ELs were logging in to online instruction. They point out "among the most significant barriers to ELs' participation were a lack of access to digital devices and broadband; parents' limited capacity to support home learning; inadequate remote learning resources and training for teachers; and school–family language barriers." The report concludes that if schools continue distance learning through the fall, many students will lose 7 to 11 months of learning. In addition, "for many families of ELs, the pandemic and accompanied school building closures have compromised their access to food and income security as well as social and mental-health supports."

There were different issues beyond access for many students. When teachers gave assignments, neither students nor their parents had had enough experience with technology to help students attend meetings online or upload assignments on platforms like Google Classroom. In addition, if there were several children in the family, the tablets had to be shared (LaFave 2020). Parents who might have helped were often absent because they were essential workers, including those working in health care, on farms, in meatpacking plants, in grocery stores, or in delivery services. For immigrant parents there was often the added problem of not reading and writing English proficiently enough to be of assistance to their children.

Even when parents or relatives in these families could help their children, other issues took priority. Family members got sick or lost jobs or both. One administrator in New York City explained in a Zoom meeting that her main priorities were not getting instruction to families but getting food to them and helping them with funeral arrangements.

During a recent TESOL presentation an administrator from a school district in Connecticut pointed out that the online plan for the district involved sending home lesson packets for students to complete (Becker 2020). Packets are not generally effective for teaching students and clearly do not provide equity for ELs. In this district, since they had materials only for mainstream students, there were no accommodations for English learners. This created a situation like that of the *Lau v. Nichols* case in 1974. Beginning-level ELs had a hard time understanding the instructions on the packets, and many parents could not read English, so they could not help. The district was able to translate the packets into Spanish, and this helped many ELs since many of them spoke Spanish, but not all did. The district made many other accommodations, such as having social workers visit homes of students who were not participating in the program, but it is evident that many challenges face school districts, even as they continue to improve services for emergent bilinguals.

Another presentation at this TESOL session involved EL specialists working in Missouri (Hellman et al. 2020). They conducted a survey of teachers with follow-up. In addition to EL families lacking internet access or devices, they found that EL families were not always informed on how to proceed after schools suspended operations. Information was provided on the school website, but it was difficult to find any EL supports. There were problems in connecting with EL families. Only 62 percent of the teachers connected with every EL family, and 43 percent did not connect with every EL student. The district also lacked good translation services for families of ELs who did not speak Spanish, such as their Karen population. Teachers made great efforts to support ELs, but many ELs did not participate in instruction because of the problems with communication and the lack of any clear plan by the district. Again, as this example shows, lack of online schooling resources for ELs in many districts across the country results in a lack of equitable education for these students.

REFLECT OR TURN AND TALK

We explained the difference between equality and equity and some examples of lack of equity during the COVID-19 pandemic. Consider your present context. Can you think of an example where equality in schools you know does not provide equity for emergent bilinguals? Do your administrators consider equity when they make decisions that affect racially, ethnically, or linguistically diverse students? How?

In a climate rife with racial and ethnic tensions and students who are not equitably served, educators need some guidance in how to approach the teaching of emergent bilinguals. They also need some practical suggestions for what they can do as they teach these students. We present two different frameworks from Cummins that look at how students are viewed and the policies toward them that have led to those views. The first is his societal relations, identity negotiation, and academic achievement framework and the second is his intercultural orientations framework (Cummins 2001, 2009).

Societal Relations and Equity for Emergent Bilinguals

Cummins (2009) explains that society often exerts negative power over ethnic and racial groups. These powers are evident in experiences such as police violence and frequent racial slurs and threats. These types of events negatively impact the school achievement of racially, ethnically, and linguistically diverse students. When immigrant emergent bilingual children see political figures threatening to deport their relatives and hear themselves called derogatory names, children sometimes fear even going to school (Saxon 2018). These societal conditions can influence how teachers interact positively or negatively with linguistically and culturally diverse students.

Coercive and Collaborative Relations of Power

According to Cummins (2001, 2009), when teachers interact with students, they create interpersonal spaces in which learning happens and students' identities are negotiated. What students learn and how teachers either support their identities or negate them is critical to emergent bilingual students. Teachers either reinforce the coercive relations of power that negatively affect their students or promote collaborative relations of power. Coercive relations of power develop when the school or teachers overtly or covertly view certain students as less capable and even less worthy.

Over the years we have heard teachers and administrators talk about "those children" who don't have a good home, don't have parents who care, aren't really trying, interact only with other students who don't speak English, or are *mañana* students. One hears things like "What can you expect of Pancho? His family doesn't speak English at home." In coercive relations of power, the dominant group defines the subordinated group as inferior and tends to blame the victim (Cummins 2001). Teachers have low expectations of these students and provide fewer opportunities for their academic development.

We remember observing a high school ESL class where during the entire class period, the teacher gave students five vocabulary words to work with: first they repeated the words, then copied their definitions, and then completed a fill-in-the-blanks sheet. Students were bored, tended not to pay attention, and knew they were not being challenged. It was painful to sit and watch this class. When asked about readings and other activities, the teacher pointed to some anthologies but explained, "They really can't read them. We don't use them very often. When we try activities, they don't understand." Valdés (2001) has written in detail about cases of students who are given placements and instruction that result in their never advancing academically. Many of these students simply drop out.

In contrast to coercive power relations, collaborative relations of power assume that students can be empowered learners when their identities are affirmed, and they work collaboratively with the teacher and classmates to learn together. Instead of worksheets and boring repetition, students read meaningful, grade-appropriate texts together, are encouraged to discuss and write in their home languages as well as in English, and are provided opportunities to respond in a variety of ways to show what they know and understand. This can include artwork, reports based on internet searches, and group sharing.

One teacher had her year one ESL students do a "cool country" report. They drew a map of their home country and drew and colored their flag, listed key points of interest in a travel brochure, identified products or industries within the country, and wrote about holidays and favorite foods. Drawing on the content from their reports, they made silhouettes of their faces and decorated them to make cultural visuals of themselves that included a map of their country, words in their home language, their flag, drawings of points of interest, and religious symbols. In her silhouette, a girl from India wrote in Hindi and Tamil, drew the Taj Mahal, and included an altar with an elephant with a marigold necklace. These activities helped students develop both literacy and oral language skills while affirming their bilingual identities.

As we described in Chapter 5, Mary and Elizabeth had their university students who were studying to become bilingual teachers make cultural mandalas in multicultural small groups. They asked the students to list characteristics of their identity with their culture and families. After they had completed their cultural mandalas, the whole class shared their personal characteristics on the large classroom whiteboard. This powerful cultural graffiti board, shown in Figure 6–1, celebrated and reflected the class' diversity by including drawings as well as phrases in English and students' home languages.

Francisco, a teacher from El Salvador, read his bilingual third graders a story he had written about his childhood in rural El Salvador. The students asked him about the childhood memories he described, and he provided additional details about growing up in poverty in his home country. He then asked the children to write about an incident from their own childhood or to interview their parents or grandparents and

Figure 6–1 • Cultural Graffiti Board

write those experiences. The teacher's sharing allowed students to reflect on their own experiences and those of their relatives and share them. Students spent a great deal of energy on this project, which validated who they were and, for many, helped them appreciate and celebrate their relatives' lived experiences, something they had never done before.

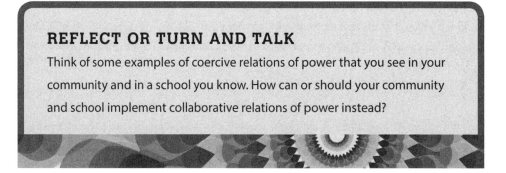

REFLECT OR TURN AND TALK

Think of some examples of coercive relations of power that you see in your community and in a school you know. How can or should your community and school implement collaborative relations of power instead?

Intercultural Orientations for Education

Earlier we discussed Ruíz's general orientations toward language. These orientations have led to the establishment of different kinds of programs that support the development of home languages for ELs. Cummins (2001, 2009) has also developed a framework based on orientations, but rather than focus strictly on language, he considers language policies as just one of the areas to consider in analyzing how schools respond to emergent bilinguals. These orientations can help educators to consider the approach their school takes toward culturally diverse students.

Cummins defines two orientations that schools can develop: intercultural or assimilationist. These two orientations differ in four areas: use of students' primary languages and cultures in the curriculum; relationships with racially, ethnically, and linguistically diverse community members; approach to teaching; and methods of assessment. Figure 6–2 outlines the key points of differences between the two orientations.

As Figure 6–2 shows, when schools take an intercultural orientation, they include students' home languages and cultures, they involve parents of racially, ethnically, and linguistically diverse students in school activities, they encourage the use of current pedagogical methods of collaborative critical inquiry, and they design assessments that allow students to demonstrate their competence. In contrast, when schools take an assimilationist orientation, they exclude students' home languages and pay little attention to students' cultures, they discourage diverse community members from active involvement in their local schools, they teach using traditional methods, and they use

Intercultural Orientations		
	Intercultural Orientation	Assimilationist Orientation
Students' languages and cultures	Add them to the curriculum.	Exclude them from the curriculum.
Racially, ethnically, and linguistically diverse community members	Involve them in the school.	Exclude them from the school.
Teaching	Use transformative methods.	Use traditional methods.
Assessment	Help students show what they know.	Use measures to justify grades.

Figure 6–2 • Intercultural Orientations   Adapted from Cummins (2001)

forms of assessment, such as tests and quizzes, that help teachers justify the grades they give students.

Generally, schools that take an intercultural orientation see student diversity as an asset. Such schools find ways to incorporate diverse students into the institution and to provide programs that promote their success. On the other hand, some schools have as their goal the assimilation of diverse students into the mainstream. In the attempt to assimilate students, such schools often operate programs that disempower and marginalize second language students and the communities they come from.

Including Students' Languages and Cultures

In schools that adopt an intercultural orientation, students' home languages and cultures are included in the curriculum. In schools with students from multicultural, multilingual backgrounds, murals painted by students can welcome all to the school with visual symbols or simply the word *welcome* in the many languages of the students and their families. Suárez-Orozco supports this kind of visual display by explaining that "hallways should be allowed to echo many languages, spoken by both students and adults" (2018, 10). One school provided a multilingual information board next to the main office with questions like "How can I help you?" "What language do you speak" "Do you want to register your child?" "Do you need to take your child home?" and "Who is your child's teacher?" The board included the questions in English, Spanish, Bengali, Urdu, Arabic, and Russian. Non-English-speaking caregivers can enter the school and indicate their home language to school staff and begin to get at their needs without being completely lost. This kind of support is in contrast to the schools where office staff intimidate non-English-speaking parents, have no translators, and offer no real way of supporting parents who cannot ask for what they need.

Individual teachers can also support students' cultures starting when the students enter US schools. Marcela teaches multiage newcomers in an elementary school in the Midwest. She knows how important it is to these students who speak very little English to share their lived experiences. One activity she assigns her students is a project where they share celebrations from their countries. Figure 6–3 shows one student's detailed Vietnamese New Year's celebration project, which includes drawings and labels of special food, lanterns, the dragon dance, the wearing of traditional costumes, fireworks, and the custom of getting money from neighbors.

Another student, from Mexico, created a page on the Mexican *quinceañera* (sweet fifteen celebration), shown in Figure 6–4. The Mexican flag in the center is surrounded

Figure 6–3 • Vietnamese New Year

Figure 6–4 • Mexican *Quinceañera*

by what people do: "We bring presents. We dance. We go to church. We eat *mole*, *virria* [goat, conventionally spelled *birria*], and *carnitas*."

Figure 6–5 shows a third detailed depiction, this time of Christmas in El Salvador, which also displays the flag in the middle. In different boxes the author shows going to church, singing, praying, preparing and eating special food, exploding fireworks, and dancing with the family. Clearly, these very recent newcomers put effort into sharing their experiences and adding the English they had been learning.

Including translanguaging strategies, as we discussed in Chapter 5, is another key way that teachers can strategically use students' home languages to affirm their identities and help them acquire English. Bilingual word walls featuring key concepts and turn-and-talks where pairs of students clarify ideas using their home languages are some translanguaging strategies teachers use to support students' acquisition of both language and content.

As we discussed in Chapter 5, dual language programs include the goals of developing bilingualism and biliteracy and of promoting an intercultural orientation. The Two-Way Immersion website of the Center for Applied Linguistics (www.cal.org/twi/)

Figure 6–5 • Christmas in El Salvador

lists the three goals of dual language programs: develop high levels of language proficiency and literacy in both program languages, demonstrate high levels of academic achievement, and *develop an appreciation for and an understanding of diverse cultures* (italics added). By their nature, well-conceived bilingual programs promote an intercultural orientation because they promote and celebrate students' home languages and validate their identity.

REFLECT OR TURN AND TALK

What are some ways that your school or a school you know is including students' cultures and languages? Be specific. What are some ideas you have to increase the inclusion of students' cultures and languages?

DRAWING ON CULTURAL FUNDS OF KNOWLEDGE

In schools that have an intercultural orientation, teachers draw on students' funds of knowledge as they plan their curriculum. Moll and his colleagues (1992) engaged both university researchers and classroom teachers in projects aimed at discovering students' funds of knowledge—the knowledge and skills that are developed in homes and communities. Their research, conducted by teachers, took place in the homes of students, many of whom were immigrants. The research was designed to learn from the students and parents and to discover their funds of knowledge. The researchers discovered the strategies and skills that families develop to function effectively. For example, families know whom to call for medical advice or whom to talk to if their car needs repair.

Two clear examples of funds of knowledge that immigrants have come to mind. In teaching about health, teachers should be aware of home remedies and community expertise and practices. Our son-in-law's mother lives in California near relatives and friends who are all from El Salvador or Mexico. She is known as the woman to call for a *sobada* (massage) when one has aches and pains. She knows how to vary her massages to the condition of the person, what salves to use, and when to use heat. She even knows how to use cupping, originally an ancient therapy developed in Asia. She does the massages, but she turns to others in the community to find who will repair her car or solve her plumbing problem at minimal cost.

Sandra, who was teaching in a farming community in the central valley of California, knew how to draw on funds of knowledge in her teaching. She developed a unit on seeds, plants, plant growth, and nutrition. She began the unit by having students bring in seeds their parents used in their work and home gardens. Then, students interviewed their parents about how to plant and cultivate the seeds. One mother came to class and talked to the students about her large garden, which included tomatoes, chiles, squash, chayote, and beans. She also talked about herbs she grew to make teas that were used when family members got sick.

Bennett (2020) has suggested that teachers can draw on their students' funds of knowledge by making home visits and by having conversations with students about what they and their families do at home, having students bring in artifacts that connect to what the class is learning, having students interview family members and write about them, and having students share about their countries of origin. Teachers who do these kinds of activities show they are teaching using an intercultural rather than an assimilationist orientation.

REFLECT OR TURN AND TALK

Explain in your own words what funds of knowledge are and why they are important for teachers. How have you or teachers you know drawn upon your emergent bilinguals' funds of knowledge?

Involving Racially, Ethnically, and Linguistically Diverse Community Members in the School

A second characteristic of schools that adopt an intercultural orientation is that they involve racially, ethnically, and linguistically diverse community members in school activities. These schools develop programs that encourage collaboration between the school and the community. In the United States over 25 percent of the children under eighteen, or 18.7 million children, have a parent who is an immigrant (Suárez-Orozco and Marks 2016). With these numbers in mind, schools should take an intercultural orientation and foster strong relationships with all parents, including parents of emergent bilinguals.

All parents want their children to be successful. However, some parents of English language learners do not appear to show interest in their children's school lives. Francisco provides us with some insights into why teachers and administrators might develop the impression that the parents of emergent bilinguals just don't care.

In 1989, at age fourteen, Francisco came to the United States from El Salvador, during its period of civil war. Francisco, like many young men his age, was in danger of being conscripted by the army of either side and forced to fight. Concepción, his mother, viewed his arrival in Fresno as the end of her long struggle to get him to the United States legally. Concepción spoke no English and had not been educated in El Salvador. She saw her responsibility as making sure Francisco was safe in the United States, and providing food and shelter for him.

Once Francisco was in the United States, his job was to succeed here—to accomplish the American dream. His mother certainly cared about his schooling, but she was not prepared to approach his teachers to discuss his schoolwork and progress. The large inner-city high school of over three thousand was overwhelming to her. She assumed that the school was educating Francisco, and she believed it was the teacher's job to teach and hers to be sure that Francisco was *bien educado*, meaning respectful and polite. In Concepción's worldview, it would have been presumptive for her to interfere.

In his first year in college, Francisco found the coursework very difficult and was at the point of giving up when his college soccer coach, who could speak Spanish, came to Francisco's home to talk to Concepción about Francisco's academic struggles. After this visit, Concepción talked to her son long and hard about the sacrifices she had made to give him this opportunity for an education. Francisco still remembers thinking, "You don't know how hard it is. You have no idea." He did not lack respect for his mother. He was simply living in a world that she was not part of and did not understand. She was not a negligent parent. She was just not able to help him with his academic school subjects. Instead, she saw her role as raising him to be respectful, caring for his physical needs, and providing strong encouragement for him to continue his education.

Tou, the Hmong student we described in Chapter 2, came from an immigrant family that had suffered greatly because of the move from Southeast Asia to the United States. Tou's parents had separated, and he lived with his father, who could not find work and who did not speak English. His father only came to school for a conference at the request of school personnel. He would probably not have felt comfortable coming to parent meetings or participating in parent groups.

José Luis, Guillermo, and Patricia, the three teens from El Salvador, lived by themselves. Their only relative in the United States was their aunt. Unlike Francisco's mother, she was very well educated, studying for a doctorate. She was a wife, a graduate student, and a teacher of Spanish at both the university where she studied and the local community college. Like Tou's father, she would come to a school meeting, but only if a serious problem arose. She provided the teens with family, love, and shelter. Her niece and nephews knew what they needed to do to succeed, and it was up to them to do it. Even though she was involved in education, she had not attended public schools in the United States. In El Salvador, where she had been educated, parents were not expected to be involved in their children's schooling. As a result, she did not see her role as helping her nephews and niece with their schooling.

Parents of English language learners like Francisco, Tou, and the three siblings from El Salvador realize that school may be the only road to success for the young people. Sometimes they do not know how to help their children succeed, especially if they do not speak English and have had very little schooling themselves. Even if they received an education, it may have been in a school system very different from the system in this country, and they might not understand the expectations of their role as parents here.

For that reason, in schools with an intercultural orientation, extra efforts are made to involve parents. This includes hiring liaisons who visit the homes and encourage the families to come to parent meetings at the school, conducting parent meetings in the students' home languages, and sending out notices and invitations to meetings in the home languages of all the students. In addition, these schools have a plan for welcoming the parents at the school. Individual teachers make it a point to meet the parents and maintain contact with them. For example, in one school, a second-grade bilingual teacher provided coffee and donuts for parents before school on Mondays. She found that her Spanish-speaking parents came and talked to her and they were able to solve many issues through this dedicated time.

RESEARCH ON TEACHER ATTITUDES TOWARD IMMIGRANT PARENTS

In many cases, teachers do not realize that parents of emergent bilinguals may not see their role as becoming involved in their children's schooling. In their research, Suárez-Orozco, Suárez-Orozco, and Todorova (2008) conducted interviews with seventy-five teachers in seven school districts in different areas of the country to determine their perception of the parents of immigrant adolescents. They asked questions such as, "How do you expect parents to support their children's education?" They found that many teachers felt that most immigrant parents were not as involved as they should be and that they held low expectations for their children's academic future. The researchers summed up their findings by commenting,

> *Parents who came to school and helped with homework were viewed as concerned parents, whereas parents who did neither were thought to be disinterested and parents of poor students. A teacher shared with us: "Only a minimum percentage of parents get involved in their kid's education and usually the parents that are concerned and get involved are the parents of the students that are doing well in school. Parents that have kids with problems prefer to hide and not get involved." (77)*

While the Suárez-Orozco team found that teachers perceived that parents held low expectations for their children, interviews with the students painted a different picture. The researchers wrote:

> *While overall teachers' assessments of immigrant parents were often patronizing at best and hostile at worst, looking into the eyes of immigrant youth, we found a very different perspective. The vast majority of the children had internalized very high parental expectations for their students' performance. (77)*

The researchers asked students to complete the question, "For my parents, getting good grades is _____?" (77). Seventy-one percent of the students responded "very important" and another 22 percent responded "important."

Even though their children's academic success is important for parents of emergent bilinguals, often they do not understand how school works and how to help their children with school. Gándara and Contreras, in their study of Latinx students, found this to be the case, even with middle or upper class parents:

> *Latino parents also have less access to information about schooling, even when they are ostensibly from the same social class as white parents. And if they are undocumented, they have much less access to social and health services than a similarly low-income white family. (2009, 83)*

Valdés (1996), in her study of ten migrant families over a three-year period, found that the gap between home and school was, indeed, wide. The school did not understand the families, and the families did not understand the school. She explains the problems in communication from the school's perspective:

> Schools expected a "standard" family, a family whose members were educated, who were familiar with how schools worked, and who saw their role as complementing the teacher's in developing children's academic abilities. It did not occur to school personnel that parents might not know the appropriate ways to communicate with the teachers, that they might feel embarrassed about writing notes filled with errors, and that they might not even understand how to interpret their children's report cards. (167)

REFLECT OR TURN AND TALK

What are the attitudes that teachers you know have expressed about emergent bilingual students' families? What did the stories about Francisco's mother, Tou's father, and the Salvadoran students' aunt tell you about immigrant parents? What did the researchers explain about parents of immigrant students?

PARENT EDUCATION PROGRAMS

Schools have found it difficult to reach out to immigrant parents in particular, in part because of the issues discussed previously and in part because they do not know what to do or how to do it. Yvonne remembers a rural school district with many migrant children that decided to try something different. The school invited her to give a workshop for parents on how to support their children in reading and present it all in Spanish. The response at the parent meeting was overwhelming. So many Spanish-speaking parents showed up that the officials had to move them to a bigger room. White English-speaking parents complained that they didn't get the same information that the Spanish-speaking parents were getting and resented getting moved to a smaller room.

One South Texas border dual language school we worked in provided a classroom especially for parents. There was coffee available and parents brought snacks. At tables the parents and young children sometimes helped teachers with art projects and sometimes talked to the bilingual teachers and administrators who stopped by. The school also provided a Spanish-speaking parent liaison who worked with parents, role-playing scenarios for interacting with their children and with the school. At all times, younger children not yet in school were welcome with parents.

Marcelo Suarez-Orozco (2018) encourages schools to offer workshops and webinars on topics of interest to immigrant parents in particular. He describes how one Spanish–English bilingual school held weekly meetings in Spanish where staff members discussed with parents adjustments to life in the United States and gave parents tools to help their children navigate their schooling. This could be especially helpful as technology becomes more important in schooling in this country. If parents see that technology is beyond them and something they cannot do, that leaves students completely on their own at home. To combat this challenge, schools could hold discussions and workshops virtually once they've provided families with the technology they need. With home responsibilities, sessions from home might be more possible than attending events in person. Sessions could help parents understand the different platforms their children are using to do their work.

HOME VISITS

We discussed earlier how teachers conducting home visits discovered the funds of knowledge that families had. Doing home visits can be part of parent involvement in a school's intercultural orientation. The home and the school can really be two different worlds. To bridge that gap, teachers can carry out home visits.

Katherine was in her first year of teaching when she visited her students' homes at the end of the first grading period. Before she went, she complained about the time and effort the visits were going to take. Afterward, however, she realized how much she had learned. Her students' homes were modest, located around the small farming community where she taught. She came away from each visit with respect for both the parents and the children. She saw that many parents were struggling to get food on the table for their children. She found out that many of her first-grade children often took on responsibilities at home while parents and older siblings worked extra hours to make ends meet. Perhaps what touched her most, however, were the eagerness and respect with which she was received in homes, and the interest, pride, and hope parents showed for their children's futures.

Even when it is not a school requirement, several teachers we work with have made home visits because this has helped them understand their students and parents so much better. Two weeks before school starts, Peter sends an introductory letter to all the children in his class and to their parents. He tells them in the letter that he will be visiting their home to get to know them in the following week. Then he makes short visits to as many homes as possible. Even though he does not speak the first languages of many of his students, he is welcomed into the homes and has a chance to see something of his students' home lives.

Peter has found that those visits have a made a big difference for students during their first days of school, and that after meeting their children's teacher, parents are much more comfortable with both him and the school. The visits have often given him ideas about how parents can become involved in his class. One parent, for instance, played a musical instrument, and another did wood carving. Peter would never have known this had he not been in the students' homes, and since the parents had met him, they were more responsive to his invitations to come and share their skills. This personal contact, undertaken before school even starts, has made a big difference for Peter in the home–school relationship.

In some districts, teachers go out on home visits in pairs to support each other. After the visits they share what they have learned with their partner and other colleagues. This approach has been quite successful.

ACTIVITIES FOR BOOSTING HOME-LANGUAGE LITERACY

In the past, some schools have encouraged parents to speak English to their children at home. However, when parents talk to their children and read and write with them in their first language at home, communication is more natural. We discussed translanguaging in Chapter 5. Encouraging translanguaging draws on students' linguistic repertoire and leads to more school success. For example, a good activity to encourage children to do at home is to make books in the home language. Especially as students are doing work virtually from home, making books on different topics allows students to develop language and at the same time creates home–school connections.

Teachers could ask students to notice what people read in their homes. This could include conventional things like magazines and books but also ads, packages, letters, recipes, spice jars and cans, and cell phones. Students could take pictures of people in the household reading those things and create a book to share online with the teacher and classmates. They could make a similar book by taking pictures of places in the neighborhood or parts of an apartment building, labeling the pictures, and assembling them into a book.

Yvonne has developed some practical suggestions for what parents can do with their children in their home language, even when parents are not literate in their native language. These suggestions can be worded in ways that give parents ideas for what they can do with their children at home in the home language to support their children's literacy development in the home language and English.

1. ***Talking.*** Parents who have conversations with their children help them to think and to explore their world. Parents should talk to students as they shop, explaining why they are choosing different products, or they could point out plants in the neighborhood or in the garden. They can discuss a phone conversation with a family member or talk about a job they have. In this process children learn to use language for a variety of purposes.

2. ***Reading.*** Parents who read with their children and take them to the library give them experiences with books that they need for school success. If parents are not confident readers, they can ask their children to do the reading, or parents and children can follow a story while listening together to a recorded reading or audiobook. Some websites have read-alouds available in different languages. See, for example, Audible (https://stories.audible.com/discovery) and click on any of the languages listed across the top.

   If the children read a book in English to their parents or if the children and parents listen to an English audiobook, the children can then explain the story to the parents, and they can discuss it in their home language as they look at the pictures. A study conducted in six inner-city schools in London (Tizard, Schofield, and Hewison 1982) investigated the benefits of having children from two schools take books home each day to read to their parents. They compared the reading improvement of this group with another group from two different schools that received extra reading support from a well-trained literacy coach and with a third group from two other schools that received no extra help.

   Many of the parents of the children who took books home were illiterate or did not speak English. Despite this, the children who read to parents at home made greater gains in reading than the other two groups. The gains were greatest among children in the group who were having initial problems with reading. This group also showed greater interest in school and were better behaved. This study clearly demonstrated the benefits of having children take home books to read to their parents.

3. ***Writing.*** Parents who encourage their children to draw and write teach them to express themselves in writing. Parents can also make children aware that adults use writing for a variety of purposes every day, including writing letters, making out checks, jotting notes, and making shopping lists. Even if parents do not write frequently themselves, they can have writing materials including paper and marking pens around for children during playtime.

Educators at schools that take an intercultural orientation try different approaches to involve the parents of emergent bilinguals. A good first step is to listen to the parents and encourage them to voice their concerns and what their needs are either during meetings at school, through check-in phone calls, or through home visits.

REFLECT OR TURN AND TALK

Yvonne had three ideas parents of emergent bilinguals could implement to support their students' literacy. Can you suggest other ways parents can support their children's literacy? Do you understand how using the home language will support literacy in English? Explain.

Implementing Transformative Pedagogy

A third characteristic of schools that take an intercultural orientation is that they implement a transformative pedagogy. As Cummins (2009) explains, there are two main components of transformative pedagogy. The first is identity investment in learning and the second involves negotiation of identity to encourage engagement.

In Chapter 5 we discussed Mary's culture mandala and cultural Venn activities. Both encouraged identity investment and engaged her students. Mary's students were older and more proficient, but Marcela engaged her lower-elementary newcomers in similar activities. The drawings of cultural celebrations was one, but she also had students make elaborate posters to display during a whole-school fair. These posters included a world map indicating their home country and the United States. Next to the map, they identified the distance from their home countries to the United States and how they traveled to the United States. They included their flag and wrote why they came to America. In a Venn diagram they compared their home countries with America. They posted a bilingual list of key words of their choice in their home languages and the English translations. On another part of the poster, students drew and listed foods from their countries. In one corner of the poster, they attached a paper doll figure in traditional dress from their country.

When Sandra had her multiage fourth-, fifth-, and sixth-grade ESL students study seeds, plants, and nutrition, she was drawing on their experiences and their knowledge as children of families that worked in agriculture. The many books they read about seeds growing into plants and their projects including growing plants and keeping a plant journal all expanded on what her students did know and gave them academic concepts and language. Their identities were validated as they learned.

Another project that Sandra used with her students resulted in a transformation for them. The project involved both students and parents. Sandra's students were from Mexico, but Sandra was an immigrant from Argentina. She told her students she did not know how to make tortillas. They were incredulous and asked if they could show her how. Sandra bought materials as directed and the mothers brought in a tortilla press, a mortar and pestle, and even corn kernels and lime to show how corn is processed and ground into flour and made into tortillas.

The students impressed Sandra as they set up two long tables and explained and demonstrated how corn is ground into corn flour and eventually is made into tortillas. This presentation by the students was so impressive that other teachers wanted them to repeat it for their classes. Sandra worked with her students to help them describe the process in English as they made their presentations. It was very empowering for these ESL students, who were usually left out and considered not important in the school. Through this activity they became sought-after presenters for the entire school. This experience gave the students confidence and was truly transformative.

Taking an Advocacy Role in Assessment

A fourth characteristic of schools that take an intercultural orientation is that they design assessments that allow all their students, including their English language learners, to demonstrate what they have learned. Often, emergent bilinguals have learned much more than they can show on quizzes, tests, and essays written in English. However, they can show what they know when teachers use alternative forms of assessment, including assessment in their home language.

When students make books, they show teachers they can organize their thoughts, and they understand how books are organized. They use language that is appropriate to talk about the pictures they choose, and they show vocabulary development through what they include in their bookmaking. When students read to their parents in English and are able to explain what the books are about in their home languages, they show comprehension in a much deeper way than if they complete a fill-in-the-blanks worksheet with one-word answers.

Certainly, Sandra's students' work, both with the plants and seed unit and with the tortilla-making presentations, was a way she could assess their progress. During the plant unit, sorting of seeds into categories, journal entries where students graphed and recorded plant growth, labeling of parts of plants, and identifying the products that come from plants all allowed Sandra to evaluate student language and academic growth. When her students sequenced their presentation of how corn becomes corn flour that is then formed into tortillas, it showed her students' understanding of process and their abilities to explain it in English to others.

According to Cummins (2009), when schools adopt an intercultural orientation, the result is students who are academically and personally empowered. Students in Sandra's class developed language and raised their self-esteem by organizing and presenting the process of making tortillas. When Marcela's students displayed their country's posters, they showed they were proud of where they came from and what they had learned. Teachers who adopt an intercultural orientation find ways to incorporate students' languages and cultures into the school program. They encourage parent involvement. They adopt transformative pedagogical approaches and use forms of assessment that allow all their students to demonstrate what they have learned.

REFLECT OR TURN AND TALK

List ways that you or teachers you know have assessed students other than traditional testing. Discuss how alternative assessments can inform teachers.

Intercultural Orientation Through Virtual Teaching

Teaching students virtually offers many opportunities for teachers to validate students' home languages and cultures. At home, using Chromebooks, tablets, or iPads, students can create books about their families and their neighborhoods. They can research the history of their home countries and compare and contrast that history with US history. For example, they can compare struggles for independence.

With the concerns about equity and the Black Lives Matter movement, students can write about how racially, ethnically, and linguistically diverse minorities are viewed in their home countries. They can explore the oppression of similar groups in the United States and around the world. They can read about how children in some countries are still forced to work and cannot go to school to learn. They can read about the rights of children that UNICEF has promoted (UNICEF 2000). They can read articles on current topics including the pandemic, immigration, and Black Lives Matter on Newsela and other sites and write about them and discuss them in chat rooms. Whether online or in classrooms, it is critically important that educators consider how projects that students are involved in reflect an intercultural orientation that is transformative.

Equity in Action

We have discussed societal relations of power in schools, supporting students as they negotiate their identities, and how to take an intercultural orientation. In this last section of the chapter we provide specific examples of what teachers can do to practice equity and inclusion. Our goal as educators for our emergent bilingual students is to have them succeed academically, socially, and emotionally. This will happen only if we provide them with an education that supports them in all these ways.

When educators acknowledge the translanguaging *corriente* (current) in their classrooms with bilingual and multilingual students and adopt a *juntos* (together) stance as they teach, they provide students with an equitable education (García, Ibarra Johnson, and Seltzer 2017). Schools that take a juntos stance work together with students, families, and communities to ensure that all students succeed. They acknowledge and value students' home languages and cultures. They see students' families and communities as valuable resources. Community members and parents work together with teachers and school leadership to ensure student success. In classrooms, teachers and students learn together, challenging traditional methods of teaching and learning, and they work toward a more just world. When schools take a juntos stance, there is equity in resources, equity in student grouping, equity reflected in the school environment, and cultural and linguistic equity in approaches to teaching.

Equity in Resources

Some schools in different parts of cities and towns have more resources than others. Despite federal efforts in the past to provide underfunded schools with adequate resources, inequities persist. Stories from teachers across the country tell of underpaid teachers spending a portion of their salaries each month to have basic supplies for their classrooms, including pencils, markers, chalk, and paper (Cohen 2019). What teachers purchase goes beyond these essentials. Weir (2019) interviewed teachers who bought their own shelving and bins and basic materials for their desks including sticky notes, whiteboard erasers, and staples and staplers.

Resources for emergent bilingual students are often inappropriate for the students and of poor quality (Heltin 2016). Teachers of emergent bilingual students need materials that are relevant to their lives and that draw on their backgrounds. And the demands on emergent bilinguals are great, especially with the Common Core State Standards. As Fu, Hadjioannou, and Zhou point out, the new standards "put pressure on EBs' capabilities and prove more taxing for their long-term success" (2019, 22). The materials should support both content learning and academic language development. At the same time, the materials should be accessible and include scaffolding for the students to access the materials written in English (Soto, Freeman, and Freeman 2020).

Administrators can make a big difference. Proactive administrators who understand the importance of supplying teachers and students with rich resources apply for grants and check classrooms often to see what teachers need. Post, a principal working in a school with large numbers of diverse emergent bilinguals, explains that equity in his school does not mean that everyone gets the same materials but, instead, that materials are matched with student and teacher needs (Freeman, Freeman, and Mercuri 2018).

Administrators can also make sure their school libraries are well stocked and consult with teachers about what books are needed. Resources should include books that support all the students, including the ELs in the school. Besides quality books, magazines, multimedia, and online resources in English, there should be materials in the home languages of the students in the school. Unfortunately, budget cuts in schools have led to loss of funding for librarians and library resources. Some teachers in one study described schools that had no school libraries at all and so they created their own classroom libraries (Weir 2019). Teachers bought books appropriate for their students to read. Weir explained, "To provide a variety of reading options for their more curious students, teachers will create their own classroom libraries by purchasing books themselves."

Equity in Resources During the Pandemic

During the COVID-19 pandemic when many schools implemented online instruction, emergent bilinguals suffered from inequity in resources. Our son-in-law was teaching third grade near Oakland, California, at the time when schools were closed on a Friday and all instruction was to be delivered online starting the following week. In his Bay Area school, many of the students lived in multifamily households with incomes dependent on jobs that suddenly had disappeared when the state shut down. Although teachers were instructed to send basic information to parents via email, it was clear to Francisco that information was not getting to all his students. Homes did not have computers or sometimes lacked internet connections. Often his only way to communicate was to visit the home or call on a cell phone.

It was clear to Francisco and the administrators in the district that the first priority was getting food to students on the free breakfast and lunch programs. Getting that information out to families required phone calls, which teachers helped with. However, some families at first were too proud to accept the help. Francisco found himself calling homes, delivering the information personally, and encouraging caregivers who were desperate.

Francisco began teaching online, but it wasn't until the end of the third month that he was able to get his whole class on a Zoom call, and that was so chaotic he had to mute students because of the background noises in the homes from other children, pets, and adults talking. He kept assignments simple but meaningful. He asked students to read and write daily and send on what they wrote. He reminded them about writing a good introduction or describing a setting, and then he asked students to include those skills in their writing. However, not many students had appropriate reading materials, libraries were closed, and few had the internet expertise to read online.

What disturbed Francisco the most was that the students who were doing well before the shutdown continued to participate in the virtual program, but the students whom he always had to encourage and sit down with and help were falling behind. Despite phone calls to encourage them, those students were not turning in any work at all. Parents sometimes called him to explain why assignments were not turned in, but in the end, they called because they needed someone to talk to about their worries and fears.

In Marcela's school in the Midwest, the response to the pandemic was even worse for her newcomer ESL students. Most students did not have computers or an email address for her to use. The district provided no tablets or internet service. The ESL coordinators put together a packet of activities for all ESL students, and if students did not have email access, the school mailed out the packet. However, the assignments were too difficult for her newcomers, and there was almost nothing that was appropriate for them to use. She called students and tried to help them identify something they could do. She modified assignments, and she visited the students' homes. By the end of the semester, she was extremely stressed. She said, "I never want to go through this again. I don't feel they learned anything. I really need to get back to school with my students." However, she understands that can happen only when the virus is under control and it's safe.

REFLECT OR TURN AND TALK

Taking a juntos stance includes being sure that students have the resources they need. What inequities of resources have you observed in your school or schools you know? How can schools begin to address these inequities?

Equity in Grouping

To provide an equitable education, teachers should consider how to group emergent bilinguals to create optimal conditions for their learning. Howard and her colleagues (2018) include among the guiding principles for dual language bilingual teaching the importance of opportunities for group work and opportunities for oral interaction.

Oral language development has been emphasized in recent curriculum standards and for emergent bilinguals. In the Common Core State Standards, students are asked to "participate effectively in a range of conversations and collaborations with diverse partners" (CCSS.ELA-LITERACY.CCRA.SL.1) and to be able to "present information, findings, and supporting evidence such that listeners can follow" (CCSS.ELA -LITERACY.CCRA.SL.4) (CCSSO and NGA Center for Best Practices 2020).

Zwiers (2014) and Zwiers and Crawford (2011) have written about how classroom conversations should be structured to promote academic language during group or pair work. Careful grouping helps students meet oral language development standards. Zwiers and Crawford suggest four key practices that promote academic language development, including being prepared for discussions, using appropriate body language, participating by taking turns, and making connections to what others have said. They provide descriptions of activities teachers can use to implement these practices. Teachers need to help their students develop oral language and participate effectively in group work, and these suggestions are good first steps. This is important whether teaching online or in a classroom. Teachers should carefully prepare students with the four key practices and put students into rooms or small groups to practice them virtually.

Wong (2016) lists "using group work strategically" first among his five fundamental strategies for bilingual learners. He emphasizes the importance of structuring groups carefully with both heterogeneous groups, so that students can communicate across languages and cultures, and homogeneous groups, to allow for tailoring instruction to specific objectives. Whether teaching remotely or teaching in person, teachers need to know their students' language strengths and organize discussion groups to enable students from different language backgrounds to work in English, or to set up same-language groups so that students can internalize concepts they are studying and report back in English.

Like Zwiers and Crawford, Wong suggests that both structured and unstructured tasks give students different opportunities for language development. A structured task might involve working collaboratively to plan for and complete a graphic organizer using specific academic language, while an unstructured task might be to discuss what students liked best about a book they just read.

Teachers organize their emergent bilinguals in different ways to support their learning. Often, teachers arrange their students into pairs with the same home language. The students, then, can do a turn-and-talk in the home language to clarify and deepen their understanding of the content and then report back in the language of instruction. At other times, an emergent bilingual is paired with a native English speaker or a bilingual whose English is quite strong. Doing this provides the emergent bilingual a strong model who can support the acquisition of English.

During centers or small groups students have many opportunities to share and to learn from one another. Centers in upper grades usually have students working together on projects. Grouping emergent bilingual students with other students who speak their home languages allows students to discuss and clarify in their home languages and then report back in English with the support of peers. Figure 6–6 shows bilingual grouping as students in science work on their circuits.

Writing workshop offers another opportunity for organizing students in pairs or small groups to support each other's writing. When students can talk together about their writing and share it, their writing improves. If teaching virtually, teachers can assign pairs of students to read and discuss each other's writing and report back using a checklist of what to look for, like the one shown in Figure 6–7.

Figure 6–6 • Bilingual Group Working on Circuits

Writing contains only one or two complete sentences.	Writing contains some complete sentences.	Most of the sentences are complete.	All of the sentences are complete.
None or few of the sentences start with a capital letter and end with a period.	Some of the sentences start with a capital letter and end with a period.	Most of the sentences start with a capital letter and end with a period.	All the sentences start with a capital letter and end with a period.
Student identifies few of the main ideas.	Student identifies some of the main ideas.	Student identifies most of the main ideas.	Student identifies all the main ideas.
Student chooses textual evidence that fits only a few of the main ideas.	Student chooses textual evidence that fits some of the main ideas.	Student chooses textual evidence that fits most of the main ideas.	Student chooses textual evidence that fits all of the main ideas.

Figure 6–7 • Writing Rubric

Equity in the School Environment

García and her research team worked with struggling schools in the New York City area to help them improve their programs for emergent bilinguals (García and Kleifgen 2010). The schools they worked in had to agree to two nonnegotiables: bilingualism was to be seen as a resource in educating the students, and the whole school needed to support a multilingual ecology.

This second nonnegotiable, the support for a multilingual ecology, is not always evident in schools with ELs. In schools with a multilingual ecology, the home languages of all the students should be visible everywhere to celebrate the students and their backgrounds. The multilingual information board in the front of the main office and the multilingual welcome murals we discussed earlier are excellent examples of what schools should have. Signs, murals, and posters in the students' languages inside and outside the school reflect a multilingual ecology. In classrooms, materials should be available in the students' languages, and student work in their home languages should be displayed as well as projects in English. Bi- or multilingual announcements of events for parents should also be displayed. Figure 6–8 shows an announcement for an upcoming parent orientation to a school's dual language program displayed in the front hall.

A multilingual ecology goes even farther than having only Spanish and English visible. The environment should reflect the multilingual student body, including languages that use non-Roman alphabet scripts like Arabic, Mandarin, Hindi, Korean, Tamil, and some indigenous languages. Even though Spanish and English are often the two languages most of the ELs in the school speak, we live and learn in a global, multilingual society, and all students' languages should be recognized.

REFLECT OR TURN AND TALK

Equity in grouping and in providing a multilingual environment involves planning and commitment. How have you observed that students are grouped in physical classrooms or virtual classrooms? What are the pros and cons of those groupings? Do schools you are in display a multilingual ecology? Explain.

Figure 6-8 • Parent Orientation Sign

Cultural and Linguistic Equity in Teaching

In schools that promote equity, the goal should be to develop a culturally sustaining pedagogy. Paris (2012) and Paris and Alim (2017) describe in detail what a culturally sustaining pedagogy consists of. It is one that moves beyond culturally relevant or culturally responsive teaching. Paris explains that a culturally sustaining pedagogy "seeks to perpetuate and foster—to sustain—linguistic, literate, and cultural pluralism as part of the democratic project of schooling" (2012, 93). He labels our society as monolingual and monocultural and argues that policies and practices in schools and society perpetuate this type of society.

Although Paris first wrote about a culturally sustaining pedagogy in 2012, it is even more relevant today. Inequities in access to health, adequate housing, and food security have become more evident during the pandemic. The lack of security and protection for people of color is being brought to the forefront by incidents of police brutality and the rise of the Black Lives Matter movement. Schools are places where students must be helped to understand and embrace cultural pluralism and cultural equality. Paris calls for a pedagogy that would do that and would develop a generation of students "who can both understand and critique the existing social order" (2012, 94).

Some teachers have implemented a culturally sustaining pedagogy. Francisco assigned his Spanish-speaking third-grade students to read an article in Spanish from Newsela (https://newsela.com). He knew students needed to be able to read informational articles and respond to them by including information from what they read in their own writing to meet one of the Common Core standards. The article described a proposal from the anti-immigrant Trump administration to deny citizenship to all children born in this country if their parents were undocumented. This astounding proposal would have affected policies that have been in place not only in the United States but across the world. The class discussed the article and then Francisco asked them to write about it in Spanish.

He gave the class a starter for their writing. They had been studying dialogue in texts. He explained their writing should start with a conversation between two women, María and Clara, who were discussing the proposal. Students were to write about what would happen next. One student showed how she would take action to fight this unjust proposal if it were ever to be put on a ballot to become law. In her writing, María explained to Clara that she was organizing a protest against this proposal. She had made posters and talked to many people, telling them about the injustice of taking away citizenship from thousands of people. Through dialogue, María inspired Clara to join her in this battle. Although the proposal never reached any ballot boxes, in María's well-written dialogue, there was an election, and the unjust proposal was voted down because of her actions. This activity certainly allowed Francisco's students an opportunity to critique the social order and even show how they would take action to change it.

When Mary was teaching ESL newcomers in the Río Grande Valley, her students had never heard of César Chávez or his struggles for the rights of migrant farmworkers. Most of her students had come across the border from Mexico with parents who worked in the fields. In fact, many of the students worked beside their parents before or after school and during vacations to supplement the family incomes. Mary had her students read about and talk about Chávez and the United Farmworkers Union he began. The students made posters about him and, with Mary's help, wrote a readers theatre piece that told about his life. They presented their readers theatre about this civil rights leader to the bilingual director of the school. They read the piece in different voices, sometimes all girls, sometimes all boys, sometimes singly, and at other times as a whole group. At the end, the director was in tears. She invited the students to present this to teachers at an upcoming bilingual conference at South Padre Island, some seventy miles from the school. The school provided their transportation and lodging at the beach resort. Most of the students had never been to the beach though it was less than two hours away from their town. After more practice, they proudly presented their readers theatre to over five hundred teachers. The enthusiastic response of the audience validated these students and their families.

Critical consciousness, another important concept within cultural and linguistic equity for schools, is based on the work of Freire (1970) and a number of other researchers. It has been advanced as a theoretical foundation for teaching emergent bilinguals in schools that apply a culturally sustaining pedagogy and an intercultural orientation. Freire applied a critical consciousness approach to teaching literacy to adults. His method, which became a method of teaching ESL called *problem posing*, begins by the teacher first listening to the students and assessing their situation to help them determine the things that truly concern them. The teacher then chooses a "code" (a picture, a story, a song, and so on) to present to students to help them take an objective look at their personal experiences and concerns. Through discussion, students identify real life problems that they can solve through specific actions.

For example, a teacher of older students might show students a photo of the substandard housing in the neighborhood where they live. The students meet in small groups that Freire calls "culture circles" to discuss the picture. In the process the students identify or "pose" what they perceive as a problem. Through their collective dialog in the culture circle they plan for social action to improve the situation. They also identify the language they will need to solve their problem. Through this approach, Freire helped oppressed, illiterate adults develop a critical consciousness of their situation and develop strategies, including developing reading and writing skills, to address the problem and to improve their lives.

In their article, "Combating Inequalities in Two-Way Language Immersion Programs: Toward Critical Consciousness in Bilingual Education Spaces" Cervantes-Soon and her colleagues explain how Freire's concept of critical consciousness can be applied in dual language bilingual education. They explain, "Critical consciousness involves the process of overcoming pervasive myths through an understanding of the role of power in the formation of oppressive conditions (P. Freire 2007). TWI teachers, students, and parents can take part and take action only to the extent that they problematize the history, culture, and societal configurations that brought them together" (2017, 419).

Cervantes-Soon and her colleagues propose that critical consciousness should be added as a fourth goal to the goals of dual language or two-way immersion programs for emergent bilinguals. The first three goals are bilingualism and biliteracy, high academic achievement, and multicultural competence. As they state, "Critical consciousness can be developed through expanding politically oriented curriculum and instruction that originate in the very knowledges and ways that students from marginalized communities experience language" (418).

Palmer (2020) outlines the components of critical consciousness in a dual language program. These are (1) continuously interrogating power, (2) historicizing schools and education policy, (3) critical listening, and (4) engaging with discomfort.

The first component, interrogating power, means questioning power relationships. Palmer suggests resisting the kinds of testing systems that marginalize some students and result in an achievement gap, systematically conducting equity audits to determine if the education students are offered in dual language programs is equitable, and supporting all the voices and perspectives in a classroom.

The second component, historicizing schools and educational policy, could involve engaging students in studying the history of dual language education that emerged from the civil rights struggles and moved through protests and court cases to the present moment. Students might research the policies governing bilingual education in their state and compare them with policies in other states. It could include reading books about immigrants like *Enrique's Journey* (Nazario 2014) and interviewing relatives who have immigrated.

The third component is critical listening. This would include discussing topics like racism, sexism, and poverty. Students could talk about their fears of deportation or worries concerning their parents losing jobs during the pandemic. It could also involve ensuring that the school conducts parent meetings in the languages of the students in the school.

Finally, engaging with discomfort means that teachers should acknowledge their power, help white and middle-class students in dual language classrooms to be allies to students of color, and take the risks required to support all students. These four components form the principles that critical consciousness is based on, and the goal is to ensure that the curriculum moves these principles to action.

What do you understand a culturally sustaining pedagogy to be? What are examples that you have seen of this in schools, or what ideas do you have to implement a culturally sustaining pedagogy? What is critical consciousness? How are the four components of critical consciousness being applied at your school or in your classroom?

In 2020 as we write this book, there is a need for culturally sustaining pedagogy that include an understanding of critical consciousness and its importance for schools. The United States experienced a lack of leadership during the COVID-19 pandemic that disproportionately affected Black and Brown people. Both Black and Latinx citizens have also been heavily affected by police violence. In LA County, nearly 80 percent of people who have been killed by police since the year 2000 were Black or Latinx, according to a continually updated *LA Times* article (*Los Angeles Times* staff 2020). The leadership in Washington during the Trump administration tried to misrepresent the positive goals of the Black Lives Matter movement, depicting it as a movement that fomented hate.

Immigrants seeking asylum in this country have been detained along the border in unsanitary compounds while unscrupulous owners of these facilities who should have maintained them took millions from government funds and did nothing. The leader of the country spent military funds on building a useless wall, a cruel symbol of hatred for those who wished to come to this country seeking a better life. The number of hate groups increased and more people openly expressed white supremacist views culminating in an insurrectionist attack on the Capitol. Emergent bilinguals and their families have been victims of the attitudes these events reflected.

Our schools have a responsibility to adopt a culturally sustaining pedagogy and to implement an intercultural orientation to teach children in ways that will change our society. When educators take a juntos stance, they work with students, families, and communities to ensure social justice. They help their students develop a critical consciousness (Freire 1970). Mary and Francisco provide us with two examples of how teachers might do this. They not only taught academic content but also helped their students understand that what they were learning was connected to their lives. They helped them to become empowered. A goal for all teachers should be to teach academic language and content in a way that empowers students to change the world.

References

Ada, Alma F. 2002. *I Love Saturdays y domingos*. New York: Atheneum Books.

Ahmed, Azam. 2019. "Inside Gang Territory in Honduras: 'Either They Kill Us or We Kill Them.'" *New York Times*, May 13. www.nytimes.com/interactive/2019/05/04/world/americas/honduras-gang-violence.html.

Asher, James. 1977. *Learning Another Language Through Actions: The Complete Teacher's Guide*. Los Gatos, CA: Sky Oaks.

August, Diane, and Timothy Shanahan, eds. 2006. *Developing Literacy in Second-Language Learners: Report of the National Literacy Panel on Language Minority Children and Youth*. Mahwah, NJ: Lawrence Erlbaum Associates.

Baker, Colin. 2006. *Foundations of Bilingual Education and Bilingualism*. 4th ed. Clevedon, UK: Multilingual Matters.

Baker, Colin, and Wayne E. Wright. 2017. *Foundations of Bilingual Education and Bilingualism*. 6th ed. Bristol, UK: Multilingual Matters.

Bakhtin, Mikhail M. 1981. *The Dialogic Imagination: Four Essays*. Edited by Michael Holquist. Translated by Caryl Emerson. Austin: University of Texas Press.

Batalova, Jeanne, and Jie Zong. 2016. "Language Diversity and English Proficiency in the United States." *Migration Information Source*, November 11. www.migrationpolicy.org/article/language-diversity-and-english-proficiency-united-states-2015.

Becker, Helene. 2020. "Supporting English Learners During Distance Learning." Paper presented at TESOL International Convention and English Language Expo, Denver, Colorado, March 21–April 3, 2020.

Beirich, Heidi, and Susy Buchanan. 2018. "2017: The Year in Hate and Extremism." *Intelligence Report*, February 11. www.splcenter.org/fighting-hate/intelligence-report/2018/2017-year-hate-and-extremism.

Bennett, Colette. 2020. "ELL Students' Background Knowledge as an Academic Fund." *ThoughtCo*, February 12. www.thoughtco.com/ell-students-funds-of-knowledge-4011987.

Bialystok, Ellen. 2007. "Cognitive Effects of Bilingualism: How Linguistic Experience Leads to Cognitive Change." *International Journal of Bilingual Education and Bilingualism* 10 (3): 210–23.

————. 2011. "Reshaping the Mind: The Benefits of Bilingualism." *Canadian Journal of Experimental Psychology* 65 (4): 229–35.

Biber, Douglas. 1986. "Spoken and Written Textual Dimensions in English: Resolving the Contradictory Findings." *Language* 62 (2): 384–414.

Bourdieu, Pierre, and Jean-Claude Passeron. 1977. *Reproduction in Education, Society and Culture*. London: Sage.

Brown, H. Douglas. 2007. *Principles of Language Learning and Teaching*. 5th ed. White Plains, NY: Pearson Education.

California Department of Education (CDE). 2015. *English Language Arts/English Language Development Framework for California Public Schools, Kindergarten Through Grade Twelve*. Sacramento: California State Department of Education. www.mydigital chalkboard.org/cognoti/content/file/resources/documents/ac/ac1376ba/ac1376ba78 a91e80241cb0e458caaa57310d0763/elaeldfmwkfeb17.pdf.

————. 2018. *Global California 2030: Speak. Learn. Lead.* Sacramento: California State Department of Education. www.cde.ca.gov/eo/in/documents/globalca2030 report.pdf.

————. 2019a. "Facts About English Learners in California—*CalEdFacts*." California Department of Education (website). www.cde.ca.gov/ds/sd/cb/cefelfacts.asp.

————. 2019b. "Multilingual Education." California Department of Education (website). www.cde.ca.gov/sp/el/er/multilingualedu.asp.

————. 2020. "State Seal of Biliteracy." California Department of Education (website). www.cde.ca.gov/sp/el/er/sealofbiliteracy.asp.

Callahan, Rebecca M., and Patricia C. Gándara, eds. 2014. *The Bilingual Advantage: Language, Literacy, and the US Labor Market*. Bristol, UK: Multilingual Matters.

Canale, Michael, and Merrill Swain. 1980. "Theoretical Bases of Communicative Approaches to Second Language Teaching and Testing." *Applied Linguistics* I (1): 1–47.

Carpeño, Eva R., and Hannah I. Feldman. 2015. "Childhood and Education in Thailand-Burma/Myanmar Border Refugees Camps." *Global Studies of Childhood* 5 (4): 414–25. https://journals.sagepub.com/doi/full/10.1177/2043610615612951.

Carpenter, Kathryn, Ivana Espinet, and Elizabeth Pratt. n.d. "Supporting Emergent Bilingual Learners Labeled Long-Term English Language Learners (LTELL)." CUNY–NYSIEB (website). www.cuny-nysieb.org/translanguaging-resources /resources-for-work-with-particular-subgroups/supporting-emergent-bilingual -learners-labeled-long-term-english-language-learners-ltell/.

Cervantes-Soon, Claudia, Lisa Dorner, Deborah Palmer, Dan Heiman, Rebecca Schwerdtfeger, and Jinmyung Choi. 2017. "Combatting Inequalities in Two-Way

Language Immersion Programs: Toward Critical Consciousness in Bilingual Education Spaces." *Review of Research in Education* 41 (1): 403–27.

Chen-Gaddini, Min, and Elizabeth Burr. 2016. "Long-Term English Learner Students: Spotlight on an Overlooked Population." San Francisco: WestEd. www.wested.org/resources/long-term-english-learner-students/.

Chomsky, Noam. 1975. *Reflections on Language*. New York: Pantheon Books.

Cohen, Max. 2019. "'Ridiculous': Teachers Spend Their Own Money to Buy Supplies for First Day of School." *USA Today*, August 29. www.usatoday.com/story/news/education/2019/08/29/teacher-first-day-school-supplies-list-target-staples-buy-shopping/2082791001/.

Cole, Michael. 1998. *Cultural Psychology: A Once and Future Discipline*. Cambridge: Harvard University Press.

Collier, Virginia P. 1989. "How Long? A Synthesis of Research on Academic Achievement in a Second Language." *TESOL Quarterly* 23 (3): 509–32.

Collier, Virginia P., and Wayne P. Thomas. 2009. *Educating English Learners for a Transformed World*. Albuquerque, NM: Dual Language Education of New Mexico/Fuente Press.

Connor, Phillip, and Jens M. Krogstad. 2016. "5 Facts About Global Somali Diaspora." *Fact Tank: News in the Numbers*, June 1. www.pewresearch.org/fact-tank/2016/06/01/5-facts-about-the-global-somali-diaspora/.

Cortés, Carlos. 1986. "The Education of Language Minority Students: A Contextual Interaction Model." In *Beyond Language: Social and Cultural Factors in Schooling Language Minority Students*, developed by Bilingual Education Office, 3–33. Los Angeles: Evaluation, Dissemination, and Assessment Center, California State University.

Council of Chief State School Officers (CCSSO) and National Governors Association (NGA) Center for Best Practices. 2020. "English Language Arts Standards: Anchor Standards: College and Career Readiness Anchor Standards for Speaking and Listening." Common Core State Standards Initiative. www.corestandards.org/ELA-Literacy/CCRA/SL/#CCSS.ELA-Literacy.CCRA.SL.1.

Cummins, Jim. 1979. "Linguistic Interdependence and the Educational Development of Bilingual Children." *Review of Educational Research* 49 (2): 222–51.

———. 1981. "Age on Arrival and Immigrant Second Language Learning in Canada: A Reassessment." *Applied Linguistics* 2 (2): 132–49.

———. 2000. *Language, Power and Pedagogy: Bilingual Children in the Crossfire*. Tonawanda, NY: Multilingual Matters.

———. 2001. *Negotiating Identities: Education for Empowerment in a Diverse Society.* 2nd ed. Ontario: California Association of Bilingual Education.

———. 2007. "Rethinking Monolingual Instructional Strategies in Multilingual Classrooms." *Canadian Journal of Applied Linguistics* 10 (2): 221–40.

———. 2009. "Transformative Multiliteracies Pedagogy: School-Based Strategies for Closing the Achievement Gap." *Multiple Voices for Ethnically Diverse Exceptional Learners* 11 (2): 1–19.

———. 2017. "Teaching Minoritized Students: Are Additive Approaches Legitimate?" *Harvard Educational Review* 87 (3): 404–25.

———. Forthcoming. "Translanguaging: A Critical Analysis of Theoretical Claims." In *Pedagogical Translanguaging: Teachers and Researchers Shaping Plurilingual Practices*, edited by Päivi Juvonen and Marie Källkvist. Bristol, UK: Multilingual Matters.

Custodio, Brenda, and Judith O'Loughlin. 2017. *Students with Interrupted Formal Education: Bridging Where They Are and What They Need.* Thousand Oaks, CA: Corwin.

de Brey, Cristobal, Lauren Musu, Joel McFarland, Sidney Wilkinson-Flicker, Melissa Diliberti, Anlan Zhang, Claire Branstetter, and Xiaolei Wang. 2019a. "Indicator 4: Children Living in Poverty." In *Status and Trends in the Education of Racial and Ethnic Groups 2018*, 38–41. NCES 2019-038. Washington, DC: National Center for Education Statistics. https://nces.ed.gov/pubs2019/2019038.pdf.

———. 2019b. "Indicator 8: English Language Learners in Public Schools." In *Status and Trends in the Education of Racial and Ethnic Groups 2018*, 60–61. NCES 2019-038. Washington, DC: National Center for Education Statistics. https://nces.ed.gov/pubs2019/2019038.pdf.

———. 2019c. "Spotlight A: Characteristics of Public School Teachers by Race/Ethnicity." In *Status and Trends in the Education of Racial and Ethnic Groups 2018*, 10–15. NCES 2019-038. Washington, DC: National Center for Education Statistics. https://nces.ed.gov/pubs2019/2019038.pdf.

Deruy, Emily, Alia Wong, and Hayley Glatter. 2016. "Learning in the Aftermath of a Divisive Election." *The Atlantic*, November 15. www.theatlantic.com/education/archive/2016/11/how-children-reacted-to-trumps-win/507518/.

Díaz, Stephen, Luis Moll, and Hugh Mehan. 1986. "Sociocultural Resources in Instruction: A Context-Specific Approach." In *Beyond Language: Social and Cultural Factors in Schooling Language Minority Students*, developed by Bilingual Education Office, 187–230. Los Angeles: Evaluation, Dissemination and Assessment Center, California State University.

Dickens, Charles. 2009. *A Tale of Two Cities.* Oxford: Oxford University Press.

Doughty, Catherine J., and Michael H. Long, eds. 2003. *The Handbook of Second Language Acquisition*. Victoria, Australia: Blackwell.

Dulay, Heidi C., and Marina K. Burt. 1974. "Natural Sequences in Child Second Language Acquisition." *Language Learning* 24 (1): 37–53.

Ebe, Ann E., and Charene Chapman-Santiago. 2016. "Student Voices Shining Through: Exploring Translanguaging as a Literary Device." In *Translanguaging with Multilingual Students: Learning from Classroom Moments*, edited by Ofelia García and Tatyana Kleyn, 57–82. New York: Routledge.

Egalite, Anna J., and Brian Kisida. 2018. "The Effects of Teacher Match on Students' Academic Perceptions and Attitudes." *Educational Evaluation and Policy Analysis* 40 (1): 59–81.

Ellis, Rod. 2005. "Principles of Instructed Language Teaching." *System* 33 (2): 209–24.

Esquivel, Paloma, and Howard Blume. 2020. "L.A. Latino, Black Students Suffered Deep Disparities in Online Learning, Records Show." *LA Times*, July 16. www.latimes.com/california/story/2020-07-16/latino-and-black-students-hard-hit-with-disparities-in-their-struggle-with-online-learning.

Faltis, Christian, and Sarah Hudelson. 1998. *Bilingual Education in Elementary and Secondary School Communities*. Boston: Allyn and Bacon.

Ferreiro, Emilia, and Ana Teberosky. 1982. *Literacy Before Schooling*. Translated by K. G. Castro. Portsmouth, NH: Heinemann.

Ferrón, Mario. 2012. "Educational Effects of Implementing a K–12 Dual Language Instruction Program in a Community with a High Percentage of Hispanics and Hispanic English Language Learners." EdD diss., University of Texas at Brownsville.

Fillmore, Lily Wong. 1991. "When Learning a Second Language Means Losing the First." *Early Childhood Research Quarterly* 6 (3): 323–46.

Fix, Michael, and Randy Capps. 2005. "Immigrant Children, Urban Schools, and the No Child Left Behind Act." *Migration Information Source*, November 1. www.migrationpolicy.org/article/immigrant-children-urban-schools-and-no-child-left-behind-act.

Frankenberg, Erica, Jongyeon Ee, Jennifer B. Ayscue, and Gary Orfield. 2019. *Harming Our Common Future: America's Segregated Schools 65 Years After* Brown. Los Angeles: Civil Rights Project. www.civilrightsproject.ucla.edu/research/k-12-education/integration-and-diversity/harming-our-common-future-americas-segregated-schools-65-years-after-brown/Brown-65-050919v4-final.pdf.

Freeman, David, and Yvonne Freeman. 2009. *Academic Language for English Language Learners and Struggling Readers: How to Help Students Succeed Across Content Areas.* Portsmouth, NH: Heinemann.

———. 2014. *Essential Linguistics: What Teachers Need to Know to Teach ESL, Reading, Spelling, and Grammar.* Portsmouth, NH: Heinemann.

Freeman, David, Mary Soto, and Yvonne Freeman. 2016. "Translanguaging Success into Practice." *Language Magazine* 16 (4): 18–21.

Freeman, Yvonne S., and David E. Freeman. 1990. "New Attitudes for New Students." *Holistic Education Review* 3 (2): 25–30.

———. 2002. *Closing the Achievement Gap: How to Reach Limited Formal Schooling and Long-Term English Learners.* Portsmouth, NH: Heinemann.

———. 2011a. "Bilingual Books, Bridges to Literacy for Emergent Bilinguals." In *Reclaiming Reading: Teachers, Students and Researchers Regaining Spaces for Thinking and Action*, edited by Richard J. Meyer and Kathryn F. Whitmore, 224–35. New York: Taylor and Francis/Routledge.

———. 2011b. "Using Culturally Relevant Spanish/English Bilingual Books with Emergent Bilinguals." *NABE News* 33 (1): 5–28.

Freeman, Yvonne, David Freeman, and Sandra Mercuri. 2018. *Dual Language Essentials for Teachers and Administrators.* 2nd ed. Portsmouth, NH: Heinemann.

Freeman, Yvonne, David Freeman, Mary Soto, and Ann Ebe. 2016. *ESL Teaching: Principles for Success.* Portsmouth, NH: Heinemann.

Freire, Paulo. 1970. *Pedagogy of the Oppressed.* Translated by Myra B. Ramos. New York: Continuum.

Fu, Danling, Xenia Hadjioannou, and Xiaodi Zhou. 2019. *Translanguaging for Emergent Bilinguals: Inclusive Teaching in the Linguistically Diverse Classroom.* New York: Teachers College Press.

Gándara, Patricia. 2017. "The Potential and Promise of Latino Students." *American Educator* 41 (1): 4–11, 42–43.

Gándara, Patricia, and Frances Contreras. 2009. *The Latino Education Crisis: The Consequences of Failed School Policies.* Cambridge: Harvard University Press.

Gándara, Patricia, and Kfir Mordechay. 2017. "Demographic Change and the New (and Not So New) Challenges for Latino Education." *The Educational Forum* 81 (2): 148–59.

García, Amaya. 2015. "What the Rising Popularity in Dual Language Programs Could Mean for Dual Language Learners." *New America* (blog), January 16. www.newamerica.org/education-policy/edcentral/duallanguageexpansion/.

García, Ofelia. 2009. *Bilingual Education in the 21st Century: A Global Perspective*. Malden, MA: Wiley-Blackwell.

García, Ofelia, Susana Ibarra Johnson, and Kate Seltzer. 2017. *The Translanguaging Classroom: Leveraging Student Bilingualism for Learning*. Philadelphia: Caslon.

García, Ofelia, and Jo Anne Kleifgen. 2010. *Educating Emergent Bilinguals: Policies, Programs, and Practices for English Language Learners*. New York: Teachers College Press.

García, Ofelia, and Tatyana Kleyn, eds. 2016. *Translanguaging with Multilingual Students: Learning from Classroom Moments*. New York: Routledge.

García, Ofelia, and Li Wei. 2014. *Translanguaging: Language, Bilingualism, and Education*. New York: Palgrave Macmillan.

Gee, James P. 1992. *The Social Mind: Language, Ideology, and Social Practice*. New York: Bergin and Garvey.

Gessen, Masha. 2019. "Trump, the Fear-Based President, Asks Children to 'Build the Wall.'" *The New Yorker*, November 4: 1–4. www.newyorker.com/news/our-columnists/donald-trump-asks-children-to-build-the-wall-on-halloween.

Gilhooly, Daniel J. 2015. "Lessons Learned: Insights into One Teacher's Experience Working with Karen Refugee Students in the United States." *Journal of Southeast Asian American Education and Advancement* 10 (1): 1–30.

Glatter, Hayley. 2017. "Massachusetts Legislature Passes Bilingual Education Bill." *Boston Magazine*, November 16. www.bostonmagazine.com/education/2017/11/16/bilingual-education-massachusetts/.

Goodman, Kenneth S. 1986. *What's Whole in Whole Language?* Portsmouth, NH: Heinemann.

Goodman, Kenneth, and David Freeman. 1993. "What's Simple in Simplified Language?" In *Simplification: Theory and Application*, edited by Makhan L. Tickoo, 69–81. Singapore: SEAMEO Regional Language Center.

Goodman, Kenneth, E. Brooks Smith, Robert Meredith, and Yetta Goodman. 1987. *Language and Thinking in School: A Whole Language Curriculum*. 3rd ed. New York: Richard C. Owen.

Goodman, Yetta M., and Kenneth S. Goodman. 1990. "Vygotsky in a Whole Language Perspective." In *Vygotsky and Education: Instructional Implications and Applications of Sociohistorical Psychology*, edited by Luis Moll, 223–50. Cambridge, UK: Cambridge University Press.

Graves, Donald. 1983. *Writing: Teachers and Children at Work*. Portsmouth, NH: Heinemann.

Greene, Jay P. 1998. *A Meta-Analysis of the Effectiveness of Bilingual Education.* Los Angeles: Tomas Rivera Policy Institute.

Grosjean, François. 2010. *Bilingual: Life and Reality.* Cambridge, MA: Harvard University Press.

———. 2012. "Bilinguals in the United States." *Psychology Today,* May 20. www .psychologytoday.com/blog/life-bilingual/201205/bilinguals-in-the-united-states.

———. 2020. "The Amazing Rise of Bilingualism in the United States." *Life as a Bilingual* (blog), PsychologyToday.com. Originally posted Sept. 11, 2018, updated and posted April 2. https://www.psychologytoday.com/us/blog/life-bilingual/201809 /the-amazing-rise-bilingualism-in-the-united-states.

Hakuta, Kenji. 2018. *The California English Learner Roadmap: Strengthening Comprehensive Educational Policies, Programs, and Practices for English Learners.* Sacramento: California Department of Education.

Hakuta, Kenji, Yuko G. Butler, and Daria Whitt. 2000. *How Long Does It Take English Learners to Attain Proficiency?* Policy Report 2000-1. Santa Barbara: University of California Linguistic Minority Research Institute.

Halliday, Michael A. K. 1975. *Learning How to Mean: Explorations in the Development of Language.* London: Edward Arnold.

———. 1982. "Three Aspects of Children's Language Development: Learning Language, Learning Through Language, and Learning About Language." In *Oral and Written Language Development Research: Impact on the Schools,* edited by Yetta Goodman, Myna Haussler, and Dorothy Strickland, 7–19. Urbana, IL: National Council of Teachers of English.

———. 1989. *Spoken and Written Language.* Oxford, UK: Oxford University Press.

Halliday, Michael A. K., and Ruqaiya Hasan. 1989. *Language, Context, and Text: Aspects of Language in a Social-Semiotic Perspective.* 2nd ed. Oxford, UK: Oxford University Press.

Hamayan, Else, Fred Genesee, and Nancy Cloud. 2013. *Dual Language Instruction from A to Z: Practical Guidance for Teachers and Administrators.* Portsmouth, NH: Heinemann.

Hatch, Evelyn M. 1983. *Psycholinguistics: A Second Language Perspective.* Rowley, MA: Newbury House.

Heath, Shirley B. 1983. *Ways with Words: Language, Life, and Work in Communities and Classrooms.* Cambridge, UK: Cambridge University Press.

———. 1986. "Sociocultural Contexts of Language Development." In *Beyond Language: Social and Cultural Factors in Schooling Language Minority Students,* by California

State Department of Education, 143–86. Los Angeles: Evaluation, Dissemination and Assessment Center California State University.

Hellman, Andrea, Ximena Uribe-Zarain, Helene Becker, and Kia McDaniel. 2020. "How K–12 Districts Served ELs from a Distance." Presented at TESOL International Convention and English Language Expo, virtual convention, July 18.

Heltin, Liana. 2016. "Quality Learning Materials Are Scarce for English-Language Learners." *Education Week*, May 11. www.edweek.org/ew/articles/2016/05/11/quality-learning-materials-are-scarce-for-english-language.html.

Hernandez, Martha. 2020. "Analysis: Educators Say Distance Learning Failed Most English Learners Last Spring. Here's 10 Ways to More Effectively Serve ELs as Schools Reopen for Virtual and Blended Learning." The74Million.org. https://www.the74million.org/article/analysis-educators-say-distance-learning-failed-most-english-learners-last-spring-heres-10-ways-to-more-effectively-serve-els-as-schools-reopen-for-virtual-and-blended-learning/.

Herndon, Astead W. 2019. "These People Aren't Coming from Norway: Refugees in a Minnesota City Face a Backlash." *New York Times*, June 20. www.nytimes.com/2019/06/20/us/politics/minnesota-refugees-trump.html.

Horowitz, Juliana M. 2019. *Americans See Advantages and Challenges in Country's Growing Racial and Ethnic Diversity.* May 8. Washington, DC: Pew Research Center. www.pewsocialtrends.org/2019/05/08/americans-see-advantages-and-challenges-in-countrys-growing-racial-and-ethnic-diversity/.

Horwitz, Amanda R., Gabriela Uro, Ricki Price-Baugh, Candace Simon, Renata Uzzell, Sharon Lewis, and Michael Casserly. 2009. *Succeeding with English Language Learners: Lessons Learned from the Great City Schools.* Washington, DC: Council of the Great City Schools. ww.cgcs.org/cms/lib/DC00001581/Centricity/Domain/35/Publication%20Docs/ELL_Report09.pdf.

Howard, Elizabeth R., Kathryn J. Lindholm-Leary, David Rogers, Natalie Olague, José Medina, Barbara Kennedy, and Julie Sugarman. 2018. *Guiding Principles for Dual Language Education.* 3rd ed. Washington, DC: Center for Applied Linguistics.

Huang, Min, Eric Haas, Niufeng Zhu, and Loan Tran. 2016. *High School Graduation Rates Across English Learner Student Subgroups in Arizona.* REL 2017–205. Washington, DC: Regional Educational Laboratory West. www.wested.org/resources/graduation-rates-across-english-learner-subgroups-in-arizona/.

Hymes, Dell. 1970. "On Communicative Competence." In *Directions in Sociolinguistics: The Ethnography of Communication,* edited by John J. Gumperz and Dell Hymes, 35–71. New York: Holt, Rinehart and Winston.

John-Steiner, Vera P., and Holbrook Mahn. 1996. "Sociocultural Approaches to Learning and Development: A Vygotskian Framework." *Educational Psychologist* 31 (3–4): 191–206.

Johnson, Karen E. 1995. *Understanding Communication in Second Language Classrooms.* New York: Cambridge University Press.

Kozol, Jonathan. 1991. *Savage Inequalities: Children in America's Schools.* New York: Harper.

Krashen, Stephen. 1982. *Principles and Practice in Second Language Acquisition.* New York: Pergamon Press.

———. 1985. *Inquiries and Insights: Second Language Teaching: Immersion and Bilingual Education, Literacy.* Haywood, CA: Alemany.

———. 1996. *Under Attack: The Case Against Bilingual Education.* Culver City, CA: Language Education Associates.

———. 2004. *The Power of Reading: Insights from the Research.* 2nd ed. Portsmouth, NH: Heinemann.

———. 2013. "The Sullivan and Brown Reading Study: New Evidence for the Power of Reading, the Effect of Reading on Poverty, and Evidence for Late Intervention." *SKrashen* (blog), September 13. http://skrashen.blogspot.com/2013/09/new-evidence-for-power-of-reading.html.

Krashen, Stephen D., and Tracy D. Terrell. 1983. *The Natural Approach: Language Acquisition in the Classroom.* Hayward, CA: Alemany Press.

LaFave, Sarah. 2020. "How School Closures for COVID-19 Amplify Inequality." *HUB*, May 4. https://hub.jhu.edu/2020/05/04/school-closures-inequality/.

Lai, Thanhhà. 2011. *Inside Out and Back Again.* New York: HarperCollins.

Lambert, Wallace E., and G. Richard Tucker. 1972. *Bilingual Education of Children: The St. Lambert Experiment.* Rowley, MA: Newbury House.

Lauer, Patricia A., Motoko Akiba, Stephanie B. Wilkerson, Helen S. Apthorp, David Snow, and Mya L. Martin-Glenn. 2006. "Out-of-School-Time Programs: A Meta-Analysis of Effects for At-Risk Students." *Review of Educational Research* 76 (2): 275–313.

Lindfors, Judith W. 1987. *Children's Language and Learning.* 2nd ed. Englewood Cliffs, NJ: Prentice Hall.

Lindholm-Leary, Kathryn. 2020. "Current Research Findings on Two-Way Bilingual Immersion Education." Paper presented at the Association of Two-Way & Dual Language Education (ATDLE), December 20, virtual.

Lomas Garza, Carmen. 1996. *In My Family/En mi familia.* San Francisco: Children's Book Press.

Los Angeles Times staff. 2020. "Police Have Killed 886 People in L.A. County Since 2000." *Los Angeles Times* online. www.latimes.com/projects/los-angeles-police -killings-database/.

MacDonald, Rita, Timothy Boals, Mariana Castro, H. Gary Cook, Todd Lundberg, and Paula A. White. 2015. *Formative Language Assessment for English Learners: A Four-Step Process.* Portsmouth, NH: Heinemann.

Major, Amielle. 2020. "How to Develop Culturally Responsive Teaching for Distance Learning." *Mind/Shift*, May 20. www.kqed.org/mindshift/55941/how-to-develop -culturally-responsive-teaching-for-distance-learning.

Marzano, Robert J., Debra J. Pickering, and Jane E. Pollock. 2001. *Classroom Instruction That Works: Research-Based Strategies for Increasing Student Achievement.* Alexandria, VA: Association for Curriculum Development and Supervision.

McNeil, Linda, Eileen Coppola, Judy Radigan, and Julian V. Heilig. 2008. "Avoidable Losses: High-Stakes Accountability and the Dropout Crisis." *Education Policy Analysis Archives* 16 (3): 1–45. https://epaa.asu.edu/ojs/article/view/28.

Menken, Kate, and Tatyana Kleyn. 2009. "The Difficult Road for Long-Term English Learners." *Educational Leadership* 66 (7). www.ascd.org/publications/educational _leadership/apr09/vol66/num07/The_Difficult_Road_for_Long-Term_English _Learners.aspx.

Menken, Kate, Tatyana Kleyn, and Nabin Chae. 2012. "Spotlight on 'Long-Term English Language Learners': Characteristics and Prior Schooling Experiences of an Invisible Population." *International Multilingual Research Journal* 6 (2): 121–42.

Miller, Beth M. 2003. *Critical Hours: Afterschool Programs and Educational Success.* Quincy, MA: Nellie Mae Education Foundation.

Mitchell, Corey. 2019. "'English-Only' Laws in Education on Verge of Extinction." *Education Week* 39 (11): 1, 11.

Moll, Luis C., Cathy Amanti, Deborah Neff, and Norma Gonzalez. 1992. "Funds of Knowledge for Teaching: Using a Qualitative Approach to Connect Homes and Classrooms." *Theory into Practice* 31 (2): 132–41.

Muñiz, Jenny. 2019. "How Omaha Public Schools Is Weaving Together Resources for Immigrant and Refugee Families." *New America* (blog), October 15. www .newamerica.org/education-policy/edcentral/how-omaha-public-schools-weaving -together-resources-immigrant-and-refugee-families/.

National Academies of Sciences, Engineering, and Medicine, Division of Behavioral and Social Sciences and Education, Board on Science Education, Board on Behavioral, Cognitive, and Sensory Sciences, Committee on How People Learn II: The Science and Practice of Learning. 2018. *How People Learn II: Learners, Contexts and Cultures*. Washington, DC: National Academies Press.

National Center for Educational Statistics (NCES). 2020 (updated). https://nces.ed.gov /programs/coe/indicator_cge.asp.

Nazario, Sonia. 2014. *Enrique's Journey: The Story of a Boy's Dangerous Odyssey to Reunite with His Mother*. New York: Random House Trade Paperbacks.

Office of English Language Acquisition (OELA). https://ncela.ed.gov/files/rcd/TO20 _DualLanguageRpt_508.pdf.

Olsen, Laurie. 2010a. "Changing Course for Long Term English Learners." *Leadership* 40 (2): 30–33.

———. 2010b. *Reparable Harm: Fulfilling the Unkept Promise of Educational Opportunity for California's Long Term English Learners*. Long Beach, CA: Californians Together.

———. 2012. *Secondary School Courses Designed to Address the Language Needs and Academic Gaps of Long Term English Learners*. Long Beach, CA: Californians Together.

———. 2014. *Meeting the Unique Needs of Long Term English Language Learners: A Guide for Educators*. Washington, DC: National Education Association.

Omaha Public Schools (OPS). 2020. "English Learners: Mission and Philosophy." Omaha Public Schools (website). https://district.ops.org/DEPARTMENTS/Curriculum -and-Instruction-Support/English-Learners#6901169-mission-and-philosophy.

Otheguy, Ricardo, Ofelia García, and Wallis Reid. 2015. "Clarifying Translanguaging and Deconstructing Named Languages: A Perspective from Linguistics." *Applied Linguistics Review* 6 (3): 281–307.

———. 2018. "A Translanguaging View of the Linguistic System of Bilinguals." *Applied Linguistics Review*, 10 (4): 1–27. https://doi.org/10.1515/applirev-2018-0020.

Palmer, Deborah. 2020. "Bilingualism, Biliteracy, Biculturalism . . . and Critical Consciousness to Support Equity in Dual Language Bilingual Education." Presented at La Cosecha Dual Language Education Virtual Conference, Santa Fe, New Mexico, Nov. 4–7.

Paris, Django. 2012. "Culturally Sustaining Pedagogy: A Needed Change in Stance, Terminology, and Practice." *Educational Researcher* 41 (3): 91–96. http://edr.sagepub .com/content/41/3/93.

Paris, Django, and H. Samy Alim, eds. 2017. *Culturally Sustaining Pedagogies: Teaching and Learning for Justice in a Changing World*. New York: Teachers College Press.

Partnership for 21st Century Learning. 2019. "Framework for 21st Century Learning." Columbus, OH: Battelle for Kids. http://static.battelleforkids.org/documents /p21/P21_Framework_DefinitionsBFK.pdf.

Piaget, Jean. 1955. *The Language and Thought of the Child*. New York: Meridian.

Pinker, Steven. 1994. *The Language Instinct: How the Mind Creates Language*. New York: William Morrow.

Ramirez, David. 1991. *Final Report: Longitudinal Study of Structured English Immersion Strategy, Early-Exit and Late-Exit Transitional Bilingual Education Programs for Language-Minority Children*. ED 300-87-0156. Dept of Education, Washington, DC. https:// files.eric.ed.gov/fulltext/ED330216.pdf.

Rao, Maya. 2019. "How Did the Twin Cities Become a Hub for Somali Immigrants?" *Star Tribune*, June 21. www.startribune.com/how-did-the-twin-cities-become-a -hub-for-somali-immigrants/510139341/.

Riley, Richard W. 2000. "Excelencia para todos = Excellence for All: The Progress of Hispanic Education and the Challenges of a New Century." Speech presented at Bell Multicultural High School, Washington, DC, March 1. ED 440 542. https:// files.eric.ed.gov/fulltext/ED440542.pdf.

Rolstad, Kellie, Kate Mahoney, and Gene V. Glass. 2005. "A Meta-Analysis of Program Effectiveness Research on English Language Learners." *Educational Policy* 19 (4): 572–94.

Ruíz, Richard. 1984. "Orientations in Language Planning." *Journal of the National Association of Bilingual Education* 8 (2): 15–34.

Sager, Rebekah. 2020. "Lawmakers Ask Trump to Protect 30,000 Frontline Healthcare Workers in Danger of Deportation." *Courier*, April 16. https://couriernewsroom .com/2020/04/16/lawmakers-ask-trump-to-protect-30000-frontline-healthcare -workers-in-danger-of-deportation/.

Samway, Katharine D., Lucinda Pease-Alvarez, and Laura Alvarez. 2020. *Supporting Newcomer Students: Advocacy and Instruction for English Learners*. New York: W. W. Norton.

Sanchez, Claudio. 2017. "English Language Learners: How Your State Is Doing." *NPR Ed*, February 23. www.npr.org/sections/ed/2017/02/23/512451228/5-million -english-language-learners-a-vast-pool-of-talent-at-risk.

Sánchez, María T., Ofelia García, and Cristian Solorza. 2018. "Reframing Language Allocation Policy in Dual Language Bilingual Education." *Bilingual Research Journal*, 1–15. www.tandfonline.com/doi/full/10.1080/15235882.2017.1405098.

Saxon, Shani. 2018. "New Report Shows Fear of Deportation Is Keeping Children Out of School." *Colorlines*, November 21. www.colorlines.com/articles/new -report-shows-fear-deportation-keeping-children-out-school.

Schleppegrell, Mary J. 2004. *The Language of Schooling: A Functional Linguistics Perspective*. Mahwah, NJ: Lawrence Erlbaum.

Selinker, Larry. 1972. "Interlanguage." *International Review of Applied Linguistics*, 10 (3): 201–31.

Slavin, Robert E., and Alan Cheung. 2003. *Effective Reading Programs for English Language Learners: A Best-Evidence Synthesis*. Report no. 66. Baltimore, MD: Center for Research on the Education of Students Placed at Risk. https://jscholarship.library .jhu.edu/bitstream/handle/1774.2/62926/Report66.pdf.

Smith, Frank. 1988. *Joining the Literacy Club: Further Essays into Literacy*. Portsmouth, NH: Heinemann.

Soika, Brian. 2020. "Steven Krashen's Seven Tips for Teaching Language During COVID-19." *Language Magazine* (July): 18–20.

Soltero, Sonia W. 2016. *Dual Language Education: Program Design and Implementation*. Portsmouth, NH: Heinemann.

Soto, Mary, David Freeman, and Yvonne Freeman. 2020. *Equitable Access for English Learners: Strategies and Units for Differentiating Your Language Arts Curriculum*. Thousand Oaks, CA: Corwin.

Southern Poverty Law Center (SPLC). 2019. "The Year in Hate and Extremism 2019." https://www.splcenter.org/year-hate-and-extremism-2019.

Stanley, Sue, and Amado Padilla. 1986. "Ethnic Minority Issues in the United States: Challenges for the Educational System." In *Beyond Language: Social and Cultural Factors in Schooling Language Minority Students*, developed by Bilingual Education Office, 35–72. Los Angeles: Evaluation, Assessment, and Dissemination Center, California State University.

Suárez-Orozco, Carola, and Amy K. Marks. 2016. "Immigrant Students in the United States: Addressing Their Possibilities and Challenges." In *Global Migration, Diversity, and Civic Education*, edited by James A. Banks, Marcelo M. Suárez-Orozco, and Miriam Ben-Peretz, 107–31. New York: Teachers College Press.

Suárez-Orozco, Carola, Marcelo Suárez-Orozco, and Irina Todorova. 2008. *Learning a New Land: Immigrant Students in American Society*. Cambridge, MA: Belknap Press.

Suárez-Orozco, Marcelo. 2018. *Children of Immigration*. Paper prepared for the Fourth Policy Forum of the Strength Through Diversity Project, New Brunswick,

Canada, May 31–June 1. Paris: OECD. www.oecd.org/education/school/Children -of%20-Immigration.pdf.

Sugarman, Julie, and Courtney Geary. 2018. "English Learners in Select States: Demographics, Outcomes, and State Accountability Policies." Washington, DC: Migration Policy Institute. www.migrationpolicy.org/research/english-learners -demographics-outcomes-state-accountability-policies.

Sugarman, Julie, and Melissa Lazarín. 2020. "Educating English Learners During the Covid-19 Pandemic." Washington, DC: National Center on Immigrant Integration Policy, Migration Policy Institute.

Svajlenka, Nicole P. 2019. "What We Know About DACA Recipients in the United States." Center for American Progress (website). www.americanprogress.org/issues /immigration/news/2019/09/05/474177/know-daca-recipients-united-states/.

Swain, Merrill. 1985. "Communicative Competence: Some Roles of Comprehensible Output in Its Development." In *Input in Second Language Acquisition*, edited by Susan M. Gass and Carolyn G. Madden, 235–53. Rowley, MA: Newbury House.

Texas Education Agency (TEA). 2019. "Enrollment in Texas Public Schools 2018–19." Document No. GE19 601 13. Austin: TEA. https://tea.texas.gov/sites/default/files /enroll_2018-19.pdf.

Thomas, Wayne P., and Virginia P. Collier. 2002. *A National Study of School Effectiveness for Language Minority Students' Long-Term Academic Achievement*. Santa Cruz, CA: Center for Research on Education, Diversity, and Excellence. https://escholarship .org/uc/item/65j213pt.

Tizard, J., W. N. Schofield, and Jenny Hewison. 1982. "Collaboration Between Teachers and Parents in Assisting Children's Reading." *British Journal of Educational Psychology* 52 (1): 1–15.

UNICEF. 2000. *For Every Child*. England: Penguin Random House.

US Department of Education. 2016. *Non-regulatory Guidance: English Learners and Title II of the Elementary and Secondary Education Act (ESEA), as Amended by the Every Student Succeeds Act (ESSA)*. September 23. Washington, DC: US Department of Education.

Valdés, Guadalupe. 1996. *Con respeto: Bridging the Distances Between Culturally Diverse Families and Schools*. New York: Teachers College Press.

———. 2001. *Learning and Not Learning English: Latino Students in American Schools*. New York: Teachers College Press.

Valentino, Rachel, and Sean F. Reardon. 2014. *Effectiveness of Four Instructional Programs Designed to Serve English Language Learners: Variation by Ethnicity and Initial English*

Proficiency. Stanford, CA; Stanford University Graduate School of Education. http://cepa.stanford.edu/sites/default/files/Valentino_Reardon_EL%20Programs_14_0326_2.pdf.

Valenzuela, Angela. 1999. *Subtractive Schooling: U.S.-Mexican Youth and the Politics of Caring.* Albany: State University of New York.

Van Lier, Leo. 1988. *The Classroom and the Language Learner.* New York: Longman.

Vygotsky, Lev. 1962. *Thought and Language.* Translated by Eugenia Hanfmann and Gertrude Vakar. Cambridge, MA: MIT Press.

———. 1978. *Mind in Society: The Development of Higher Psychological Processes.* Cambridge, MA: Harvard University Press.

Wang, Xiao-lei. 2015. *Understanding Language and Literacy Development: Diverse Learners in the Classroom.* Malden, MA: John Wiley and Sons.

Weir, Melanie. 2019. "10 Things You Didn't Realize Teachers Have to Buy with Their Own Money." *Business Insider,* November 2. www.businessinsider.com/teachers-buy-supplies-own-money-classrooms-2019-10.

Wells, Gordon, and Gen L. Chang-Wells. 1992. *Constructing Knowledge Together: Classrooms as Centers of Inquiry and Literacy.* Portsmouth, NH: Heinemann.

Wertsch, James V. 1991. *Voices of the Mind: A Sociocultural Approach to Mediated Action.* Cambridge, MA: Harvard University Press.

Williams, Can, ed. 1996. "Secondary Education: Teaching in the Bilingual Situation." In *The Language Policy: Taking Stock,* edited by C. H. Williams, E. G. Lewis, and C. Baker, 39–78. Llangefni, UK: CAI.

Wink, Joan. 1993. "Labels Often Reflect Educators' Beliefs and Practices." *Bilingual Education Office Outreach* 4 (2): 28–29.

Wong, Kevin. 2016. "Five Fundamental Strategies for Bilingual Learners." *HuffPost,* December 23. www.huffpost.com/entry/five-fundamental-strategi_b_8870038.

Yang, Pao. 1992. "Why Hmong Came to America." *The Fresno Bee,* Section B, p. 9.

Zwiers, Jeff. 2014. *Building Academic Language: Meeting Common Core Standards Across the Disciplines, Grades 5–12.* 2nd ed. San Francisco: Jossey-Bass.

Zwiers, Jeff, and Marie Crawford. 2011. *Academic Conversations: Classroom Talk That Fosters Critical Thinking and Content Understanding.* Portland, ME: Stenhouse.

Index

case studies

    Carlos (student on the Mexico–Texas border), 49

    Elena (Spanish speaker with Mexican antecedents), 31–33

    José Luis, Guillermo, and Patricia (refugees from El Salvador), 37–39, 43, 72, 76, 178

    Ler Moo (refugee from Myanmar), 32–34

    Maritza (refugee from Honduras), 36–37

    Osman (Somali Muslim refugee), 34–35

    Tou (Hmong refugee from Laos), case study, 35–36, 48–50, 132, 177–78

    value of for understanding context, 30–31

    Yvonne (impacts of COVID-19 on teaching), 104–14

Cervantes-Soon, Claudia, 196–97

Chomsky, Noam, 59, 63, 70, 73

Cloud, Nancy, 122, 154

cognates, 65–66, 130–31, 143–46

Cole, Michael, 53

Collier, Virginia P., 121, 151, 153

communicative competence, 61–63

competence vs. performance, 63–67

contextual interaction model

    dual language bilingual programs, 16

    examples, 14–18

    family and community contexts, 11–12

    immigration experience/status, 12–13

    national and state legal mandates, 7–10, 19–21

national context, 3–7

overview, 2–3

school context, 13

as two-way, flexible model, 21–22

Contreras, Francis, 12

conversational language, 44, 47–48, 58–59, 82, 153

Cortés, Carlos, 2–3, 13–14, 24–25

COVID-19 pandemic

    and educational equity and equality, 165–67

    equity in resources during, 188–89

    impacts on ELs, xiv, 21, 103–104

    impacts on teaching, 104–14

    and remote learning, 81, 87, 186–89

    and social–emotional needs, xiii–xiv, 79

Crawford, Marie, 190–91

critical consciousness, 196–97

cultural capital, cultural context, xiv–xv, 24–30, 119, 170–76

culturally and linguistically diverse (CLD) groups, 24

culturally sustaining pedagogy, 194–99

Cummins, Jim

    on coercive power structures, 168

    common underlying proficiency (CUP) hypothesis, 129–32

    conversational vs. academic language, 58

    intercultural vs. assimilationist orientations, 170–72

    transformative pedagogy, 184, 186

    two solitudes assumption, 126–28

Custodio, Brenda, 44

D

DACA (Deferred Action for Childhood Arrivals) status, xiv, 5, 32

David (examples), 89, 125

dual language bilingual programs

  benefits, xiii, 94

  and critical consciousness, 196–97

  example, 16

  goals, 175

  one-way and two-way, 154–57

Dulay, Heidi, 74

dynamic bilingualism, 128–29, 136, 139

E

Ebe, Ann, 116

Ellis, Rod, 82

emergent bilinguals (EBs)

  case studies, 31–39

  failures of, explanations for, 24–30

  intercultural vs. assimilationist orientations, 170–75

  invented spellings, 57

  and language diversity in the US, 117–18

  long-term English learners (LTELs), 41, 45–49

  potential long-term English learners, 41, 49–50

  recent arrivals with adequate schooling, 41, 43

  schooling models for, 150–57

  students with interrupted formal education (SIFE), 34–37, 41, 44–45

  student–teacher relationships, 168–70

  teacher attitudes toward, 178–79

  types of students, overview, 40

  See also bilingualism; learning; teaching techniques/methods; translanguaging

emergent/experienced bilinguals (EBs), xvii–xviii

English learners (ELs)

  cultural/linguistic contexts, xv

  impact of COVID-19 pandemic, xiv

  numbers and programs for, in California, 2–3, 19, 40

  terms used for, xvii–xviii

Enrique's Journey (Nazario), 37

equity/inclusion, educational

  cultural and linguistic equity, 194–99

  equality vs., 163–65

  equitable resources/grouping, 187–92

  promoting, 193–94

  and school demographics, 161–63

  and segregation, 160–61

  and success, 160–61, 187

ESL pull-out/push-in program models, 15–16, 150–52, 159

Every Student Succeeds Act (ESSA) legislation, xiii, 7

F

Faltis, Christian, 52–53

Francisco, 5, 13, 132, 169, 177, 189, 195

Freire, Paulo, 196

G

Gándara, Patricia, 10–12, 121, 162–64, 179

García, Ofelia, xvii–xviii, 126, 132–38, 139

Genesee, Fred, 122, 154

monitor hypothesis, 75–77

monolinguals, monolingualism, xvi, 118, 120–24, 126–27, 194

Mordechay, Kfir, 162–64

morphology, 60

multilingual ecology, 193

N

natural order hypothesis, 74–75

Nazario, Sonia, 37

O

O'Loughlin, Judith, 44

Olsen, Laurie, 46, 153

Omaha Public Schools (OPS), EL, ESL programs, 17–19

output
  and comprehensible output, 82–83
  forced, 83
  input hypothesis vs., 77, 80
  monitoring, 75–76
  Van Lier's model, 84–86

P

Padilla, Amado, 24, 86

Palmer, Deborah, 197

paraphrasing, 65

parents
  home-language literacy, 182–84
  home visits, 181
  importance, 176–78
  parent education programs, 180–81
  and teachers' attitudes, 178–80

Paris, Django, 87, 194

Pease-Alvarez, Lucinda, 40, 42

phonology, 59–60

plurilingualism, 129

potential long-term English learners, 41, 49–50

power relationships, coercive vs. collaborative, 168–70

principled teaching/orientation, 114–15

production-based teaching approaches, 82–83

R

racial diversity in US schools, 161–63

read-alouds, 148

Reardon, Sean F., 120–21

recent arrivals with adequate schooling, 37–39, 41, 43

recent arrivals with limited/interrupted schooling, 44–45

remote/online instruction, 81, 87, 186–87. *See also* COVID-19 pandemic

resources, equity in, 187–89

Riley, Richard W., 118

Ruíz, Richard, 92–94, 170

S

Samway, Katharine D., 40, 42

Sandra (examples), 176, 184–86

scaffolding, 54–55, 66, 134–35, 146–47, 188

Seal of Biliteracy, xiii, 8–10, 20

second language acquisition
  acquisition vs. learning hypothesis, 70–73
  affective filter hypothesis, 79–80
  childhood bilingualism, 67–68

second language acquisition (*continued*)
    input hypothesis, 77–78
    monitor hypothesis, 75–77
    natural order hypothesis, 74–75
    reception-based vs. production-based
        approaches, 82–83
    simultaneous and sequential bilingual-
        ism, 67–69
    stages associated with, 84
    van Lier's model, 84–86
    See also Krashen, Stephen
Selinker, Larry, 57
Seltzer, Kate, 132–33, 136–37
semantics, 60
simplified input, 78–79
simultaneous and sequential bilingual-
    ism, 67–68
social–emotional learning (SEL),
    xiii–xiv, 79
social interaction and learning, xii,
    52–59
Soltero, Sonia W., 154
spelling, 55–56
standardized tests, 9, 41, 97–98, 120, 159
Stanley, Sue, 24–25
state initiatives and mandates, 8–11
students with interrupted formal educa-
    tion (SIFE), 34–37, 41, 44–45
Suárez-Orozco, Carola, 58, 95, 178
Suárez-Orozco, Marcelo, xiii, 12, 172,
    178, 181
success, factors contributing to
    academic success, 2–3
    for emergent bilinguals, 42, 50–51
    and teacher expectations, 95
    and teacher experiences, 162–63

and two-way contextual interaction
    model, 21–22
value of case studies for understand-
    ing, 30–31
Swain, Merrill, 82
syntax, 60

T

teachers, bilingual, xiv, 13–14, 162–63
teaching techniques/methods
    attitudes and expectations, 95–102,
        178
    and changing student populations, 102
    collaborative vs. coercive approaches,
        168–70
    dual language bilingual programs,
        154–57
    early-exit bilingual programs, 152–53,
        159
    effective practices, 157–58
    ESL pull-out/push-in program
        models, 150–52, 159
    factors that influence, 88–92
    intercultural vs. assimilationist orienta-
        tions, 170–72
    involving parents, 176–82
    late-exit/maintenance programs,
        153–54, 159
    middle and high school models, 157
    principled, effective teaching, 114–15
    problem posing, 196
    reception-based vs. production-based,
        82–83
    in-school and remote, 139–50
    See also scaffolding; translanguaging
Terrel, Tracy D., 84

Thomas, Wayne P., 121, 143, 151, 153–54

Todorova, Irina, 178

transformative pedagogy, 184–85

transitional bilingual education (TBE) model, 15

translanguaging, xiii, 94, 132–37, 139–50, 174

translation, literal, 38, 65, 100, 127, 134, 144

Trump, Donald, 4–6, 164

V

vaivén students, 47, 49

Valdés, Guadalupe, 27–28, 152, 169, 179–80

Valentino, Rachel, 120–21

van Lier, Leo, 84–86

Vygotsky, Lev, 52–59

W

Wei, Li, 133, 139, 142

Weir, Melanie, 188

Wertsch, James V., 53

Wong, Kevin, 191

Wright, Wayne E., 118, 134, 152, 157–58

writing workshop, 191–92

Y

Yvonne (examples), 54, 61, 71–75, 79–80

Yvonne's story, 104–14

Z

zone of proximal development (ZPD), 53–55, 77

Zwiers, Jeff, 190–91

Continuation of credit lines from copyright page: